WATLING STREET

By John Higgs

I Have America Surrounded: The Life of Timothy Leary

The KLF: Chaos, Magic and the Band
Who Burned a Million Pounds

Stranger Than We Can Imagine

Fiction

The Brandy of the Damned

The First Church on the Moon

WATLING STREET

TRAVELS THROUGH BRITAIN
AND ITS EVER-PRESENT PAST

JOHN HIGGS

WEIDENFELD & NICOLSON

First published in Great Britain in 2017
by Weidenfeld & Nicolson
an imprint of The Orion Publishing Group Ltd
Carmelite House, 50 Victoria Embankment
London EC4Y 0DZ

An Hachette UK Company

3 5 7 9 10 8 6 4 2

A CIP catalogue record for this book
is available from the British Library

ISBN 978 1 4746 0347 8

Typeset at The Spartan Press Ltd,
Lymington, Hants

Printed and bound by CPI Group (UK) Ltd,
Croydon, CR0 4YY

MIX
Paper from
responsible sources
FSC® C104740
FSC
www.fsc.org

www.orionbooks.co.uk

For Mum and Dad, and all before.

CONTENTS

CONTENTS

I'm trying to take a stance and rise above my contradictions
But I'm just a bunch of words in pants and most of those are
  fiction.

Mike Scott, 'Long Strange Golden Road'

INTRODUCTION

A Milton Keynes solstice

I love walking down the middle of a road when there's no traffic and the street is deserted. The regular rules have been suspended and things are not in their normal place, which always feels pleasantly transgressive. It usually requires a road closure, street party or treacherous weather, but it is sometimes possible in the early hours of the morning when the traffic has dwindled away to nothing and the night is still and calm and quiet. In the words of the seventeenth-century ballad, the world is turned upside down. At times like these walking in the middle of the road feels liberating, as if anything might happen.

It is a little after 4 a.m. on Sunday, 21 June 2015, just before dawn on the longest day. I am walking down Midsummer Boulevard in the heart of Milton Keynes in Buckinghamshire. It is deathly quiet. I cannot see a single person or moving car. These are perfect conditions for a walk along the centre of the road, yet I'm finding the experience a little disconcerting. It's not the street itself that is at fault. There is something about the town.

Milton Keynes looks like a Canadian airport which has started a new life in the Buckinghamshire countryside. It is a land of squat boxy office buildings and endless roundabouts. It feels more concerned with the needs of cars than of people, not least because of the signs that declare 'Pedestrians do not have priority' in black text on a yellow background. Another common sign, found on walls near pedestrian underpasses, seems to unintentionally reveal a little too much about the town's reputation. It states simply, 'This is not a toilet'.

Pedestrians do not have priority

Poor Milton Keynes. Its notoriety is not entirely fair. For all that it is the butt of countless jokes about concrete and roundabouts, the people who live here seem to like it. It performs well in reports on quality of life and economic activity. Outsiders criticise the large amount of retail outlets and car parks, yet these are things we would value and use if we had more of them where we lived. I suspect it is not what Milton Keynes has that is the real cause of its notoriety, but what it lacks. It is a town without a past.

Milton Keynes is a new town. It was founded in January 1967, back when Harold Wilson was Prime Minister, Patrick Troughton was Doctor Who and The Beatles were recording *Sgt. Pepper's Lonely Hearts Club Band*. The post-war population boom necessitated a huge increase in home building, and the simplest way to achieve this was to construct about a dozen new towns from scratch. Milton Keynes was the largest of these, intended to provide homes for a quarter of a million people. In the years that followed, our housing shortage became a problem for the private sector to tackle, rather than grand centrally planned government schemes. This hasn't worked well, and in 2017 the government announced plans to build 14 brand-new 'garden villages'. These will be much smaller than the new towns of the 1960s, and Milton Keynes's unhappy reputation is part of the reason for this. The town is perceived as unattractive and not an experiment to repeat on the same scale.

Midsummer Boulevard is at the heart of the city, nearly a couple of kilometres long and unnaturally straight. The original design assumed pedestrians would get about by means of a monorail, although this was never built. A central strip, planted with a row of trees, separates the westbound and eastbound lanes. The trees are a sycamore hybrid called London Planes. They are beloved by town planners due to their ability to thrive in polluted air with compacted roots, and for being the sort of high-branched tree that is almost impossible for children to climb.

A half-dozen crows launch themselves from the branches of a London Plane as I approach. They break the silence with their cries. This feels worryingly like an episode of *The Walking Dead*.

It's not the zombie-movie atmosphere that robs the simple act of walking down the middle of the road of its pleasure. I have not yet acclimatised to my surroundings. Milton Keynes is only four years older than I am, so there is nothing here that feels like history. In a country as old as Britain, being entirely surrounded by the modern world takes getting used to.

Our surroundings give us context. In modern business districts, such as Canary Wharf or central Milton Keynes, the present is all that matters and the near future is all that is thought about. In a medieval city such as Oxford or Cambridge, the backdrop is different and that alters how we see ourselves. There is more to life, in places like that, than the immediate future. If we go to a place that is thousands of years old, such as the

Giza pyramids or Stonehenge, then the shift in our sense of ourselves is even more pronounced. As individuals we become insignificant, but at the same time the story we are part of becomes much greater.

This is why, at the same time as I am walking along this deserted Buckinghamshire road, 23,000 people are gathered at Stonehenge a hundred miles to the south-west. They are waiting to greet the sunrise of the longest day. This massive crowd is remarkable because, beyond those old stones in that Wiltshire landscape, there is nothing else there. It is not like a festival, with bands and tents and exciting things around every corner. It is simply thousands of people standing in a field over-night, waiting for the sun. The only attraction is the age of the stones the crowd congregates around, which puts their lives in the context of 5,000 years of history. Seeing yourself in those terms affects you.

Five thousand years is a long time. Kingdoms, languages and empires have come and gone, stories have flourished and been forgotten, gods have been worshipped and discarded. And yet, throughout that time, people have always returned to those stones to watch the sunrise on the longest day. The size of the crowds may be a modern phenomenon but what evidence we have suggests that visitors have always gone to those stones at midsummer. If you were looking for some defining behaviour of the inhabitants of these islands across that great stretch of history, then this would be a strong contender.

Milton Keynes was also designed as a temple to the sun, exactly like Stonehenge. For all the town's reputation as a dull, lifeless place, it has a far stranger heart than is usually recognised. Its major streets were laid out in a sensible grid pattern, with horizontal roads labelled H1 to H9 and vertical roads named V1 to V11. But these roads do not run directly north–south and east–west, as you might expect. They have been deliberately tilted at an angle. Amazingly, this was done so that the rising sun on midsummer's morning shines directly down the length of Midsummer Boulevard, just as the rising sun in Wiltshire shines over the Heel Stone directly into the heart of Stonehenge.

The Chief Architect and planner of Milton Keynes was a man named

Derek Walker. He was not immune to the strange currents of the 1960s and '70s counterculture as he designed the town. His obituary in the *Guardian* quotes him as describing those times as 'very kinky'. Late-night planning meetings were soundtracked by Pink Floyd albums, and John Michell's 1969 book about ley lines, stone circles and archaeo-astronomy, *The View over Atlantis,* was a big influence. Many street names in Milton Keynes linked Walker's new town to the ancient past described in Michell's book; Midsummer Boulevard, for example, runs between Silbury Boulevard and Avebury Boulevard, and Silbury and Avebury are prominent Neolithic sites of great importance to Michell.

At this hour and on this morning over forty years earlier, Derek Walker and his team were on this very spot, waiting to check the position of the midsummer sunrise. Whereas I am surrounded by concrete and glass, they were in the middle of a muddy field staking out the route of the central boulevard with ropes and posts. From this, the rest of Milton Keynes followed.

Walker discovered that the intended route ran past a mature oak tree, which was then around a hundred years old. He altered his designs to include this tree. His modern town would have an old English oak at its heart, and be positioned to face the rising sun on the eastern horizon on the longest day. That sunrise would shine directly along Midsummer Boulevard like torchlight down a pipe. It would reflect off the glass-fronted train station at the western end of the road, illuminating the link between Milton Keynes and the rest of the country. Derek Walker was working on the principle that our modern future and our deep past need not be separated, like two sides of a coin, but could work together.

In his epic novel *Jerusalem*, Alan Moore, the author of such ground-breaking graphic novels as *Watchmen*, *V for Vendetta*, *Lost Girls* and *Promethea*, describes the physical shape of a tree as a solidified record of time. A tree's past is not lost with passing years but remains visibly present in its shape. It expands as shoots bud and branches grow, but it always physically contains the younger tree it used to be. The unique fractal shape of the Milton Keynes oak, when seen in this light, becomes a map of its history and a physical summation of its past. Perhaps Walker was on to something when he chose it as a symbol for the heart of a town.

I was talking to Alan Moore about this recently and he happened to mention that he had personally built Milton Keynes.

'Yes, I built Milton Keynes. Not single-handedly. No, I had some help,' he admitted. 'But yes, I was one of the mythical builders of that town. I was working for the contractor who had the contract to lay the gas mains. This was about 1975, I think. I was in the office ordering equipment and dealing with time sheets and invoices and so on. The planners were young, and heavily into John Michell's books. They didn't really seem to know what they were doing.

'I remember once I was in the office and one of the planners came in. A couple of the labourers accosted him, an Irish guy and a Polish guy. These were the guys who were out in the mud digging trenches. They asked him to explain the blueprints, because as far as they could tell they showed that all the fire hydrants should be connected to the gas mains. The planner told them not to be daft. He spread out the blue prints, and stared at them, and went white. At which point he grabbed the blueprints and ran out of the office.

'So they changed the plans, which was sensible. If there had been a fire, then having the fire hydrants connected to the gas mains wouldn't have helped.'

I asked him if the solstice alignment was public knowledge back then, and he said it was fairly well known. 'You'd get a bunch of pagans turning up, and a mob of born-again Christians turning up to heckle them, and the police turning up to keep them apart. But all that faded away pretty quickly.'

The shopping centre Walker designed around the oak tree was opened in 1979 by the new Prime Minister, Margaret Thatcher. She praised 'the imagination of the private sector' in her speech and no one corrected her, for the centrally planned nature of Milton Keynes was already falling from memory. New towns had already lost their utopian, collectivist façade and were starting to be seen as soulless and bleak; for example, in songs like 'Newtown' by The Slits (1979). The 1980s were around the corner, and a town with no visible past could only be understood as a product of the present. Paul Weller wrote the unhappy song 'Welcome to Milton Keynes' in 1985, in which he sang about slashing his wrists on this 'fine Conservative night'. Milton Keynes had become something inherently Thatcherite, a place that was industrious, corporate and heartless. The town's name was taken from an old village, but some suggested it also honoured the economists Milton Friedman and John Maynard Keynes. Ancient English oaks and solstice celebrations did not really fit into that story.

In the year 2000, the shopping centre expanded. It crossed over Midsummer Boulevard and blocked the solstice alignment. A covered food court now stands where the road was, offering you the choice of Pret A Manger, Burger King, Starbucks, Baskin Robbins or Ed's Easy Diner. Friendly signs by the exits read 'Come back again soon – it's just not the same without you'. The oak tree was entirely surrounded by the shopping centre. Concrete cow sculptures were placed around its trunk.

Milton Keynes oak

The tree did not do well in its new surroundings. As the 2000s rolled on it became increasingly clear that the oak was far from healthy. Attempts to reinvigorate the tree, by cutting it back and feeding it nutrients, came to nothing. In March 2015 it was pronounced dead. It remains in place with its branches cut away, leaving little more than the trunk. When the shopping centre was extended, drainage pipes were removed by mistake and the oak technically drowned.

After its death, a new concrete cow was added to the sculptures that surround the trunk. This cow has been painted in bright colours by local schoolchildren, who also drew the Harry Potter 'Deathly Hallows' logo on its chest. The symbol is a representation of the three gifts of death. This was presumably not an intentional statement, yet it was horribly apt. Derek Walker died a couple of months after the tree. He remained proud of Milton Keynes even though, as his obituary notes, he was 'often in disagreement with more recent development plans'.

It is nearly 4.42 a.m., the time of sunrise, but there is not a single person here to witness it. I keep heading east, along a path that extends beyond Midsummer Boulevard and into parkland. Ahead, I see a silver pyramid at the point where the sun is due to rise. This turns out to be a six-metre-high sculpture called *Light Pyramid*. It was built in 2012 to replace a beacon destroyed by lightning not long after the shopping centre was extended. The sculpture lights up at night, and the position of this light at the exact point where the sun rises on the solstice seems like a heavy-handed reminder to the people of Milton Keynes to pay attention to this spot. But if this was the intention, it has not been a success. Of the 230,000 people currently living in the town, only thirteen have gathered at the pyramid to watch the solstice sunrise.

As I walk up to the sculpture, the path becomes an artificial hill which gives unimpeded views to the far horizon across Buckingham-shire and Bedfordshire. It is a dramatic sight, but it is clear that I am not going to get the sunrise I hoped for. A band of stubbornly static low cloud sits over the eastern horizon and does not look like it will be moving anytime soon. The sky is starting to lighten, but the sun is not going to show itself.

Milton Keynes Pyramid

Of the thirteen people who have come to witness the dawn, eight are a group of students, one of whom is strumming an acoustic guitar. They are eating bagels and talking about ketamine, and they do not seem enthused by the experience. Following a period of silence one of them announces, 'We could be playing Xbox.' But the other five observers seem to find the experience more valuable. They watch the horizon silently and I join them, for even with the sun obscured by cloud it is still a very beautiful dawn. Shades of lilac edge the clouds above, framing occasional patches of blue. The fields, woodland and villages ahead are slowly revealed in the growing light, forming out of the grey into differing shades of green. The seven white turbines of a wind farm stand in a row to the north. Their blades turn out of sync with each other, like infant schoolchildren trying to perform a dance in a school play. I don't think I will ever understand how anyone can describe a wind farm as an eyesore. Daylight spreads and the longest day begins.

One by one, the gathered witnesses drift off to start their morning. I walk back along Midsummer Boulevard, disappointed to have failed to see Milton Keynes perform its role as a modern sun temple. But the experience has confirmed something for me: Derek Walker was right to attempt to use the ancient and the modern simultaneously. The contemporary world, by itself, is not enough.

At the shopping centre I look back over my shoulder, hoping to find that the clouds have lifted and the sun is able to shine along Midsummer Boulevard. But the clouds are stubborn. The first rays of dawn do not trouble the food court or warm the buildings that hide the dead oak. Perhaps the small band who gather next year will have better luck.

As I walk back along Midsummer Boulevard, I walk towards the road that brought me to this town. According to the town's grid system, it is called V4. But the street signs themselves include its older, more familiar name. They read 'Watling Street V4'. It is the reason why the Milton Keynes road grid does not run directly north–south or east–west. Watling Street was here first. The town was laid out to fit around it and this, by happy coincidence, meant that the town could be aligned with the solstice.

The route of Watling Street is far older than recorded history. It was formed by prehistoric feet walking across an untouched landscape, back when this island was owned by everyone and no one. And yet, as the alignment of modern Milton Keynes shows, that route still affects the world around us in surprising ways. It may be ancient history, but it is far from dead.

It is not just our immediate surroundings, be they Milton Keynes, Oxford or Stonehenge, that give context to our lives. The country as a whole frames us also. Its influence is more complicated, and considerably messier, than that of a single town. There are times when the story it tells isn't up to the job of providing a unifying context for all the people of this island, and the result is a population estranged and divided. This is one of those times, as I'm sure you've noticed.

For this reason we're about to undertake a journey, from Dover up through London and the Midlands to North Wales, along this ancient road called Watling Street. I realise that embarking on this journey might be something of a leap of faith. Not many people have given Watling Street much thought over the years. Even those who know where the road is, or where it goes, are unlikely to have had any desire to journey along its full length. Many hundreds of thousands of people travel along Watling Street every day but few realise the extent to which the grey tarmac underneath their feet has been shaping our history, culture and personal identities for thousands of years. The most enchanting and significant road in the country doesn't advertise its importance. It's a very British road like that.

Long ago, a path was created through endless forest. Gradually that path became a trackway, and the trackway became a road. It connected the White Cliffs of Dover to the druid groves of the Welsh island of Anglesey, across land that was first called Albion, then Britain, Mercia, and eventually England. Armies from Rome arrived and straightened 444 kilometres of that meandering track. They called the route *Iter II* and *Iter III*. In the Dark Ages it gained the name Watling Street, after the name of a local warlord whose territory it passed through. In the twelfth century it was one of the four royal highways, roads so import-ant to the realm that travellers along them were under the protection of the king. More recently, this ancient track has been given names like the A2, the A5 and the M6 Toll. Watling Street is a palimpsest. It is always being rewritten.

It is a road of witches and ghosts, of queens and highwaymen, of history and of fiction. Dickens and Lord Byron wrote about it. The road which the pilgrims of Chaucer's *Canterbury Tales* travelled along is the same road alongside which the *Star Wars* movies were filmed; there is no road anywhere in the world that has produced so many stories.

Along this route Boudica met her end, the Battle of Bosworth changed royal history, Bletchley Park codebreakers cracked Nazi transmissions and Capability Brown started the English landscape tradition. Watling Street was the boundary between Saxon England and the Viking-ruled Danelaw. It marked the path of the Great Fire of London and it boasts both the oldest pub in Britain and the first Indian restaurant. The body of Queen Eleanor travelled southwards down this road, her final journey marked by crosses built at each place her body stopped, while the body of Diana Princess of Wales travelled the route northwards. The road connected St Paul's Cathedral, the location of Diana's marriage, with the Althorp estate, where she was buried.

A location with a story to tell, such as a castle or a battlefield, will typically be roped off by the National Trust or a similar organisation. They will add a tea shop and charge a tenner to enter, and that money will be used to preserve the place as it was at a specific moment in history. This can be a wonderful way of teaching us about our shared past, but when a place is preserved like this, unchanging and eternal, it is to all intents and purposes dead. If history is understood as the roots that nourish us, then we are in effect saying that those roots are dead too.

It's not possible for the National Trust to put a fence around Watling Street. It's not possible to freeze it in time. It is constantly changing yet always the same – a simple trackway offering passage over a particular piece of landscape. It is past and present combined in a way that Derek Walker, I think, would have appreciated.

We have a choice of histories in these islands. Those that are focused on royal houses or social movements are inherently political. Accounts that begin with military victories, such as the Roman or Norman Conquest, follow a victor's script. Watling Street is more neutral, because a road does not care what those who travel along it are planning. As a result, the history of this particular road tells a story quite unlike the histories we are used to.

By travelling from South-East England to North Wales we will miss the West Country and the North-East, and of course Scotland. This may seem a poor way to look at the history of this island, but think of this more like a surgical incision than an exercise in open-cast mining. By retracing this fine line across the landscape, we are acting like a surgeon tracing a scalpel across the skin in order to gain access to what lies beneath. The surgeon wields her scalpel in a well-chosen line at times of illness or disease, because sometimes you have to go inside the body to fix the problem. Our sense of national identity is fearful and troubled in these days of uncertainty, austerity and blame, and we are going to have to go in deep if we want to cure this division. At least a neat line will leave less of a scar.

We are seeking a better sense of national identity. Not one that is imposed on us by the state, monarchy or military, but one which bubbles naturally out of the land – an identity that is welcoming, not insular; magical rather than boorish; creative rather than triumphant. It is out there, waiting for us, and if we head out of the front door and follow the road, we will find it. It is an identity fit for those would live nowhere else in the world, but who wince at jingoism and flag-waving. It should not make anyone proud to be British; it should make them delighted to be British.

Watling Street is simultaneously mundane and extraordinary. It facilitates movement, which generates stories, which create history. We are about to travel from one end to the other, stopping off at significant points along the route. Our one rule is that we will never stray more than five miles from the road. This divided island has lost a workable sense of identity but, because so much of the British story is connected to this one single road, perhaps retracing all those uncountable journeys along Watling Street will help us understand that division. So we are not travelling as tourists, but we venture out with purpose. When you lose something, you retrace your steps until you find it again.

of Sheppey

Whitstable

Margate

Broadstairs

Ramsgate

Canterbury Cathedral

Tales

CANTERBURY

Watling Street

Deal

DOVER

Shakespeare Cliff

Folkestone

The White Cliffs of Dover

STRAIT of DOVER

New Romney

Calais

Spanish Armada

France

I.

THE WHITE CLIFFS OF DOVER

How much history is too much history?

'Lia,' I ask, 'do you ever worry that there's too much history?'

Lia is my daughter. It is 18 October 2015 and we are twenty-three metres below ground in a Second World War tunnel system carved deep within the White Cliffs of Dover. The only light comes from the torches mounted on the front of our white hard hats. I am looking up at hundreds of thousands of tonnes of pure white chalk a few inches above my head. It appears dazzlingly white in the weak torch light.

Lia gives me the look that teenagers give their parents. She is fifteen and has been obsessed with history since she was about six. History means more to her than Harry Potter posters, Fall Out Boy CDs and the Fitz/Simmons relationship in *Marvel's Agents of SHIELD*. She has never once worried that there was too much of it because her brain is still a sponge, soaking up whatever it encounters. 'Why would you say that?' she asks, my question being too stupid to warrant an answer.

'I've been rereading an old novel, from the nineties, about a nineteen-year-old kid called Tyler,' I explain. 'He's from Washington State on the American Pacific coast. He grew up surrounded by untouched landscape where there was very little history, or at least very little Western history. And, in the book, he visits Europe and it freaks him out because there's so much history. He finds it oppressive and controlling, as if the sheer weight of the past was pushing down on him and he couldn't escape.'

'What book is that?' she asks.

'*Shampoo Planet*, by Douglas Coupland.'

'Oh, I've heard of that.'

This takes me by surprise. 'Really?'

'Yes, it's mentioned in some Panic! At The Disco songs. I was thinking of reading it one day. I won't bother now, if that's what it's like.' She returns her attention to the tunnels.

It was the daunting physical presence of these cliffs above my head that had caused me to ask. Tyler's reaction to the past had stuck with me, ever since I'd first read the book. My visit to Milton Keynes had convinced me that the presence of the past was important. And yet, as I looked up at the countless tonnes of chalk above my head, I did wonder if Tyler had a point. Do we have too much history weighing down on our lives? Is British history controlling and oppressive?

The chalk above me dates back to the age of dinosaurs. It was originally under the sea, where single-cell algae called coccolithophores lived and bred in the warm, shallow waters. The coccolithophores had the ability to form tiny round calcium carbonate shields, called coccoliths, which they surrounded their bodies with for protection. When they died these coccoliths fell away and floated down to the seabed, where they slowly accumulated. In time, and under pressure, they became the thick white rock above my head.

The amount of time this took is difficult to grasp. Each coccolith was only a few thousandths of a millimetre in size. To form a single centimetre of chalk took a thousand years and uncountable billions of algae. A metre of chalk would have taken a 100,000 years to form. These cliffs took over a million years. The White Cliffs, then, are history solidified, the past in physical form. Deep underground, with the bare rock only inches from your head, the weight of the past is hard to ignore.

The chalk was raised up above sea level by the same geological movement that created the Alps, back when the lands we now call Britain and France were continuous. The English Channel formed around 8,000 years ago, when sea levels rose after the last ice age. That rush of water also revealed the White Cliffs, so their arrival in history and the birth of the island of Britain were one and the same event. They are thought to be the reason for the name 'Albion', the earliest known name for these islands, which means 'white island'.

To reach these tunnels, the Fan Bay Deep Shelter, Lia and I walked a mile and a half east, across the coastal headlands, from the White Cliffs car park. At the entrance we joined a guided tour and descended a concrete staircase, 125 steps deep, that led down into the ground. At the top it was pleasantly warm, as the midday October sun slowly burned away the morning haze. As we descended our breath became visible in the thin light of our head torches. In the cooler air at the bottom of the staircase, beads of condensation hung from the cast-iron roof supports.

Second World War tunnels

The tunnels were built in late 1940 and early 1941. They originally contained rows of bunk beds and were designed to quarter 150 soldiers. It was part of a gun battery built on the order of Winston Churchill, who visited Dover shortly after the Dunkirk evacuations and discovered that enemy shipping was using the English Channel unopposed. The tunnels were filled in after the war, and the National Trust had no idea they existed when they acquired this stretch of the cliffs in 2012. After the importance of what they now inadvertently owned was realised, teams of volunteers spent eighteen months removing the 100 tonnes of spoil from the entrance shaft.

We turn off the torches on our hard hats. The blackness is total, and our other senses sharpen to compensate. From deep within the chalk cliffs I try to imagine the first humans arriving on the landscape high above, following the retreating glaciers to the north as the virgin landscape of this cold northern territory was slowly revealed, thousands of years before the English Channel formed.

Would it have been possible, I wonder, to hear their movement on the turf twenty-three metres above our heads? Would we have heard the scuffling of animals, or the first human footprints on the landscape as the passage of feet sought out the driest, easiest routes? Down here, would we have heard as the accumulation of those feet formed the first paths, which became the first trackways, which became the first roads?

Standing in total darkness, I can imagine that those first footsteps on the Southern English countryside above did indeed echo all the way down into this cold silence. According to *Puck of Pook's Hill*, Rudyard Kipling's 1906 book of children's stories, the first person in England was Puck, 'The oldest Old Thing in England'. This is the same Puck from *A Midsummer Night's Dream*, a mischievous woodland spirit and 'merry wanderer of the night'. Puck, also known as Robin Goodfellow, was here to ensure that those who followed didn't take the pompous seriously. He is best known for turning the weaver Nick Bottom's head into that of an ass.

Others will insist that those first footsteps belonged to a stoic Palaeolithic wanderer rather than a scampering prankster sprite and, who knows, they might even be right. But, regardless of their owner, those footsteps still mark an origin for these islands every bit as important as the flooding of the English Channel. The British Isles, that slow-shifting dance of ice and rock, had been observed. Once they had been seen, and judged, they now existed as an idea.

In the 1920s the French Jesuit priest Pierre Teilhard de Chardin coined the marvellous word noosphere, which refers to the world of human thought. It is the end product of a hierarchy of earthly spheres. At the bottom of these is the geosphere, the physical inanimate world of rock, ocean and mineral. From the geosphere arises the biosphere, the world of all living things. The biosphere moves and evolves faster than the geosphere, and can also change it. The noosphere, in turn, arises from the biosphere. This sphere is the realm of thought, and contains all our myth, history, science, law, religion and culture. It is more fluid and changeable than the biosphere, and it can also affect it. For example, men and women in the UK are on average 4.3 inches taller than they were a hundred years ago, due to changes in our understanding of health and nutrition. This understanding resides in the noosphere, so the noosphere in this example has physically altered the biosphere.

When the first man or woman arrived in this landscape and looked out, the idea of Britain sparked into being. Britain now had qualities and character. Those qualities were probably 'damp' and 'unpromising', but it was a start. The immaterial aspect of Britain, that slippery notion of national character or identity, had been born in the noosphere. And, having been born, it started to grow.

We turn our lights back on and continue to walk the tunnels of the Fan Bay Deep Shelter. The world of the Second World War feels incredibly close.

The soldiers left behind physical traces which were small but telling, from spent ammunition to a football pools coupon or a needle and thread. A carved face in the chalk wall, only an inch or so high, looks like it could be a soldier's self-portrait. Among the graffiti, one soldier had written 'Russia bleeds while Britain blancos'. The reference dates it ('blanco' refers to keeping items of a soldier's kit spick and span, when it isn't being used), but the underlying sense of political frustration is still clear. Elsewhere, the left-hand side of a piece of more poetical graffiti has been lost, yet the soldier-poet's talents are still evident in the side that remains:

[…] IT IN SUCH A CAPER HAVING SHIT AND GOT NO
[…] PARADE IS DUE I DARE NOT LINGER
[…] HERE GOES I'LL USE MY FINGER.

You can get a sense of what life was like under constant shelling from occupied France in a 1944 Pathé Gazette newsreel called *Hellfire Corner*. It began, after the crowing cockerel logo, with shots of a crowd of people running towards a Dover air-raid shelter. This opening scene was clearly staged for the benefit of the cameras, as all those people, from children to the elderly, were grinning and merry as if dashing to get ice cream. But what followed was genuine: rubble, destroyed houses, the bloodied legs of a dead body being covered over with what looked like offcuts of carpet.

The film showed the people of Dover celebrating at the end of years of bombardment. Canadian forces pushing through Normandy had captured the German guns and gunners who pounded this part of the English coast, giving it the nickname 'hellfire corner'. One of the German gunners was Jakob Nacken, at 7'3" the tallest man in the German army. He was photographed surrendering to the 5'6" tall Corporal Bob Roberts of the North Shore New Brunswick Regiment. It's hard to say, from the film, which of the pair found the situation funnier. It is not often you see a prisoner of war enjoying his capture. Their good-natured enjoyment of that surreal situation, together with the grinning faces re-creating the dash into the air-raid shelter, are striking when shown alongside the realities of bombed cities. This collision of horror and tomfoolery makes a telling portrait of the spirit of the 1940s.

Our tour concludes and we begin the slow trudge up 125 steps to the surface, leaving the 1940s behind and emerging into the present day. Outside, the sun is high and warm. The green and white turf-covered cliffs look out upon a featureless hazy void, where the blue-grey sky merges with the grey-blue sea. Thanks to the height of the cliffs the sound of the crashing waves is distant, a subtle background warning easily drowned out by the cries of the circling gulls.

I have never been to the White Cliffs before, but they are incredibly familiar. I grew up hearing about them in songs, in particular Jimmy Cliff's 'Many Rivers to Cross' and Vera Lynn's 'White Cliffs of Dover'. These are both songs about struggle and the promise of a brighter tomorrow, with powerful vocal performances all the more extraordinary when you realise how young Lynn and Cliff were when they recorded them.

Lia at the White Cliffs

We walk as close to the edge of the cliffs as good sense allows, and then go a little further. We have to, really, for the temptation to look over is too strong. The wind toys with us, saving its sudden gusts for when we are at our most secure and complacent. On the other side of the harbour to our right, past the medieval castle where Jon Pertwee's *Doctor Who* battled the Master back in 1971, stands Shakespeare Cliff. This is said to be the cliff in *King Lear*, in the scene where Edgar described the view over the edge to his father, the blinded Earl of Gloucester:

Come on, sir. Here's the place. Stand still. How fearful
And dizzy 'tis to cast one's eyes so low!
The crows and choughs that wing the midway air
Show scarce so gross as beetles. Halfway down
Hangs one that gathers samphire – dreadful trade!
Methinks he seems no bigger than his head.
The fishermen that walk upon the beach
Appear like mice. And yon tall anchoring bark,
Diminished to her cock, her cock a buoy
Almost too small for sight. The murmuring surge
That on th' unnumbered idle pebbles chafes
Cannot be heard so high. I'll look no more,
Lest my brain turn and the deficient sight
Topple down headlong.

This was all a ruse. Blind Gloucester had been heading to the Dover cliffs to commit suicide, but Edgar had diverted him to flat ground to prevent him from doing so. But the vividness of Edgar's description of his pretend elevated perspective, with its rushing sense of uncertain vertigo and details such as the man picking the herb samphire from the cliff face, suggests that Shakespeare once stood on these cliffs with his cloak flapping erratically in the wind, inching forward warily as we do now, unable to resist the dangerous need to look over the edge.

I step back from the cliff and look to the left, where the coast flows down to St Margaret's Bay. This was where the naval spy turned author Ian Fleming lived, after he bought a cottage from his friend Noël Coward in the early 1950s. His 1955 James Bond novel *Moonraker*, which has little in common with the film of the same name, was almost entirely based around this part of Kent. Bond's codename, '007', it is said, is taken from the number of the coach which ran from London to Dover via Canterbury. The 007 coach is now operated by National Express but still runs along the same route with the same number. That Dover–Canterbury–London 007 road is commonly known as the A2 these days, but there are places where it retains its older name: Watling Street.

A thousand years ago, along the coast to our right, the conquering army of the Normans landed at Pevensey. Two thousand years ago, along the coast to our left, the invading Roman army are thought to have landed at Richborough. Across the water in front of us, from right to left, Sir Francis Drake chased the burning and scattered remains of the Spanish Armada. Above us, Spitfire pilots risked everything in the skies during the Battle of Britain, when freedom hung in the balance and Britain, in the words of Winston Churchill, faced its 'darkest hour'. This ancient flooded landscape, which separated Britain from the wider world after the last ice age, has witnessed the same symbolic drama play out time and time again; this island is separate, it is a sanctuary, and it will fight to remain that way.

In the back of my head, a warning bell is ringing. Having the ghosts of Shakespeare, Churchill, James Bond, Francis Drake, Doctor Who and the Battle of Britain in one panorama is catnip to the British, and to the English in particular. These are intoxicating stories of bravery, romance, genius and of always being right. This is the song of the sirens on the rocks, threatening to seduce us through the wondrous unthinking romance of our island story into falling hopelessly in love with ourselves. The British noosphere has evolved greatly since the first arrival, our Palaeolithic Puck, gazed at this damp, inhospitable wilderness. It can be quite overwhelming.

A place like the White Cliffs of Dover illustrates how powerful the British noosphere is. It is almost impossible to see this landscape as simply a nondescript line of cliffs. The history and fiction that wash around this place have as great an impact on the visitor, if not more, than the physical cliffs themselves. Standing here, it is easy to see why Tyler from *Shampoo Planet* was so disturbed by his experience of overdosing on the past.

The associations of these cliffs are pushing us into the territory of those slippery concepts 'national identity' and 'British values'. In 2016 both of the politicians David Cameron and Jeremy Corbyn justified their politics by appealing to national identity and British values. Those British values must be a broad church indeed if they include the opposing and contradictory worldviews of those two men. In truth, what was happening was that Cameron and Corbyn were projecting their own values onto the idea of Britain. This is something we all tend to do, and as a result national identity is always seen as a positive thing. Magically, it fits with and reinforces our own personal beliefs and prejudices no matter what they may be. You can understand why advertisers and politicians are so keen on it.

National identity is like a rainbow; it only exists at a distance. We've all glimpsed it, out there on the horizon, so we think it is something real and concrete when it is used to push our buttons. Yet when we approach it to nail down the details of what it really is, it becomes vague and uncertain, then evaporates.

This is not just a British phenomenon, as you can see when you look at the books, films and essays about defining national character that have been produced in other countries. These can be sweet and funny, like Rob Cohen's documentary *Being Canadian*, or wilfully deranged, such as Hunter S. Thompson's quest for the American Dream *Fear and Loathing in Las Vegas*. We can be confident that if such a thing as a fixed and clearly defined national identity ever existed, the French would have found it by now. They have certainly written enough about it.

National identity can be manipulative. It can be a mirage used against you, a spell like that of the Pied Piper of Hamlyn which seduces you into getting in line and marching behind the patriotic tune. It is a spell woven out of the more seductive strands of our history. We have a lot of history to work with in Britain, so this gives us the raw materials to create a powerful enchantment indeed.

The danger, of course, is that national identity can lead to the drug of nationalism. With nationalism, the country of your own kin is viewed as self-evidently superior while the homelands of others are automatically inferior, and the result of this is the endorphin rush of pride. Like other addictive drugs, the user of nationalism gradually requires greater and greater doses to achieve the same hit of pride. A sense of pride is valuable, of course, but the whole point of pride and self-worth is that they need to come from our own actions and relationships. To feel good about yourself because some long-dead people did extraordinary things is to miss the point quite spectacularly.

I try to break that spell, if just for a moment, because if history teaches us anything it is that nationalism never ends well. I try to ignore the associations and spirits of this landscape and see these cliffs free from the stories that have attached themselves to them over the centuries. I try to look with the eyes of Palaeolithic Puck and see the landscape as a simple physical thing, devoid of connections and myth. I focus on the geosphere and the biosphere, and ignore everything else. I almost succeed.

The sun finds a way through the haze. The dazzling white chalk matches fluffy cumulus clouds hanging in the sky, the blue of which contrasts pleasingly with the bright green turf. The effect is harmonious, peaceful and just a tiny bit magical. For a split second, the cliffs are simple and solid and real, and the sunlight has caused the noosphere to evaporate. But my mind snags on the whiteness of the cliffs and how enchanted they look, and another story about them jumps to mind.

An old Mercian legend tells of an eighth-century monk who encountered an angel at Golgotha, the hill outside Jerusalem. The angel presented him with a stone cross and bid him carry it to 'the centre of his land'. The monk dutifully accepted this command, and travelled back to Britain carrying the heavy cross. He landed on the shore below, at Dover, and headed up the route of the 007 coach, the Roman road of Watling Street, heading for the heart of England.

This is a fitting landscape for a medieval monk with a holy quest. The landscape feels uncanny and special. Perhaps this is because of the whiteness of the rock. Intuitively, we think that rock shouldn't be white. Chalk was used in writing, learning and language and these, we like to think, are our gifts to the rest of the world. These white cliffs, the manifest ancient past that created this island and gave us the name Albion, can also be said to represent our idealised attributes.

It's all too seductive.

The thought of Albion brings to mind William Blake, the author and illustrator of the epic prophetic book *Jerusalem: Emanation of the Giant Albion* (1804–20). Blake's poem 'Jerusalem' (the preface from *Milton*, another of his prophetic books) was written when Blake lived further along the coast to the west in Sussex, in the direction of Kipling's Pook Hill. It was these Southern English chalk downlands that he had in mind when he wrote of building a 'Jerusalem', a divine, eternal place unrelated to the troubled modern city, in 'England's green and pleasant land'. 'Did those feet in ancient time walk upon England's mountains green?' the poem asks. Did Jesus once visit England, as certain legends suggest? If that was the case, then this country was a Holy land.

Blake's 'Jerusalem' was set to music by Hubert Parry during the First World War. Parry assigned the copyright to the National Union of Women's Suffrage Societies, and it became the rallying hymn of the Votes for Women movement. It has not dated like other martial imperial hymns of the era and has the rare ability to resonate with people from every part of the political spectrum, making it something of an unofficial English national anthem. It is used by England at sporting events, such as the Commonwealth Games, where the nations of the United Kingdom compete separately. It is equally at home at a patriotic establishment celebration like the Last Night of the Proms as it is being sung by the socialist punk folk singer Billy Bragg. Blake and Parry's 'Jerusalem' is like the mirage of national identity; all who look at it see the best part of themselves reflected back.

Bruce Robinson's 1989 film *How to Get Ahead in Advertising*, which starred Richard E. Grant, ended with a recital of 'Jerusalem'. Grant played Bagley, an advertising executive wrestling with his conscience about the morality of his profession. At the end of the film, all that remains of Bagley's conscience survives as a sentient, fading boil on his neck.

Bagley rides a horse up a Kentish hill in that final scene, elated and victorious after his personal battle with morality, and loudly proclaims a triumphant soliloquy. He is dressed in tweed trousers and waistcoat with a silk tie, leather gloves, a long coat and riding boots. Following the defeat of his conscience, he now wears a neat moustache. Bagley delivers an impassioned monologue about how marketing convinces people they live in an elevated, wondrous world. By the end of his soliloquy, Bagley has dismounted his horse and stands on a stone pillar. There is endless countryside in all directions, he has his arms outstretched and the sun is behind him. Here Bagley quotes 'Jerusalem': 'I shall not cease until Jerusalem is built on England's green and pleasant land.'

Or at least, that's how the scene plays out in the film. In Bruce Robinson's original screenplay, Bagley's speech starts differently. It began with this dialogue, which failed to make the final cut:

BAGLEY: And did those feet in ancient time walk upon England's mountains green? The answer to that question is 'No'. Jesus did *not* shuffle up the Weald of Kent. Can you hear me, boil? No, I don't imagine that you can. But you've got to admit, that's one of the most graceful pieces of propaganda this nation's ever produced. A magnificent blend of Christianity and Conservatism. And Conservatism is capitalism, and capitalism *sells*. Did Jesus land at Margate? Ah yes my boi! For millions and millions of school kids, the answer to that question is 'Yes'.

Bagley makes a good point. Deep down, does anyone genuinely believe that Jesus travelled from Nazareth to this remote Atlantic island? Blake doesn't claim that he did. He just teases us with the idea. 'Jerusalem' is an example of what is known in journalism as Betteridge's Law, which states that for any headline that asks a question, the answer is always 'no'. And yet, Jerusalem is still an incredibly affecting work. History is not the only ingredient in the spell of national identity.

The white cliffs are not pure chalk. They are peppered through with lumps of flint, an incredibly hard black rock almost the exact opposite of soft, white chalk. Chalk is used for writing and education, but flint is used for cutting tools and lighting gunpowder. No one is sure exactly how flint forms, or why the same pressures and conditions that produce chalk should also produce such a contradictory rock. When we hold up these white cliffs as a symbol of our higher selves we focus on the chalk and ignore the hard dark flint. But the Pathé Gazette newsreel only captured the spirit of the Second World War by including both the horror and the tomfoolery. When we are dealing with the tricky notion of national identity, in a country undergoing a visible surge in nationalist sentiment, we should not forget the flint when we talk of the chalk.

'Dad, do you have that book? Could I have a look at it?'

'Sorry, Lia, I was miles away. What book?'

'*Shampoo Planet.*'

I fish the battered silver paperback out of my bag as we start to walk back towards the car. I notice the author's photograph on the back as I hand it over. Young and handsome, he is lit by slanting light through a window blind, as was the way in the late eighties. I recall a more recent picture that I saw of him, bald with a distinguished white beard. I try to reconcile those different portraits of the author with what feels like the short amount of time that has passed since I first bought the book.

Lia flicks through the pages. 'Would I like it?'

I screw up my face. 'I don't know. Maybe. It's very nineties, and people usually say his other books are better. But it's one of my favourites.'

'It's good?'

'Yeah, I think it's really good.'

'That's the important thing.'

She's right, of course. That is the important thing. Blake's words and Parry's music are good. They are, I think the consensus agrees, very, very good. They are able to march past all our rational critical filters and stir up powerful emotions within us, regardless of who we are or in which circumstances the song is played. Those emotions may be ill-defined and mysterious, but a thing is no less valid because it has not been labelled. 'Jerusalem' shows us that we're capable of creating something like 'Jerusalem'. That in itself is amazing.

I think back to the various attempts people from other nations have made to define the mirage of national identity. For all they claimed to have failed, there is something telling in the differing approaches they took. The heady arguments of French intellectuals are by themselves intrinsically French, just as Hunter S. Thompson's unapologetic individualist hedonism is very American. Rob Cohen's approach of travelling around talking to other Canadians strikes me as very Canadian because Canada is one of the few countries where people seem to like each other, and they certainly like talking. National identity cannot be defined to anyone's satisfaction, and yet, there it is.

I remember how amused people are when I travel abroad and attempt to get a good cup of tea. In the eyes of the people whose country I am visiting, I am being so stereotypically British that it is funny. To my eyes, a desire for tea seems self-evidently reasonable, a choice that I as an individual make based solely on the innate brilliance of tea. As I see it, who wouldn't want a cup of tea? Yet it seems unlikely that my stereotypical fondness for tea comes entirely from me alone, or that I would hanker after a cuppa to quite the same extent if I'd been raised in a different part of the world.

A part of what I think of as 'me' is this mysterious illusion of national identity, which bolts onto my own identity like a bionic limb. To deny national identity, in these circumstances, is to deny a part of myself. Part of my own identity is an ungraspable, undefined mirage, and that's just something I'll have to make the best of. If the stories, myths and histories of these islands are part of us, then that includes the characters of Shakespeare, James Bond, Doctor Who and Winston Churchill who are all linked to these cliffs. We would be different people without them. It is perhaps not surprising that we focus on the chalk and fail to see the flint, or that we find stories of bravery, romance, genius and of always being right so seductive. We want to think well of ourselves.

Politicians from both the left and the right don't fully understand this part of us. The left see themselves as internationalist rather than nationalist. Traditionally, they had no time for national identity and focused instead on class. More recently, they have become less invested in class and now see race, sexuality, gender and religion as the markers of our personal identity. This has been useful for highlighting inequality and systematic bias, but these are unsatisfactory categories to define ourselves by. They fail to get to the heart of who we are, and we feel belittled when we are seen only in those terms. The recent rise of the populist right has been greatly strengthened by the left's infatuation with this kind of identity politics, and when commentators remark that the Labour Party has 'lost touch' with its traditional voters they have recognised that, for ideological reasons, it has been unable to acknowledge the core of its voters' identities.

The right, in contrast, are all over national identity. They are active promoters of flags, anthems and patriotism. Yet the type of national identity they offer does not truly reflect this part of us either. A nation state is a political construct, and most of the world's current nations were created in the nineteenth and twentieth centuries. We are old in comparison: our current United Kingdom dates back to 1801, and the individual nations within the UK are far older. This longevity makes it easy to forget that our nations are also abstract political entities.

We are a product of our environments and an echo of the places we have lived, but it is the people, culture, landscape and cities around us that shape us, not the political state. To define that part of us as 'national' is akin to confusing the menu with the meal, or mistaking the map for the territory. Yet this is what the right habitually do: they recognise and flatter our sense of belonging but then hijack it for their own ends by detaching it from the physical world and attaching it to the political. When politicians call on us to support a war, they use our deep attachment to this land as reason to do so. But it is not the land itself – the hills and rivers and streets and houses – that wants the war.

The part of us that the left denies and the right subverts is not 'national' identity at all. A better name for it would be geographic identity, because it is the physical places that surround us, and not a political abstraction of that territory, that makes us who we are.

I can see how all this would terrify Douglas Coupland's Tyler. If history is part of us, then too much history becomes a larger and larger part of what we are. You can imagine how controlling and oppressive that would seem to a twentieth-century teenager from the American north-west.

'Are you really interested in reading that book,' I ask Lia, 'or are you doing that thing where you show interest in something I like to put me in a good mood before asking for crisps?'

'There is a café down by the car park and there will be a long drive home, and we could get some crisps.'

She hands me the book back.

'You're not going to read it?'

Lia shakes her head. 'Not if it's about someone who doesn't like history.'

'Why do you like history so much?' I ask.

She thinks hard. 'A place is better with history,' she says. 'I don't mean it's better than other places that don't have history. I mean it's more interesting than it would be if it didn't have any history.'

For a young mind like Lia, the presence of the past is exciting. For Tyler, the same presence is oppressive. In Gothic literature, the weight of the past presses down on the present and offers only the certainty of death. In the works of William Blake, the weight of the past presses down on the present and offers the certainty of immortality. We have contradictions ahead.

To our left, a steady stream of ferries enter and depart from the Port of Dover. I look down at the innocent-looking road that heads north out of the port, the start of Watling Street, a road older than history. For all we know of its origins, it may well be Puck-formed. Gulls hover silently in the updrafts, and the autumn sun is low and warm. I walk across England's green and pleasant land with my daughter, and we go and get some crisps.

2.

DOVER TO CANTERBURY

First English, then England

It is the morning of Thursday, 23 June 2016. I have returned to Dover.

It seemed appropriate; today is the day of the referendum on the UK leaving the European Union, and Dover seems to sit at the heart of the debate. The symbolism surrounding the White Cliffs and the town's transport links to the continent have placed Dover at the centre of both pro- and anti-immigration arguments. It has attracted far-right political marches and the corresponding anti-fascist counter-demonstrations that come with them. A walk around Dover this morning could prove revealing, I thought, and might even provide insights into the strange, dark mood that hangs over our seemingly divided country.

But the weather has other plans. Wild storms hit the south-east of England last night, flooding homes and cancelling trains. The storms came in unpredictable, sporadic waves. Periods of calm gave way to sudden rain that didn't so much fall from the sky but seemed hurled down in anger. There were many disturbed nights last night, with those awake lying still and helpless in their beds while lightning lit their rooms and torrents of water shook their windows. The morning air is humid, as if in denial about the night before and still waiting for a good thunderstorm to come and clear it. Intermittent fierce showers continue, so I have ducked into a newsagent's to keep dry. If there are any telling insights about the state of the nation to be found in Dover this morning, they are not daft enough to be out in the streets.

I look at the racks of daily newspapers. Something about them strikes me as odd, and it takes me a moment to work out what is wrong. A display of the daily papers is normally a barrage of large, black, capitalised letters in authoritative serif fonts. Every day when we pass newspaper racks, their words shout at us, demanding attention or angry emotional reactions. Today, the text is secondary. Images dominate.

The Times has a large satellite photo of Europe at night on its cover, dark save for the light of cities and civilisation. So does *The Guardian*, or *theguardian* as it now calls itself. The *Sun* also has a picture of the Earth from space, but one focused on Britain, with a blinding light above it like a sunrise. Beneath this are the words 'Independence Day', in a dramatic movie-poster font. If you've seen what happens to countries from space in the film *Independence Day*, this sends something of a mixed message.

There's no confusion over the *Daily Express*'s message. Its cover is a Union Flag with the words 'VOTE LEAVE TODAY' written on it. It seems strange to see a *Daily Express* front page that does not include the word 'migrant', but, on a hunch, I open the paper and, sure enough, the word 'migrant' is there in a page-three headline. The *Daily Mirror*, in contrast, has the words 'vote REMAIN today' in white letters underneath what looks like a full-page image of a black hole. It's not immediately clear what that image is meant to represent, although looking closer I decide that it's probably a photograph of the bottom of a well. It may be the only piece of tabloid pro-Remain propaganda we have, but you could hardly call it effective.

I buy a copy of each paper, and they make a useful makeshift umbrella as I run back to my car. The rain makes the *Daily Telegraph* unreadable, unfortunately, but based on the cover image of Big Ben and a Union Flag, I think I can guess their angle. Flicking through the papers as the rain drums on the car roof, I realise that only the *Daily*

Mail seems unaffected by the significance of the day. It has kept its normal level of text and features on the cover. Its front-page headline – 'NAILED: FOUR BIG EU LIES' – makes its opinion on the referendum clear, but for much of the rest of the paper it is business as usual. It includes articles about Taylor Swift's relationship with Tom Hiddleston, and the problem with a new Nike dress for tennis players. The hem of this 'flutters way up above the waistline', the article tells me, and there are pictures to prove it. Then there is a two-page photo spread illustrating the difficulty festival goers are currently having travelling to Glastonbury. Of the nine photographs on the page, eight are of young, long-haired, thin women in tiny shorts, and the ninth is of a traffic jam. All this is in contrast to the *Sun*, where it is impossible to forget the day's referendum. Pages four and five are dominated by a photo of a roaring lion in front of the Union Flag, underneath the words 'LET THE LION ROAR'. Turning the page, I find a full-page photograph of Jean-Claude Juncker, President of the European Commission, on which are the words 'STICK IT UP YOUR JUNCKER!'

EU referendum day newspapers

The press no longer take credit for influencing British democracy in the way they once did. We no longer wake on the day after general elections to find headlines like 'IT'S THE SUN WOT WON IT', as we did in 1992. But newspapers still influence the mood and opinions of the country. While a single headline in itself might not have much impact, the unending drumbeat of daily accusations and alarm is hard to shrug off. Years of endless negative press stories about immigrants have helped create an anti-migrant atmosphere that is the backdrop to today's referendum. Words are like the rain currently beating on the car roof, and dripping from my clothes onto these newspapers. A single shower is hardly important but a constant, lengthy downpour can sweep away our familiar, ordered world, as the residents of towns like Hebden Bridge or Burrowbridge discovered these past winters.

Thoughts of those recent floods highlight one of the stranger aspects of our tabloid newspapers' obsession with immigration. Immigration will become a serious, society-shaping problem according to reports on the impact of climate change. Water scarcity and environmental changes will be far more pronounced in areas like Bangladesh and large parts of Africa than they will in Britain. As a result, a common estimate predicts that around 150 million to 200 million people will become climate refugees by the mid twenty-first century. Figures like this cast a sobering light on our current levels of migration and the political fallout they have produced. You might think that the coming wave of climate refugees would be an important part of any discussion about migration, but the subject is almost entirely absent from the newspapers. What our culture ignores can be as revealing as what we obsess over.

Words, despite their capitalisation and angry accusations, can seem such slight things. They surround us throughout our waking day, printed on every surface and displayed on screens, pushing opinions on us and shaping how we see the world. They are so familiar that it can be hard to imagine this island without the English language, but the actual native tongue of this country was Common Brittonic, known more simply as 'British'. This was the language that Welsh and Cornish descended from, and it was spoken for far longer than English has been. Even here, in this most English of towns, it is still possible to find the influence of the British language. A number of local place names reveal their Common Brittonic origin, including Dover (which was long thought to derive from the word *Dubrās*, which means 'water', although a more recent theory suggests its origin may be from the British term for a 'double-bank') and Kent (which is derived from *Cantus*, or 'borders').

Common Brittonic was an oral language, rather than a written one, so much of what we know about it is inferred from later sources. It remained in use during the Roman occupation and in the years that followed, when the country became lawless and dangerous. But it would not survive the next wave of immigration into this Kent landscape. The English words that daily damn migrants on the front of newspapers have their origins here in Kent, and they developed because of invasive migration. The Anglo-Saxons were coming.

Vortigern was a British king in the fifth century who ruled shortly after the Romans had departed. This was an unruly, violent time, and Vortigern needed help defending his people from attacks by the Scots and the Picts. The Scots were people from what is now Ireland, who would in due course invade the north of Britain and create Scotland. The Picts were people who then lived in what we now call Scotland, but who would be pushed back into the Highlands by the invading Scots. A map of Britain dating to the fifth century, which labels Ireland as containing 'Scots' and the majority of England as 'Welsh', can usually be relied upon to make any attempt at English or Scottish nationalism appear totally ridiculous.

Historians think that Vortigern was a real king although they are not convinced by some of the stories told of him, not least his adventures with Merlin. Nevertheless, it is generally accepted that he hired a tribe of Jutes, from modern-day Denmark, and that they arrived in 449

CE and successfully repelled the Scots and the Picts. As a reward, Vortigern gave them the Isle of Thanet in Kent. This is now the eastern-most part of Kent, but it was still an island at the time.

With hindsight, the gift was unwise. The Jutes were so taken by the fertile Kentish landscape that word of it quickly spread back home. More and more Germanic tribes began arriving, including the Angles and the Saxons. Many battles followed, and many of the Celtic British were massacred or forced to flee their land. The historian Bede wrote that the invading Anglo-Saxons 'swarmed over the island and they began to increase so much that they became terrible to the natives themselves who had invited them'.

The Common Brittonic language had survived Roman rule, but it was not so resilient against the invading Germanic speakers. There is some speculation that the language of southern Britain may have differed from Common Brittonic and contained signs of Germanic influence back into prehistory, but it is generally accepted that the birth of the English language was the linguistic result of the Anglo-Saxon invasion. This remarkable language would in time leave these shores and become the international language of the world; not the most common native language, for it trails both Mandarin and Spanish in terms of native speakers, but by far the most common second language.

Old English, the version of our language spoken in the Dark Ages, was poetic and creative but looks entirely foreign to us today. In Old English poems, such as *Beowulf*, we find evocative descriptions such as the sea called a *hwæl wag* ('whale way'), or the human body called a *ban hus* ('bone house'). The arrival of Viking settlers in the north-east from the eighth century onwards led to Old English adopting around 1,400 Norse words. These include words that live up to the barbarous Viking image, such as 'slaughter' (*slátr*), 'ransack' (*rannsaka*) and 'die' (*døyia*), but also words that show the more settled side of Norse life, such as 'sister' (*systir*), 'husband' (*húsbóndi*) and 'birth' (*byrðr*).

The Norse word for a place was 'by', which we see in place names like Whitby and Grimsby. The word 'law' is also Norse. Viking-controlled parts of the country had laws which only applied locally, which is where the modern word 'bylaw' comes from. The part of the country under Viking law was called the Danelaw, and the boundary between the Danelaw and Saxon law was defined as Watling Street.

To the immigrant Anglo-Saxons, with no hint of irony, the native population were *wealhas*, or 'foreigners'. It is from this word that we get the English world 'Welsh'. The Welsh, in contrast, call themselves *Cymraeg*, a word derived from the Brittonic word for compatriot or fellow countryman. So although the word 'Welsh' translates as 'Cymraeg', it actually means the opposite. Geographic identity is always going to be complicated on an island where 'us' translates as 'them'.

Old English fell from grace after the Norman invasion. William the Conqueror's coronation as king of England on Christmas Day 1066 may have been conducted in both Latin and Old English, but William himself spoke French throughout. French was imposed as the new language of court, of law and of the ruling classes. Neither the new king nor the Norman knights who replaced the Saxon nobility had any interest in the local language. English was demoted from a courtly written language to a largely unwritten peasant language. It lost the more formal standardisation of Old English, and evolved into multiple dialects. This was Middle English, and it was essentially a patois of the common people. English, once a language of power and poetry, had fallen on hard times. It could easily have become extinct, just as Common Brittonic did after Anglo-Saxon migration, leaving Britain a French-speaking country.

Instead, it adapted. It absorbed about 10,000 words from French. Many of those new words referred to the nobility, the feudal system and the aristocracy, including 'government', 'parliament', 'money', 'tax', 'judge', 'jury', 'diplomacy' and 'justice'. French-derived words often became used to refer to a better-quality version of the Saxon equivalent. The word 'stool' was Old English, whereas the word 'chair' was borrowed from the Normans. Saxon farmers used the words 'cow', 'sheep' and 'swine', while the ruling elite at their feasting tables referred to 'beef', 'mutton' and 'pork'.

To modern British ears, encountering Middle English is like hearing the broad Baltimore street dialect in the HBO series *The Wire* for the first time. The characters initially seem incomprehensible and, while you might catch some familiar words, you struggle to follow the conversation. But then, perhaps after a couple of episodes, something clicks and it suddenly makes sense. Once you are familiar with the context and the rhythms of their speech, characters can mumble about 're-ups' and 'the corners' as much as they like and you not only understand them, but you experience their world far more vividly than if they spoke in standard American English. Reading an original Middle English text such as Geoffrey Chaucer's *The Canterbury Tales* has a similar effect. The atmosphere of the medieval world comes sharply into focus when you get used to the rhythms, idiosyncrasies and logic of its words. Middle English seems to bounce along, chivalrous yet cheeky and pleasingly child-like. The stereotype of 'Merry Olde England' suddenly makes sense.

Reading Middle English, like watching *The Wire*, helps us appreciate the extent to which our awareness of the world is shaped by language. The Greek, for example, define what English-speakers would think of as 'blue' as two separate colours, *ghalazio* and *ble*. These correspond to light blue and dark blue respectively. This might not seem significant but, neurologically, it changes the way Greek brains are wired. Brain scans of Greek and non-Greek speakers show that Greeks recognise light and dark blue faster than non-Greeks. Language physically shapes the way their brains comprehend the world.

In almost all ancient languages, blue is the last primary colour to be named. There was no word for it when Homer wrote *The Odyssey*, which explains some of his strange descriptions such as the 'wine-dark sea'. Typically, languages gave names to white and black first, then red, and then yellow and green. The only ancient culture that we know had a word for blue was the Egyptians. Some languages still don't have a word for blue, such as the Himba tribe in Namibia. Members of the Himba tribe were shown a picture of eleven green squares, one of which was a slightly different shade, and asked to identify the odd one out. They had no difficulty in identifying the green square which differed subtly from the rest. But when they were shown a similar picture, where one square was blue and the rest were green, they could not identify which square was different. There was nothing wrong with their eyes, but having no word for blue they had no concept of it.

A language is an operating system for the brain. It is not just a means of communication but also a way of cataloguing, seeing and understanding. Whether we speak English or Welsh dictates whether we see 'us' or 'them', for example. The English language also gave birth to the idea of England, by binding together separate tribes in a shared culture. The word 'English' is older than the word 'England', which doesn't appear until the tenth century. As the Old Testament states, 'In the beginning was the Word.'

There are concepts from other languages that English lacks. There is no English equivalent for the Welsh word *cwtch*. A *cwtch* translates as both a small cupboard or a cubbyhole, and also as a hug or cuddle. It essentially means an embrace that makes you feel safe, and protected, and home. There is no English word for the French term *jouissance*, which means a form of enjoyment, caused by a mischievous intellectual game, which has an almost sexual, transgressive edge. Nor is there an English equivalent to the Finnish word *sisu*, which refers to a particularly stoic ability to endure and overcome pain and difficulty. The Finnish see *sisu* as one of their defining national characteristics.

Perhaps more importantly, there is no English equivalent to the German word *Mahnmal*, which means a monument to national shame. Lacking this concept in their mental operating systems, English-speaking cultures have a notable problem discussing aspects of their own history, such as the treatment of aboriginal cultures in North America and Australia or the worst excesses of the British Empire and the Atlantic slave trade. English-speakers can get quite angry when these subjects are raised, which contrasts with the Germanic willingness to discuss the two world wars.

English, then, is not perfect. It would be a better language if it would allow English-speakers to express, and conceive of, concepts like *cwtch*, *jouissance*, *sisu* and *Mahnmal*. But no language is perfect. Our mongrel tongue that emerged through the chaos of conquest and submission, which ruled a country and then was pushed into the shadows, is nothing if not adaptable. Messy, illogical and cobbled together English may be, but it is eminently practical, especially in comparison with the more elegant and refined Romance languages of Latin or French. English can describe things that no other language can. What other language has a specific verb for tricking people into watching a Rick Astley video?

Different languages have different weaknesses. It is very difficult to make a pun in Polish, for example, and the indigenous Pirahã language of Brazil is useless for mathematics, having no numbers. English is a jack-of-all-trades language, flexible enough to adapt equally well to beautiful sonnets, street slang, theoretical physics, innuendo and legal contracts. As computer people would say, it is pleasingly hackable. English is the Swiss-army knife of languages: an imperfect hotch-potch that no one could think of as elegant, but which is surprisingly interesting, curiously flexible and, above all, endlessly useful. The British noosphere runs on a solid operating system.

It's probably not just its innate quality that caused English to rise again, when it could easily have died out after the Norman Conquest. A political reaction against the French during the Hundred Years War was a factor, as perhaps was the sheer bloody-mindedness of the English. But regardless of the reasons, English did slowly resurface. It became a written language again, a language used by nobility, trade, law and eventually even church. French was overthrown as the official language of the establishment.

English was only just getting started. From out of this Kent landscape grew the first language to be spoken on the moon.

It is time to get going. I start the engine.

*

Watling Street starts in dramatic fashion. Emerging from the round-about outside the east docks, it elevates into a suspended dual carriage-way, lifting us up away from the town, out onto the clifftops and away across the downs. This is a relatively recent section of the A2. It was built in 1977, the year of the Queen's silver jubilee, and named Jubilee Way accordingly.

Once we are up on the downs, the road becomes a straight, single-carriageway road. 'Drive on left. *Tenez la gauche. Links fahren*,' declare the multilingual signs on the right-hand side of the road. They act as a reminder to motorists that they are not on the continent now.

Perhaps it is the unusual straightness of this road that makes those signs necessary. Everything else about this first section of our jour-ney drips with Englishness. This twenty-mile stretch from Dover to Canterbury is almost entirely rural, a line cut through the Garden of England, the sight of which reaches out into the far distance on both sides when the trees lining the road allow.

By travelling along Watling Street to Canterbury, we are re-enacting that pivotal text in the story of England, Geoffrey Chaucer's *The Canterbury Tales*. Before the end of the medieval period, Britain was a remote, unimportant and backwards group of islands of little concern to the larger world. But in the fourteenth century Chaucer, then a minor court official, decided to write his epic cycle of stories in English rather than the expected French or Latin. From that point onwards, literature was something that these islands did very, very well.

Britain now prides itself on being a creative country, the land of Banksy, The Beatles and Benedict Cumberbatch. In Danny Boyle and Frank Cottrell Boyce's opening ceremony to the 2012 London Olympic Games, they presented Britain to the world as a fountain of stories, music and comedy. When the Queen's Diamond Jubilee was marked by a pop concert on The Mall, organised by Gary Barlow, this display of culture felt entirely natural because Britain punches above its weight in Hollywood, the art world, fashion, music, theatre and video games.

Given all this, it's easy to forget that creative Britain is a recent development, the result of post-war art schools, the welfare state and the Arts Lab movement. Historically, Britain was always an also-ran in terms of the creative arts, especially in music and painting. We were seen as a country of merchants, which the French called 'an island of shopkeepers', and then later as an island of industry, the 'workshop of the world'. Literature was the one exception to this rule. It was the first creative thing that we were any good at.

From Chaucer onwards, through John Milton, William Shakespeare, Jane Austen, Charles Dickens and massive-selling twentieth-century authors like Agatha Christie, J. R. R. Tolkien or J. K. Rowling, British literature is globally revered. Our inelegant, cobbled-together tongue has proved capable of expressing the human imagination at a popular level above that achieved by other languages.

Chaucer's tale was about a group of fourteenth-century pilgrims who tell each other stories as they make their way to the shrine of Thomas Becket in Canterbury Cathedral. This was one of the most popular shrines in medieval Christendom. It housed the bones of the sainted martyr, and travelling to be with them was to see an immaterial myth, whispered and gossiped across the shires, as something material and real. The large number of pilgrims it attracted brought a lot of money to the Norman cathedral, and to the surrounding town. Canterbury Cathedral was the Disneyland of its day, a destination visitors were drawn to that physically represented the stories of their culture.

There was a socially accepted pace for a pilgrimage to Canterbury. The labouring class were expected to work every day, except when they had permission to take time off for religious reasons. These were 'holy days', the origin of holidays. Time away from labour was granted for a pilgrimage, but it was important not to dawdle. Yet the journey had to be taken solemnly, so it was also not acceptable to rush it in order to get it over with. Those riding to Canterbury, then, went at a speed between a trot and a gallop. This was the 'Canterbury pace', the probable origin of the word 'canter'. Those on foot would 'saunter', a word derived from 'Sainte Terre', or 'holy land'. The holy land was the pilgrim's destination, and also the pilgrimage itself. The moment you embarked on a pilgrimage your feet were on holy ground.

The pilgrims in Chaucer's tale span the social scale. They range from a knight and a prioress at the top, through middle-class characters such as a merchant and a clerk, down to working-class characters like a cook and a miller. Each character tells their own story in a distinctive style, from courtly romances to moral fables or bawdy jokes. There is no favouritism on display, for Chaucer portrayed all classes of people with the same amused respect. They are a snapshot of Britain as a whole, thrown together for their journey, competing to amuse the rest of the group by telling their best stories during their journey from London to Canterbury. As John Dryden summed up *The Canterbury Tales* in the seventeenth century, 'Here is God's plenty.'

The Canterbury Tales was in many ways the first great British achievement. It utilised our most useful asset, this strangely adaptable language, to make the first distinctively English mark on the world stage. English not only produced England, it made England noteworthy. And it did this by taking the full breadth of English society and saying that, together, all these differing types of people make up a larger story. Perhaps this is why the current divided culture which our newspapers portray seems so troubling. When we first defined ourselves, no one was excluded.

Words usually contain more information than you might expect. For example, consider the name 'Watling Street'.

Although you see Watling Street referenced in many histories of Roman Britain, the name dates from the Dark Ages, centuries after the Romans had left. It was originally known in Old English as *Wæclinga Stræt,* which means the well-built street of the *Wæclingas,* where the *Wæclingas* were the people of Wæcla. Very little is known about the warlord Wæcla, except that he or she was a tribal chief in post-Roman Britain who ruled territory around modern-day St Albans.

The *Wæclingas* did not build the road but, because it ran through their territory, it would have been considered their property and their responsibility. But although the name 'Watling Street' is a post-Roman one, it still suggests the Roman presence in this land. The word 'street' comes from the Latin *strata via*, or paved way.

Watling Street, like Jubilee Way, is just one of countless local names for a particular stretch of this old route. For some curious reason, that name spread along the length of the road in a way that other local names didn't. It's still used as far south as Canterbury, and as far north as Telford, both places far outside of Wæcla's territory. The name, evidently, possesses some charm or power that other local names lacked. That the name jumped the Thames and spread to the southern leg of the road is a reminder that, although we now mentally view the A2 and the A5 as separate roads, it was still a single route to our medieval ancestors. This is evident in the first pictorial representation of the road that we possess, a diagram drawn in the thirteenth century by the St Albans monk Matthew Paris. He drew the road running from Dover to Chester.

Like other medieval scholars, Paris described Watling Street as one of the four royal highways, together with Icknield Way (from Wiltshire to Norfolk), Ermine Street (also known as the Great North Way, from London to Lincoln or York) and the Fosse Way (from Exeter to Lincoln). These roads were given this status in pre-Norman times, when the Laws of Edward the Confessor stated that the 'King's Peace' applied to them. Anyone travelling along them was under the protection of the king and any crime committed on them would be tried by the king's own officers, not by local courts. These royal highways inspired the 'Kingsroad' in the fantasy saga *Game of Thrones*.

Paris said that Watling Street was pre-Roman. He claimed that it was built by the British king Belinus, who ruled in the fourth century BCE and whose story was recounted by the Welsh cleric Geoffrey of Monmouth. Geoffrey tells us how Belinus the Great fought bitterly with his brother Brennius until they teamed up, took their armies across Europe and invaded Rome. Historians now consider Belinus and Brennius to be fictional characters, although Rome was attacked by a Gaulish king named Brennus in 390 BCE, so there may be a spark of fact underneath the myth.

When we peer into the darkness of prehistory in search of Watling Street's pre-Roman history we leave archaeology behind and enter the fog of myth. This fog is untrustworthy but it is not entirely dark and, in the absence of any concrete facts, the light within it can't fail to attract our attention. The name Belinus is related to the Celtic sun god Belenus, who is celebrated at the Beltane festival we now call May Day. When Paris says that Watling Street is the creation of Belinus, he is pointing us at a road created by a mythical personification of the blazing sun itself. That Watling Street dictated the orientation of Milton Keynes, and aligned its streets to the summer solstice sunrise, suddenly seems entirely appropriate.

What is interesting about Paris's description is the idea that Watling Street was planned as a long-distance route, in a similar manner to Roman roads. According to Paris, it was more than a series of meandering local routes that happened to become connected. An undertaking like this suggests a degree of planning and national consciousness not usually associated with Celtic tribes, but there is evidence for it from the road itself. Both the southern and northern routes of Watling Street were originally aimed at what is now Westminster, where the Houses of Parliament today stand. Before the Romans built the first bridge over the Thames, this was the most practical ford over the River. Many long-distance British routes that were thought to be prehistoric, such as the Ridgeway and the Pilgrim's Way, are now suspected of being more recent, but the Westminster alignment makes a strong case for Watling Street being pre-bridge, and therefore pre-Roman. A practical, long-distance route like this raises the intriguing possibility of a design grander than the work of local tribes, but we cannot say any more about this because here the light in the fog goes out, and we find ourselves groping about in darkness again.

The Romans, being eminently practical, based their long, straight roads on local routes that naturally followed firmer ground and more passable territory. Before the land enclosure acts of the eighteenth and nineteenth centuries, British roads were not as neatly defined as we think of them now. They were more like the paths you follow when walking in the countryside. A route may be reasonably well defined for much of the journey, but on muddier or rougher ground mini-paths branch away from the primary route for short periods, and the traveller takes whichever path seems the most practical at the time. Even as late as the great age of coach travel in the eighteenth century, it was normal for a coach to travel across neighbouring fields, and through any crops planted there, when the road itself was impassable. Parts of the Icknield Way, to give one example, are thought to have once been up to a mile across. The exception to this were Roman roads, which were physically constructed on a raised bed of stones, often to a strictly defined width of 8 *pedes*, or Roman feet, and 12 *pedes* on bends. For a Roman road to follow a pre-existing native road was to fix a straight, clearly defined line through a meandering, fuzzy, constantly evolving route.

English poets have never really forgiven the Romans for bringing straight lines to Britain. 'Before the Roman came to Rye or out to Severn strode / The rolling English drunkard made the rolling English road,' wrote G. K. Chesterton in 1913. His appreciation of 'A reeling road, a rolling road, that rambles round the shire' would no doubt have made sense to William Blake. 'Improvement makes strait roads,' Blake wrote in *The Marriage of Heaven and Hell*, 'but the crooked roads without Improvement are roads of Genius.'

The poets may well be right in thinking that straight roads are out of character for this island. After the Romans left, there were no more attempts to build arrow-straight roads until the first section of the M1 motorway opened in 1959. This section, between junctions 5 and 18 of the current road, was designed to be as straight as the pre-war German autobahns or the American interstates then being built. It fulfilled the modernist motorway dream of a landscape-defying race to the vanishing point of the horizon. But the British motorist was deeply unimpressed. A straight line may be the fastest route between two points, but it was also the least interesting. As an *Observer* journalist noted at the time, driving along the M1 was like 'riding in a train without a book [...] safe, comfortable, relaxing and a dreadful bore'. This lesson being quickly learnt, the country's next motorway, the M6, was instead designed as continuous flowing curves. This proved to be much more satisfying to the British motorist, and all subsequent motorways have followed this pattern.

But none of this helps us discover how old Watling Street is. For all we know, the feet that first marked out the route could have belonged to Puck, our first man. It may even be older than that. Many paths were created by animals, snuffling through the undergrowth, seeking a route through the woodland. Humans may simply have followed the best routes that boar or deer laid down.

All we can really say about the age of Watling Street is that it is older than history.

The Canterbury Tales was the inspiration for the 1944 wartime film *A Canterbury Tale*, by Michael Powell and Emeric Pressburger.

It begins with a re-creation of Chaucer's pilgrimage, with his merry band of laughing medieval travellers making their way on horseback through the idyllic Kent countryside. One character launches his hawk and watches the bird fly high into the summer sky. A jump cut causes the hawk to change into a Second World War fighter plane, and we suddenly find ourselves in the same countryside 600 years later. This was the shot that inspired Stanley Kubrick's famous jump cut from *2001: A Space Odyssey*, where a bone weapon thrown by an early hominid cuts to an orbiting space station.

The film then introduces us to three characters – a British sergeant, a land girl and an American sergeant – who befriend each other when they stop in a small Kent village one night on their way to Canterbury. Under the darkness of the blackout, a dark figure rushes up and pours glue over the land girl's hair. The villagers are not surprised when they hear about this, for the 'glue man' is a known local nuisance and has poured glue on girls' heads on eleven previous occasions. Our three new friends decide to work together to solve the mystery of the glue man.

To watch *A Canterbury Tale* now is to be transported back to a long-vanished era, a land of tight-knit rural communities in the pre-television era, and also a time when filmmakers could actually pitch a story as weird as the glue-man mystery and still get their film made. Our heroes encounter a local magistrate called Thomas Colpeper, played by Eric Portman, who gives lectures about the unchanging spirit of the English countryside along the 'Old Pilgrim Road' to Canterbury. Here he confuses Chaucer's Watling Street with a walking route from Winchester that was romantically given the name 'The Pilgrim's Way' in Victorian times. Nevertheless, the characters in the film hear the shaking of bells, the sound of hooves and the laughter of the pilgrims when they are out on the road and, as Colpeper explains, 'those noises come from inside, not outside'. Chaucer's pilgrims echo down the ages, part of the subconscious of every English-speaker.

For Colpeper, to walk through the Kent countryside is to be connected with the long-vanished characters of *The Canterbury Tales*. 'When you see the bluebells in the spring and the wild thyme, and the broom and the heather,' he says, 'you're only seeing what their eyes saw. You ford the same rivers. The same birds are singing. When you lie flat on your back and rest, and watch the clouds sailing, as I often do, you're so close to those other people, that you can hear the thrumming of the hoofs of their horses, and the sound of the wheels on the road, and their laughter and talk, and the music of the instruments they carried. And when I turn the bend in the road, where they too saw the towers of Canterbury, I feel I've only to turn my head, to see them on the road behind me.'

After our three main characters solve the mystery of the glue man, they complete their journey to Canterbury by taking a train with

Colpeper. Here the story abruptly changes from a quirky mystery to a spiritual fable. Colpeper remarks that 'a pilgrimage can be either to receive a blessing, or to do penance'. Each character discovers which of these fates awaits them in the bombed-out streets of wartime Canterbury.

The odd tonal mix of *A Canterbury Tale* is strange for an audience used to the conservative narratives of modern cinema, but the combination of farce, mystery, rural romanticism and spiritual fable is entirely in keeping with Chaucer's invocation of 'God's plenty'. The original *Canterbury Tales* was never finished, because Chaucer did not live long enough to give his pilgrims all the stories he originally planned. What Powell and Pressburger did in 1944 was to pick up the open-ended, incomplete nature of Chaucer's work and declare that all journeys to Canterbury are part of the same continuing story, even those that are set 600 years later, and even those that are occurring now.

All travellers to the city are pilgrims, whether they realise it or not. This is a striking thought, as the A2 crests the North Downs and the spires of Canterbury Cathedral are briefly revealed through the trees, just as they had been to Colpeper and to Chaucer before him. Seeing Canterbury approach through the windscreen as I drive north on a modern A road, I suddenly understand that what is happening now is as much a part of the story of Britain as any long-gone pilgrimage.

A message has been passed down via Chaucer, Powell and Pressburger, encoded in our ever-useful language, informing me that this journey is no different to any journey that has come before. When I started my travels, I was looking at history as something external. I thought of it as a block of events which I could wander round and peer at from different angles, like a critic in an art gallery. In truth, we are inside history, shaping and forming it, not outside and judging it. We are not separate. We have responsibilities.

English is a powerful tool, and the advantage that put these islands on the map, but powerful tools need to be used responsibly. Words can bring us together and they can push us apart. I glance again at the capitalised words on the front of the papers on the seat next to me, wondering to what extent they reflect our divide or create it. The relative lack of text on the front pages, today of all days, is strange. It is as if this referendum is not taking place on the rational, logical level of language.

On this referendum day the future is unknown, but it's clear we are a troubled and divided country. There is a suspicion that the steady progress of globalisation may have peaked, that we are entering a time of walls rather than bridges, and that like dinosaurs our political organisations have become too big and must now fall back.

I arrive at Canterbury. Whether I'll receive a blessing or do a penance remains to be seen.

3.

CANTERBURY

A saint ranks higher than a king

If you're looking for an example to shed light on why there is so much political disillusionment in this country, then you can't get much better than the privatisation of the Royal Mail.

For nearly 500 years the postal service was an important part of our national infrastructure. The cost of sending a letter was the same, regardless of whether it was sent to someone a few streets away or whether it went from the coast of Cornwall to the highlands of Scotland. This strengthened our sense of geographic identity because, in the eyes of the Royal Mail, we were all equal. Their postcode system unified the country.

There was no public or democratic call for Royal Mail to be sold off, but sold off it was. It was done methodically, over many years and over a number of parliaments, by politicians from the Labour, Liberal Democrat and Conservative parties. It happened because a European Union Directive required the postal sector to be fully open to competition. The British people, who technically owned the Royal Mail, had no say in this. There was no way in which we could have prevented it from happening.

The first stage on the road to privatisation was called deregulation.

This allowed private or foreign state-owned companies to bid for the simpler, more profitable parts of the service, such as the bulk mail trade from large organisations. This post did not come in random sizes and wasn't hand-addressed, so it could be sorted by machines. This meant that companies like TNT, UKMail and CityMail could do this work cheaply and still make a profit. Once sorted, this mail was then returned to the Royal Mail for the more difficult job of delivering it to people's homes. The Post Office pension scheme was taken over by the government, in order to make the company more attractive to private investors. Casual agency staff gradually replaced full-time workers.

During this time insider accounts of Royal Mail deregulation appeared in publications including *The Guardian* and the *London Review of Books*, detailing the gulf between what politicians were saying and what was actually happening. These were the work of a postman who, in order to protect his job, wrote under the pen name 'Roy Mayall'.

Roy Mayall also wrote a wonderful short book called *Dear Granny Smith*. 'Granny Smith' is the nickname that postworkers use for the people they deliver mail to. 'Granny Smith' is everyone, but especially old ladies, isolated and perhaps infirm, for whom daily contact with their postman was a lifeline. In his book, Mayall recounts the time he and his fellow postal workers were taken into a 'team meeting' and told their emphasis was now on pleasing corporate clients. One postman raised a hand and asked, 'What about Granny Smith?' The management's response was, 'Granny Smith doesn't matter any more.'

Mayall joined the Royal Mail when the post was still delivered at breakfast time, people knew their regular postman and every village had a post office. He saw being a postal worker as a privilege and a responsibility, for postmen know when people are on holiday, and know when they are out of their routines. Like many postal workers, he had raised the alarm when an elderly 'Granny Smith' on his round had fallen ill, and saved her life. This doesn't happen with mail delivered by self-employed couriers who arrive in the evening, driving their own cars and rushing their deliveries to make minimum wage.

Privatisation occurred because a European committee believed in neoliberal economic theory, a political ideology that requires a constant supply of new markets to function. If new markets don't appear as they are expected to do then they must be created by politicians, as the alternative is to accept that neoliberal economics does not work. So the 500-year-old Royal Mail was taken to market, and there was nothing we could do about it. It was sold for £180 million less than it was worth, angering taxpayers but making the city investors who advised on the sale extremely wealthy.

Roy Mayall's true identity is Whitstable-based writer C. J. Stone, who is possibly best known for the Housing Benefit Hill column he used to write for *The Guardian*. 'You can out me, if you like,' he told me. 'What are they going to do? I'll be retiring soon.'

C. J. Stone

Although I must have read his writing in *The Guardian* and *The Big Issue*, I first consciously encountered Chris's work when I read his book *Fierce Dancing* in the early nineties. This was an account of his travels in counterculture and began with a memorable quote from an underground fanzine: 'We shall celebrate with such fierce dancing the death of your institutions.' I have vivid memories of losing myself in that book back when I lived in Liverpool. I can still see the book on my shelves and recall how its strong blue spine looked against the cheap red shelving unit I kept books on. But the book was not released until 1996, after I had left Liverpool and my red shelves behind. My recollection of reading the book before then is very strong, but it must be a false memory. The alternative is that a copy of the book fell back through a crack in time. I consider this extremely unlikely, but, knowing Chris, I can't entirely rule it out.

CJ, or Chris, became acutely political while watching the privatisation of the Post Office from the inside. Yet he is also a pilgrim who regularly walks the Pilgrim's Way. This rare combination of political and spiritual interests makes him a perfect guide to Canterbury. He is, if nothing else, the only person I know who has suffered the embarrassment of being caught praying by a Marxist.

The history of Canterbury goes back a long time. It was originally the Kentish stronghold of a Celtic tribe called the Cantiaci. After the Roman conquest it was rebuilt as a city with a temple, a forum, public baths and streets in a grid pattern. A wall was built around the city to prevent the Cantiaci from reclaiming their home. There were seven gates in this wall, and the one in the south-east was called Riding Gate. It was attached to a guard tower, was wide enough to allow two carriageways to enter and had a wooden drawbridge which lowered over a defensive moat. This was how Watling Street entered Canterbury.

After the Romans left, the city was known by the Welsh name *Cair Ceint*, which translates as the Fortress of Kent. The city was conquered by the Jutes, who gave it the Old English name *Cantwareburh*. The Roman gate was replaced by a medieval one, which gradually became neglected. The growing volume of traffic entering the city became too much for the narrow medieval gate and was diverted to another entrance. For a period Riding Gate was only really used to take rubbish out of the city. It was eventually widened, and it is now the city entrance used by Park & Ride buses.

Walking in through the gate, you immediately see street name signs that read 'Watling Street'. This is the southernmost part of this road that still uses the old name. A few yards further on, and we find Watling Street car park, which is where I meet Chris Stone.

Chris is in his early sixties, with gleaming white hair and a white goatee beard. His native Birmingham accent has gained a rural twang over the years, giving him a voice that matches his smiling face. He greets me with his usual cheery welcome and takes me through the streets of Canterbury towards the cathedral. As we walk he explains what brought him to prayer.

'The reason I started praying was that a friend of mine's son died,' he says. 'I couldn't imagine anything worse and I was trying to think of the most meaningful way I could to send my condolences. I had all these clichés in my head and none of them seemed adequate. The words "you are in my thoughts" just felt shallow somehow. So I wrote "you are in my prayers". That seemed to be the deepest and most meaningful thing I could say under the circumstances.

'But that set me thinking. What I decided was that prayer is sacralised thought. It is thought directed at a higher being, however you conceive that to be. To a Christian, that's Christ, of course. To a devotee of Krishna it is Krishna. It doesn't matter who you pray to, the point is you are praying to someone, or something, higher up than yourself, that has a wider perspective than you, that can see further.

'Perhaps it is your own higher self, your future self, generations down the line, when you have more wisdom than you have now. You are praying for guidance on your life's journey to someone who is able to see where it is all leading.

'So that's how I started praying. I had a little shrine in my room, with an icon of the Madonna above it, with a picture of some of my ancestors and a totem of an African river god. I was covering all the bases. And I would get down on my knees and pray, in the devotional manner, with my hands held together in front of my face. But I shared my flat with a Marxist for a while. This was someone who had once been in the Socialist Workers Party. He had pictures of Leon Trotsky on his wall. I lived in dread of my Marxist friend catching me at it. I thought there can be nothing more humiliating than being caught praying by a Marxist except, maybe, being caught masturbating by your mum.'

He laughs as he says this, but then winces again at the memory.

'That was exactly how it felt: as if I was doing something grubby and obscene, something you would be ashamed to let your mum catch you at. That's strange isn't it? People have been praying for thousands of years, maybe since the beginning of history, but in our modern, secular world being caught praying feels almost as transgressive as masturbating in public. Which is a good reason for doing it in my book.

'I've always lived in the weird space between the spiritual and the political. I have political friends, like my flatmate, the Marxist, and I have spiritual and countercultural friends: Druids and Wiccans, Buddhists and Pagans, even a few Christians, but they are very rarely in the same room at the same time.

'Most people actively avoid both subjects. It's not considered polite to talk about either in public. Spirituality is dismissed as airy-fairy, self-indulgent stuff, and politics is often seen as this amoral, corrupt, tribal thing. But I think the problem is that they both need each other. Politics needs to be grounded in morality, and spirituality needs to actually be of value to society. I think spirituality can redeem politics, and politics can redeem spirituality. Look at this...'

Chris points out a large-breasted, cloven-hooved gargoyle with a wild, gleeful grin that looks down at us from the otherwise respectable building we are passing. 'That's great, isn't it? It's a lovely city, is Canterbury.'

Despite the horrific damage done by German bombs in the Second

World War, the old town is still recognisable from the black-and-white footage in *A Canterbury Tale*. It is a busy, eccentric city, where modern chain shops mingle with old, leaning buildings and the sort of curiosities you only find in truly ancient places.

Canterbury gargoyle

Canterbury Cathedral is part of a UNESCO World Heritage site, because of the magnificence of the building itself and its importance in the story of British Christianity. The cathedral stands on the site of a church built in the early seventh century by Saint Augustine, an Italian missionary sent to Britain by the Pope. Augustine landed on the Isle of Thanet in 597 and made his way to Canterbury, with the intention of converting Æthelberht, the local king, to Christianity. Although Britain had previously been Christian in the later part of the Roman period, the religion had not survived in areas settled by pagan Anglo-Saxons.

Augustine knew that converting a king was the best way to establish his religion on this island, because a king could impose a religion on his people. He achieved this with help from Æthelberht's Germanic wife, Bertha, who was already a Christian herself. In doing so he began this island's problematic relationship between political authority and the spiritual authority of the Church.

In July 1174 King Henry II, the great-grandson of William the Conqueror, landed at Southampton. He had left his beloved continental lands to return to England because the country faced rebellion and invasion. Philip of Flanders had landed an army in East Anglia, having sworn on a holy relic that he would lead a full-scale invasion of England, and the Scottish king, William the Lion, was mustering forces and attacking from the north.

Instead of heading straight to East Anglia to tackle Philip, Henry rode to Canterbury. He dismounted outside the city and walked the last part of his journey to the cathedral barefoot.

The previous Archbishop of Canterbury, the murdered Thomas Becket, had been canonised by the Pope a year earlier. Becket had been cut down by four knights in his own cathedral in 1170. Henry didn't specifically order the knights to kill him, but they committed the act after he exclaimed in frustration, 'What miserable drones and traitors have I nurtured and promoted in my household who let their lord be treated with such shameful contempt by a low-born clerk?' Popular legend prefers to shorten this to the infamous question, 'Will no one rid me of this turbulent priest?'

When the four knights arrived at the cathedral, they left their weapons underneath a tree and hid their chainmail armour under cloaks before they entered. They confronted Becket, but he refused to submit to the king's will. So they went back outside, and reclaimed their swords. When they returned, the monks were chanting vespers, the sunset prayer, which is now more commonly known in the Anglican tradition as evensong.

The four knights killed Becket in the north-west transept. The top of his head was sliced off. An eyewitness account of the attack by Edward Grim, a man who was also injured in the attack, recounts how 'the crown of his head was separated from the head in such a way that the blood white with the brain, and the brain no less red from the blood, dyed the floor of the cathedral. The same clerk who had entered with the knights placed his foot on the neck of the holy priest and precious martyr, and, horrible to relate, scattered the brains and blood about the pavements, crying to the others, "Let us away, knights; this fellow will arise no more." '

Monks rushed forward to collect Becket's blood in vessels while it still flowed from his body. It would prove to be a lucrative asset in the pilgrim trade to come. Canterbury monks would sell 'Becket water' to the devout; it was said to contain a trace of the martyr's blood, and to have miraculous healing properties, although it would only work if the patient was sufficiently devout.

The four knights were not arrested, but they were excommunicated and ostracised. They travelled to Rome to seek forgiveness from the Pope. He ordered them to undertake a pilgrimage to the Holy Land for fourteen years, then spend the rest of their lives living alone in prayer and lamentation on the Black Mountain near Antioch.

Many thought that the sin of Becket's murder was on the king; it's possible Henry thought so himself. His pilgrimage to the shrine of Becket – once a friend, later an enemy and now a saint – was to cleanse himself of that sin, both in his own eyes and in the eyes of the world.

Crowds lined the streets to witness the penitent king. He walked into the cathedral and, with 'streaming tears, groans and sighs', knelt before the martyr's tomb, his arms outstretched, praying for forgiveness. He asked the assembled bishops for absolution, and was stripped to the waist and beaten. Each of the bishops and the dozens of monks present gave the king between three and five blows with a rod. Cut and bleeding, he spent a vigil at the tomb, then fasted for three days. Flagellation and pain are now seen as sexual fetishes and not heavily promoted by the modern Church of England, but in medieval Christianity they were all part of the practice of the pious. After he was killed Becket was discovered to be wearing a rough hairshirt crawling with lice underneath his Archbishop's robes, and this was seen as evidence of his devout spirituality.

If the aim of the king's public humiliation was to cleanse himself and bring God back onside, it worked. The king was still in bed at Canterbury when an exhausted messenger, who'd ridden all the way from Northumberland, arrived and informed him that William the Lion had unexpectedly been captured. Delighted, and thanking God and Saint Becket, the king soon defeated the forces of Philip in East Anglia and brought stability back to his English realm. Becket, clearly, was a powerful saint to invoke.

Before we pay our respects to the martyr Thomas Becket, Chris and I rest in the window seats of The Old Buttermarket, a dark wooden pub on the opposite side of the square from the elaborately carved Gothic cathedral gate. We talk about the conflict between political and spiritual ideas.

'Many people would say that the two things are incompatible,' I say to Chris. 'People tend to gravitate to one or the other.'

He shakes his head. 'Both are unavoidable,' he says. 'I always think it's a joke when people tell me they're not interested in politics. So, you're not interested in life? Politics is everywhere. Whenever you put a group of people together, there's politics going on, and that applies whether you're in the Socialist Workers Party, the Labour Party, the Tory Party, a meditation group or a knitting circle. There's always some vying for attention. There's always some jostling for position. You either become conscious of that, and attach your politics to a greater cause, or you allow your life to be controlled by the kind of petty politics that drags us all down to the lowest common denominator.

'At the heart of politics is the question of authority. If someone puts a tollgate across a road, by what authority do they do so? Why is it that I have to give them money, rather than they give me money? Obviously the usual answer is the law, but laws are things we've made up, they could be anything. Who frames those laws, and who do they benefit?

That's where politics comes in. Political argument is a clash between those who want to broaden out the benefits and the ones who want to control the tollgate, as it were, for themselves.'

Chris looks out of the pub window, past the medieval stone cross in the centre of the square, and at the Gothic entrance to the cathedral grounds opposite.

'The world we live in is a politically constructed world and to be able to see beyond it takes a great effort,' he continues. 'There's very few people who examine things like claims to authority, and to property, and to who owns what. I think these are fundamentally spiritual questions because they relate to how we think of ourselves and who we think we are.

'I know there's a lot of people who would disagree with my use of the word "spiritual" in this context. I get that all the time because when I say "spiritual" I'm meaning something different to "religious". Religion is weaponised spirituality. It's political. The role of religion is to harness people's natural spirituality in service of the State. Historically the priest was a propagandist for the establishment: his role was to inculcate the values of the State into the minds of the congregation. Everyone must know their place. The King is on the top, as the representative of God on Earth, and you are on the bottom, and it is your job to serve God by serving the King.

'At the same time, there is a battle going on between different ideas of spirituality. It's a battleground. This is where the dissenting tradition comes from. Quakers, Baptists, Levellers, Diggers: they have different beliefs than the State-sponsored religion. They believe in a higher power than the King and a different way of accessing the truth than from the pulpit. It is this different tradition that leads to people like Martin Luther King, Gandhi, Tolstoy: politically engaged figures who argue from the spirit to politics and not the other way round. Did you know that Tolstoy developed his ideas from corresponding with Quakers in America and that he was also in correspondence with Gandhi? Gandhi influenced Martin Luther King, so there's a direct line from the dissenters of the English Civil War to the civil rights movement in America, via an aristocratic Russian novelist and an anglicised Indian barrister. Gandhi and Tolstoy both rejected their backgrounds and dressed in peasant clothes to signify that their authority came from a different source.'

I head to the bar and, when I return, Chris has remembered a more recent example to illustrate what he is talking about; one who, like Chris, had lived only a few miles north of Canterbury.

'Look at Brian Haw,' he says. 'He spent his teenage years in Whitstable. He was an evangelical Christian and he couldn't live with all the deaths of the children in Iraq caused by the UN sanctions in the late nineties. He was camped out on Parliament Square before the war in Iraq even started but, obviously, once it had he was against that too. It was just morally unacceptable to him, all those dying children, and he had to do something. So he left home, he left his own wife and his own children, his job, his home, his security and went out to live on the street. He said he wouldn't live in a house again until the killing stopped.

'See, you don't get political activists as motivated as that, do you? You don't get members of the Conservative or Labour Party giving up their whole lives in defence of a moral position. Brian Haw was willing to die for his beliefs, that's the difference.

'I often think of him and Tony Blair as like the two faces of spirituality. They both declared themselves to be Christians, but one was willing to start wars and see the slaughter of innocents for a political end, while the other became like a street hermit, a modern-day version of those medieval saints living in caves that people would make pilgrimages to visit and be blessed by. People made pilgrimages to see Brian Haw too, only he didn't bless you, he activated you. He made you want to go out in the world and make a difference, like he had.

'Tony Blair must have hated him. He was like this constant admonishment on the pavement below, reminding him of his moral duty as a Christian, making him aware of how short he fell of his own stated ideals. Haw defined Blair as the hypocrite he was.

'And his life was hard. People need to know that. He suffered out there, on the streets. He was on his own. He was beaten up and arrested many times. He was a fixture, so the authorities knew where he was, and once he was alone, late at night, when everyone else had gone home, he was very vulnerable. They would send people in to get him, to bust his tent, to throw away his placards, to trash his site. And he was a radical pacifist like Martin Luther King and Tolstoy before him, so he couldn't defend himself. But he was fierce. He was like John the Baptist roaring out his truths to the world, rock-solid, like this monument to moral certitude carved out of the spirit, awesome and awe-inspiring at the same time. No amount of intimidation would move him. It's a pity he's hardly known outside the UK, while Blair, of course, has a world-wide reputation.

'So the politicians made new laws to outlaw protests on Parliament Square and said it was because of terrorists or that the protest camp looked untidy for the tourists. They tried to get rid of him that way, but they weren't able to apply the laws retrospectively, so he remained where he was. But the real reason they wanted him gone is that they knew he was backed by another authority than their own, one that they were ultimately unable to argue with. Theirs was a political authority, the authority of the State, but his was a spiritual or moral authority, and it doesn't matter whether you believe in God or not, the one trumps the other every time.

'That's the ultimate standoff between the political world and the spiritual world. Politics is pragmatic and self-serving. More often than not people are in it for what they can get out of it, for themselves and their class. It's ruthless, occasionally violent. If something stands in your way, you get rid of it. In certain extreme circumstances, you kill it.

'It's the other way round in the spiritual realm. If you are a truly spiritual person, you recognise everyone as part of yourself. Thus you can't stand back and allow the innocent to suffer. You have to get engaged. You have to sacrifice. Ultimately you have to be willing to die for your beliefs. So when political authority confronts spiritual authority, and neither will back down, that's when bloodshed occurs. The political authority kills the spiritual, and at this point the spiritual authority wins, because the people make him a saint and he continues to inform us for generations to come.

'It's an old, old story this. It's Jesus on the Cross. It's the Christian martyrs being thrown to the lions. It's Saint Sebastian and the arrows, as well as Thomas a Becket and the murder in the cathedral. And then it's Martin Luther King and Brian Haw in the modern world as well. Even when the person sacrificing themselves for the greater good is a Marxist atheist, like Che Guevara, they take on some of the patina of spirituality in the process. Che is virtually a secular saint these days. All those icons of him everywhere you look. I'd be surprised if people aren't praying to his image even now.

'Spiritual authority speaks to us from beyond the grave. That's its power. The grave becomes an object of veneration and the destination of our pilgrimage, a place where even the highest political authority in the land has to humble himself, to get down on his knees to pray, as Henry II humbled himself before the shrine of Thomas a Becket, and as Tony Blair may one day have to humble himself before the grave of Brian Haw. Who knows?'

Thomas Becket was not the only Archbishop of Canterbury to be murdered. In the year 1012 the Archbishop Ælfheah was killed by Vikings at Greenwich, after he refused to allow anyone to pay his ransom. As the *Anglo-Saxon Chronicle* told the story, the Vikings 'were very drunk, because there was wine brought from the south. Then they seized the bishop, led him to their hustings on the Saturday in the octave of Easter, and then pelted him there with bones and the heads of cattle; and one of them struck him on the head with the butt of an axe, so that with the blow he sank down and his holy blood fell on the earth.' Ælfheah's bones were later brought home to Canterbury Cathedral, and Becket himself prayed to them before he himself was killed. Yet Ælfheah is all but forgotten now. The thousandth anniversary of his murder in 2012 produced little in the way of remembrance. In contrast, the relationship between Becket and Henry remains the most famous story of the twelfth century. This tells us that the resonance of the story is not solely down to the horror of an archbishop's murder. The power and longevity of the story comes, it seems, from the relationship between Henry and Becket itself.

Becket was born on Cheapside in London, the son of a merchant turned landlord. He was born to a Norman family and hence was a member of the ruling elite, but his background was humble for a man who would become such a close confidant of the king. Their social gulf tends to be stressed in accounts of his story, which portray him as a devoted man of the people. The lavish, Oscar-winning 1964 film *Becket*, which starred Richard Burton as Becket and Peter O'Toole as Henry, went as far as making him a Saxon. It portrayed their relationship as a bromance, with the pair 'drinking and wenching' together in the happy years after Henry raised Becket to the position of his Lord Chancellor. Burton portrayed Becket at this point in his life as an amoral opportunist, comfortable with betraying his Saxon kin for the privilege of the king's favour. As he says, 'Where honour should be, in me there is only a void.'

In the film, Peter O'Toole portrays Henry II as a heartbroken man jilted by Becket, the only person he ever truly loved. O'Toole's Henry is consistent with most English portrayals of Normans, in that he plays him as cruel, unloved and slightly camp. The film starts with his penitent vigil in front of Becket's tomb. His opening lines are, 'Well, Thomas Becket, are you satisfied? Here I am stripped, kneeling at your tomb, while those treacherous Saxon monks of yours are getting ready to thrash me. Me! With my delicate skin!'

Their problems began when Henry nominated Becket for the position of Archbishop of Canterbury over the fury of his bishops, who knew that Becket's loyalty was to the king and not Rome. Neither the bishops nor Henry expected that Becket would devote himself to the church and allow that devotion to override his friendship with the king. In the church, Becket discovered the honour he needed to fill his void. He was in the service of a higher power than the king of England.

The central issue in the dispute between Henry and Becket, that of ecclesiastic freedom from secular courts, is clearly not the reason for this story's lasting appeal. Becket was a man from Cheapside. He rose to become first a courtier and trusted friend of the king of England, then his equal (in Becket's eyes, if not Henry's) and finally his superior. The king was prostrate and beaten in front of Becket's shrine, because a saint ranks higher than a king. The man of noble blood bowed before the boy from the streets of London. The story resonates because it tells us that political power is not absolute.

Becket's shrine no longer exists. It was destroyed nearly 500 years ago as part of the dissolution of the monasteries. Henry VIII ensured that all Becket's bones were destroyed and that all mentions of his name were obliterated, for he knew the power of those relics to members of the Roman faith. Henry VIII also summoned the long-dead Saint Becket to court, in order to face an accusation of treason. Here he was mocking the Catholic belief in saints. Saint Thomas failed to appear, as Henry correctly guessed he would. He was found guilty in his absence.

The original position of the shrine is now marked by the flame of a single candle. Like the idea of a saint, it is immaterial and delicate and it should be easy to snuff out, and yet still it illuminates. As the modernist poet T. S. Eliot would later write in *Murder in the Cathedral*, his verse drama about Becket, 'the blood of thy martyrs and saints shall enrich the earth, shall create the holy places, for wherever a saint has dwelt, wherever a martyr has given his blood for the blood of Christ, there is holy ground. And the sanctity shall not depart from it, though armies trample over it, though sightseers come with guidebooks looking over it.' Even Henry VIII was unable to obliterate the spot where Becket was killed. Chris and I head there now, like the countless thousands who have travelled here before us, safe in the knowledge that two more curious heathen sightseers will not harm it.

The north-west transept is now known as the Martyrdom. Cold flagstones lie beneath a tower of stained glass and soaring, heaven-bound stone pillars, separating a pair of staircases on their way down to the crypt. The place of the murder is marked by a modern altar and a jagged, brutal metal sculpture. The sculpture represents swords bearing down on their victim with their sharp tips stained red. If you kneel at the altar, the swords seem to hang suspended above your head.

The Martyrdom

Placing twentieth-century art in traditional Christian settings is never straightforward. The film director George Hoellering, who directed the T. S. Eliot-scripted Becket film *Murder in the Cathedral* (1952), also made a short film called *Shapes and Forms* (1950) that explored how modern art resembles pagan, rather than Christian, imagery. Modernist sculpture can seem like intruders in churches, sneaking into the rarefied religious space like the stone imps, gargoyles and Sheela-na-gigs added by mischievous medieval masons. During the Second World War, Hoellering also shot a film called *Message from Canterbury* which has many echoes of Powell and Pressburger's *A Canterbury Tale*. Both films feature idealised scenes of land girls, shepherds and Kent country life, with the towers of Canterbury Cathedral visible in the distance between the branches of blossom-heavy trees. Both films also feature almost identical footage of Canterbury itself, with the cathedral looming untouched over bombsites and destroyed houses, while barrage balloons hang in the air.

Most of *Message from Canterbury* is taken up by a sermon delivered by Dr William Temple, the then Archbishop of Canterbury. The archbishop placed the German air raids in a wider historical context, comparing them to previous 'decisive climaxes in the spiritual history of our nation'. He includes Becket's murder as one such spiritual climax. He talked about Canterbury's church as the 'most magnificent in Christendom', where 'pilgrims wore the new stones smooth with their knees', and used the past as a promise that the cathedral would endure. Canterbury marked the site where Augustine planted Christianity in English soil. 'Even if these sacred stones had not been preserved, the spirit of Saint Augustine and Saint Thomas [Becket] would still inhabit this holy ground, inspiring us to new devotions and to new works,' he tells us. His message was that if the cathedral was reduced to rubble by the Luftwaffe then the sacredness of the ground would remain, just as Henry VIII could not wipe away the holiness of the ground where Becket was martyred.

Dr Temple then spoke of the future. When the war would be over, there would still be 'evils nearer home, which we as Christians should acknowledge, and strive to remedy. [...] As a general principle upon which alone the solid foundations of peace can be built, we should recognise that the resources of the earth should be used as God's gift to the whole human race.' The archbishop explained that, as Christians, they 'must demand dignity and decency of housing for every family, we should demand equal opportunity of education for every child, we should insist that every worker has a voice through his representative. [...] These are the requisites of a natural order, of a Christian social order.' The push towards what became the welfare state did not just come from the political world; it came from the spiritual too. A sermon like his seems unthinkably political today.

When a *Vanity Fair* journalist asked Tony Blair about his faith in 2003, Blair's director of strategy and communications intervened to insist that 'we don't do God.' Blair later converted to Catholicism, but did not feel he could do so when he was Prime Minister. He notified the Pope of his desire to convert on 23 June 2007, four days before he left office. For Blair, it seemed politics was more important than faith. The two could never mix. Faith had to wait until his political term was over.

We are now, in the words of the previous Archbishop of Canterbury, Rowan Williams, a 'post-Christian' country. This is a fairly uncontroversial statement, given the decline of church attendance over the last century. But, more significantly, we have now reached the point where we have stopped *pretending* to be a Christian country. This is a very recent phenomenon. In the 2001 Census, 14.8 per cent of British people said they had no religion while 71.7 per cent still described themselves as Christian, even though most were non-practising and non-churchgoing. Ten years later, in the 2011 census, the 'no religions' had grown to 25.1 per cent of the population while 59.3 per cent population still described themselves as Christian. But by 2014, according to a study by St Mary's Catholic University in Twickenham, the 'no religion' group had reached 48.5 per cent while those claiming to be Christian were only 43.8 per cent of the population. 'No religions' are now the majority, and Christians are the minority. We are finally admitting that we are not a Christian country. We are a country that happens to have some Christians in it.

If any single incident can symbolise the moment Britain stopped pretending to be a Christian country, it would be the defeat in parliament of a 2016 bill that sought to take in 3,000 Syrian children, orphaned or unaccompanied, who had fled the civil war in their own country. It was not just the defeat of the bill that was so striking, but the tone of the coverage the debate received in the newspapers. It is not spiritual morality that guides our political decisions, and it was not possible to follow that story and still cling to the illusion that Britain was a Christian country. As with the wider EU referendum debate, the fact that Christians are commanded to 'love thy neighbour' was not a factor.

Commenting on the political rise of Donald Trump in America, the *Daily Mail* remarked how the 'wails of disbelief' from politicians and the 'massed ranks of luvvies (Madonna, Lady Gaga, the Archbishop of Canterbury, Lily Allen, etc.) lay bare their utter incomprehension and contempt for the ordinary people whose interests they profess to hold dear'. In the eyes of this quintessentially middle-England newspaper, the Archbishop of Canterbury's words are no different to that of pop stars. His status or reputation no longer adds any credibility to his words.

It is strange to look back on Archbishop Temple's wartime sermon and realise that during that period of shared national purpose and post-war reconstruction spiritual and political authority did work together harmoniously. They can, on occasions, put aside their traditional antagonism. It does not always have to end in violence. It just needs both the political and spiritual worlds to put aside their land-grabs and accumulation of power, and dedicate themselves to the needs of the wider population. If it happened in the 1940s, then it can happen again.

Britain has now shrugged off Christianity, just as it shrugged off the French language when that was imposed by the Normans. Back when this cathedral was built, Christianity was the dominant feature of the noosphere. It overshadowed the rest of British thought, just as the medieval St Paul's Cathedral dominated the London skyline. But just as other buildings grew up around St Paul's and began to overshadow it, so too did other systems of thought grow in immaterial Britain. While Christianity remained largely static, science, culture, art and law all continued to evolve and expand. Our noosphere became more complicated and interesting. To put it simply, it became richer. Christianity remains, of course, but only as a smaller and smaller part of the greater whole. If there is still a moral authority out there somewhere, able to shame the political sphere, then it does not look likely that it will come from Christianity.

Chris leads me down the stone steps into the crypt. Rows of stone arches run the length of the underground chamber. Our footsteps echo differently down here.

Hanging suspended from the ceiling is a sculpture called *Transport*, by Antony Gormley. It is a life-size figure of a man, laid out stiffly but peacefully, floating in mid-air above head height. The figure represents Becket. It hangs above the space where his tomb originally sat, which is directly underneath the lit candle that marks his shrine in the chapel above.

Looking closely, I realise that no actual figure is present. Becket is just a shape suggested by the linked and connected nails that make up the sculpture. The nails themselves came from the lead roof tiles of the south-east transept, so they were part of the fabric of the cathedral itself. Gormley has used the material of the cathedral to plant the idea of this long-gone man in our minds. Those sharp nails which surround and define him echo the rough hair shirt that became a symbol of his devotion. By hanging in the air, the figure is eternally in the act of ascension, too much a part of this building to ever rise up to the candlelight above. I look at the sculpture and consider the name the artist gave it. Twentieth-century artworks have sat awkwardly in buildings like this, but Antony Gormley's has no such problems. It is a wonderful piece.

The persistence of an authority which doesn't materially exist hangs in the air. It is capable of lasting longer than the religion that formed it. It is an authority based in the other, which no one has been able to wipe out and no country has been able to shrug off.

Powell and Pressburger told us that everyone travelling to Canterbury was a pilgrim who would receive either a blessing or a penance. Not being a Christian, I had not expected to receive either from the relics of this historic religion. I had not anticipated stumbling upon a work by a living British artist who is able to succinctly reignite the story of this holy ground and pass that flame on directly. T. S. Eliot was right. Sanctity has not departed from this spot, regardless of whether armies trampled over it or sightseers with guidebooks came looking over it. It's amazing what you can create with the human imagination and a few old nails.

Like Chris, I stand in silence. Christianity was long seen as a unifying factor in British geographic identity. It had been capable of bringing morality into politics: for instance, in its role in the abolishment of the slave trade. The current political animosity towards refugees is as clear an example as any of our slow abandonment of Christianity over the course of the twentieth century. It's hard to imagine another state-sponsored religion being imposed to take its place. It's doubtful a modern-day Saint Augustine would get very far attempting to impose a foreign religion on these islands.

Yet, as Chris reminded us, religion is just weaponised spirituality. Religions may fall, but spirituality remains. This is, of course, incredibly frustrating for atheists. But it does mean that there is always the potential of a moral authority arising, one which is capable of confronting political authority.

I know that it's unlikely that Tony Blair will ever prostrate himself at the grave of Brian Haw. But following this visit to Canterbury, I can't entirely rule it out.

4.

CANTERBURY TO LONDON
The moonlit road of dreams

When I was a small boy, my dreams were always set in the same house. It was a huge, rambling collection of passages, doorways, nooks and stairwells that bore no relation to any house I had been in at that age. I remember it feeling incredibly old, with small windows and rough whitewashed walls. It was a house that had stood for a long time before I arrived and would be there a long time after I was gone. My dreaming hours were spent exploring that unending old house, climbing out of windows and over rooftops, discovering new passages and hidey-holes. Physically, the geography of the building made no sense at all, but in dreams that is not a concern. It was a house of delight, discovery and *cwtch*.

Those dreams stopped as I got older. Details were lost, or perhaps overwritten. But a memory lingered that was, like most dream memories, more a feeling than a concrete image. That house felt like a lazy Sunday afternoon in late spring.

I'm not sure at what age I first read Charles Dickens's *Great Expectations*, but at some point my old dream house and Satis House, Miss Havisham's rambling, decaying home in the book, became linked in my mind. Miss Havisham's house, Dickens wrote, 'was of old brick, and dismal, and had a great many iron bars to it. Some of the windows had been walled up; of those that remained, all the lower were rustily barred. There was a courtyard in front, and that was barred.' Inside, the house was always dark. When Dickens's hero Pip was first taken through those dark passages, he was guided by the light of a single candle. My dream house was not dark or foreboding like the one described by Dickens, so I wonder now why I ever connected the two.

It's possible that *Great Expectations*' horror was not apparent to me when I was young. Because children have yet to develop the full range of adult emotions, they are often unable to understand what adults are experiencing. The image of old Miss Havisham, still wearing her fading wedding gown years after being jilted before her wedding, can be funny to a child. It's only when you get older that you realise how disturbing it is.

Perhaps I recognised that the house was not so much a real building but a physical extension of its owner's mind. The isolated Miss Havisham rattled around a symbol of her own decayed soul in much the same way that I as a fresh, undamaged little dreaming thing tried to make sense of the world I found myself in. It may also be that I caught sight of the house as part of a TV adaptation years before I read the book and, paying little attention to the story, saw the building only as an exciting place to explore, or perhaps as a building that was also impossibly old. Whatever the reason, the house in *Great Expectations* is a place that now resonates with me in odd, personal ways. All buildings from fiction are immaterial, but Miss Havisham's house seems more dreamlike than most.

I am now standing in front of that house, looking across the courtyard at its red Elizabethan bricks and its dozens of tiny windows, crisscrossed with diamond-shaped strips of lead. Being here and seeing it in the real world is an odd experience, to put it mildly. It is even stranger when you know that the building only still exists because of the efforts of the children's entertainer Rod Hull, of Rod Hull and Emu fame.

Dickens based Miss Havisham's home on the building in front of me, which he knew from his childhood in Chatham, Kent. This is Restoration House in nearby Rochester, an Elizabethan manor house about 100 yards from Watling Street. It stands behind a red brick wall with a small courtyard in front and three-quarters of an acre of formal Tudor-style gardens behind, facing a public park called The Vines.

Restoration House

On 25 May 1660 the future King Charles II landed at Dover. He was in the process of reclaiming the throne that was taken from his father by Oliver Cromwell. Charles progressed up Watling Street, reached Rochester on 28 May and spent the night in this building. The house was later named Restoration House in his honour. The following day, 29 May, Charles reached London and was proclaimed king. It was his thirtieth birthday.

There was something very British about the Restoration. Both Britain and France had revolutions, and we both cut the heads off our monarchs. Both revolutions led to power vacuums and political instability, the rise of a military dictator in the form of Cromwell or Napoleon, and what would now be classed as a military coup. Both revolutions produced incredible bloodshed, as revolutions seem destined to do. The solution, in Britain, was to back-pedal, admit that the situation had got worse instead of better and find another king to replace the now unusable headless one. Charles's son was duly placed on the throne and a form of watered-down, less problematic monarchy was restored, one that was constitutional rather than absolutist. It's difficult to imagine the French ever doing something like that, whether for reasons of intellectual purity or just pride, no matter how much blood ran through the streets of Paris during the Reign of Terror. Unlike France, Britain is comfortable with making a mistake and fudging a solution. We don't mind a system that is irrational and indefensible, just as long as it works. This is not a sensible island, but it is a practical one. In the fallout from the referendum to leave the European Union, that can be helpful to remember.

By the late twentieth century Restoration House was in dire need of repair and was very nearly bulldozed in order to build a car park. It was saved by Rod Hull, who bought it for £275,000 in 1986. Hull was the man who carried an anarchic Emu hand puppet which attacked talk-show hosts and nibbled the Queen Mother's bouquet at the Royal Variety Show. But he was also a lifelong fan of Dickens and took pride in being a self-made Kent boy able to save such a historic building. Only one half of one wing of the building was then habitable, so he and his wife moved into those rooms as scaffolding was erected and restoration of the building began. He spent half a million pounds on repairs before his ITV series was cancelled and his income dwindled. With terrible timing, the late-eighties property crash and recession meant he was unable to sell the house, and a huge tax bill pushed him into bankruptcy.

Rod Hull was now penniless, and the house was taken from him by the receiver. His wife left him and took their children to Australia. He found that many of his showbiz friends stopped calling. 'You could just see the sadness in his eyes,' remembered Debbie Davidson, his daughter from his first marriage. 'He was quite sort of broken really.' A friend offered him a small, run-down National Trust cottage near Rye in Sussex, whose rent was an affordable £20 a week. He lived there with Emu until his death in 1999, when he was killed falling off the roof and into the greenhouse. He had been attempting to adjust the TV aerial to get better reception for a Champions League quarter-final football match.

Standing in front of this house is strange enough, but imagining Rod Hull wandering around inside its walls is a real challenge. I am unable to imagine him without the oversized blue bird underneath his arm, forever pecking away at Miss Havisham's decaying wedding cake or yanking at her disintegrating veil. Yet this building would not be here now if it was not for him. He is an integral part of its story.

When he took the property on in the 1980s, Restoration House would have looked more like Miss Havisham's Gothic home than it does now. It has been beautifully restored and is open to the public a couple of days a week for four months a year. The present owners have uncovered fashionable wall decorations from the seventeenth century, possibly added to the house for Charles II's visit, and large parts of the building have been restored to show how the house would have looked during this period. The formal garden, meanwhile, has been beautifully maintained with immaculate topiary, brick archways, statues and a pond shaped by Portland stone. Perhaps a house named Restoration was always destined to return to its former glory. It is wrong of me, no doubt, to wish that it had remained untouched and uncared for.

Rather than visit the house when it is open to the public during the summer months, I would prefer to stumble upon it one late autumn night, when a light fog obscures a low moon and a single candle in an upstairs window is the only sign of life in the dark building. That building, the one in my imagination, is the house I wish to explore. This is a foolish, romantic notion, I know, far removed from the necessity of saving such a property from car-park developers or other modern dangers. We may be a practical people on this island, but part of us swims against that practical nature. If anything can stimulate that part of us, it is childhood dreams and the strength of our fiction.

Watling Street is a road of dreams, imagination and stories, especially on this stretch between London and Canterbury. Given this it seems inappropriate, as you drive along in daylight, that the physical road is so regular and straight.

The Roman obsession with straight lines is apparent during much of this section of Watling Street. There is a distinct rhythm you experience when driving down an old Roman road in Britain. The vanishing point of the horizon remains stubbornly ahead, like in an American road movie, but you bob up and down as you drive, like a small boat approaching the mouth of an estuary, as your car travels over gently rolling countryside. Other roads don't ignore the landscape in this way. They follow its contours and let it lead them through the landscape. But the Romans were deaf to what the landscape was telling them. They single-mindedly aimed their roads straight, regardless of whether the land was flat, rolling, marsh or hilly.

The Kent landscape, even today, has a distinctive charm. This is the Garden of England. It is a place of extensive agriculture, and in particular of hops and fruit trees. Large estates of regularly spaced crops line the old road. They are interspersed with traditional Kentish oast houses, which were buildings used for drying hops. They have tall, conical roofs topped by what looks like the prow of an upturned row boat, which turns with the wind to provide ventilation for a fire below. This keeps all the hops hung inside at a manageable temperature; 'oast', essentially, means 'kiln'.

The road runs parallel between the coast and the North Downs, which is a high, long ridge of chalk topped by the Pilgrim's Way. The modern A2 is a road of traffic lights, small shops and bus stops adorned with ads for property apps. It remains largely faithful to the route of the old Roman road it is built over, occasionally swerving away to bypass a town centre or join up with other, more modern routes, but always returning to its straight-ahead origins like a snake winding its way along a telephone wire. It cuts through Boughton-under-Blean, Faversham, Sittingbourne, Rainham, Chatham and Rochester before crossing the River Medway at the Rochester Bridge. These were originally resting points for medieval pilgrims riding from London to Canterbury, and prospered during the age of the stage coach in the seventeenth and eighteenth centuries, only to see road traffic dwindle after the arrival of the railways. The rise of the motor car in the mid-twentieth century brought the traffic back in such numbers that it had to be syphoned away by new dual carriageways and motorways. Nowadays, these towns prosper from the same rail link that took away their traffic. It makes them convenient commuter towns for London workers.

Most of the Dover traffic now travels along the M20 or the M2 but, as I crawl through the slow-moving traffic outside Chatham, it's clear that there are still more than enough vehicles for Watling Street. It reminds me of the repeated complaints about Kent traffic, particularly around Maidstone, in Ian Fleming's James Bond novel *Moonraker*. A traffic jam does become more bearable if you know that James Bond was once stuck in it as well.

Bond, needless to say, remained unflappably and sleazily Bond-like throughout his journey. He drove along the same stretch of Watling Street we've just visited in a considerably more Bond-like manner than I just have. 'Bond took the short cut out of Canterbury by the Old Dover Road and looked at his watch. It was six-thirty,' Fleming wrote. 'The visibility was bad and he switched on his lights as he motored slowly along the coast-road, the ruby-spangled masts of the Swingate radar station rising like petrified Roman candles on his right. The girl? He would have to be careful how he contacted her and careful not to upset her. [. . .] The photograph on her record-sheet at the Yard had shown an attractive but rather severe girl and any hint of seductiveness had been abstracted by the cheerless jacket of her policewoman's uniform. Hair: Auburn. Eyes: Blue. Height: 5 ft. 7. Weight: 9 stone. Hips: 38. Waist: 26. Bust: 38. Distinguishing marks: Mole on upper curvature of right breast. Hm! thought Bond.' Fleming's novels are now politely referred to as 'a product of their time'.

It is hard to avoid fiction when you travel along this road. This is the same stretch of Watling Street used by Chaucer's pilgrims. Lord Byron and Charles Dickens made specific references to this route. We've already found links to it in books as diverse as *Great Expectations* and *Moonraker*. Further along, when Watling Street exits London from the north-west, it passes Elstree studios, which is the home of the *EastEnders* set. This is where many hundreds of British-made films were shot, from the 1920s to the present day, including Batman, Superman, The Muppets, X-Men, Dracula, Tarzan, Monty Python and Sherlock Holmes movies. It was here that Stanley Kubrick directed Jack Nicholson in *The Shining*, and here that Steven Spielberg directed Tom Hanks in *Saving Private Ryan*. Most bewitchingly of all, to someone of my generation, Elstree was where the original Indiana Jones and *Star Wars* films were shot. The Well of Souls from *Raiders of the Lost Ark* was the same piece of land as the Dagobah swamp from *The Empire Strikes Back*.

It amazes me to think that the road ridden by Chaucer's pilgrims in *The Canterbury Tales* is the same road alongside which George Lucas's *Star Wars* movies were shot. No other road anywhere in the world, I am certain, can claim to be more drenched in stories than this.

On some levels, stories tell us more about the past than physical archaeology. The second story told by Chaucer's pilgrims on their journey is a bawdy yarn called 'The Miller's Tale'. It followed the opening chivalrous romance recounted by a knight, because the miller, who was already drunk despite it being morning on the first day of the pilgrimage, disrupted the intended order of stories. The pilgrims were supposed to tell their tales in order of social rank, with the monk following the knight, but the miller was having none of it. He insisted on telling a crude, funny story which was the opposite of the knight's tale of courtly love.

The miller's story was about a beautiful, unfaithful carpenter's wife named Alisoun, who was having an affair with her lodger, Nicholas, while also being wooed by a student. To get her husband out of the way for a night she convinced him that God was sending a second flood, and that he would only be saved if he hung a boat from the barn roof and slept inside it while waiting for the coming waters. Alisoun and Nicholas hoped that this would give them an uninterrupted night in the carpenter's own bed. As Chaucer wrote in his still-comprehensible Middle English, 'Withouten wordes mo they goon to bedde, ther as the carpenter is wont to lye. Ther was the revel and the melodye; And thus lith Alison and Nicholas, in bisynesse of myrthe and of solas.'

At this point the student arrived at the house and called up to the bedroom window. He refused to leave without being granted a kiss, which gave Alisoun an idea for a joke. Taking advantage of the darkness of the night, she told him she would lean out of the window and grant him that kiss. She then turned round and stuck her naked backside out of the window. The student couldn't see this, and 'with his mouth he kist hir naked ers'.

Realising the deception, the student departed and returned with a red-hot poker, intent on revenge. He called again for another kiss, and for a laugh Nicholas stuck his bottom out of the window and farted a greeting. For his trouble, he received the red-hot poker 'amid the ers'. Burned, he called out for water, and was overheard by the carpenter, who thought that the flood was coming. The carpenter cut his boat loose and it crashed to the ground. The deception was uncovered, and the carpenter became a public laughing stock. A gang of students mocked him and, as a modern English translation puts it, 'Everyone among them laughed and joked. And so the carpenter's wife was truly poked.' 'The Miller's Tale' ends memorably by noting, 'And Nicholas is branded on the bum, and God bring all of us to Kingdom Come.'

We're currently travelling towards Shooter's Hill in south-east London, which is all the excuse we need to compare 'The Miller's Tale' to the 1974 British movie *Carry On Dick*. Shooter's Hill was a notorious haunt of highwaymen, either emerging masked from the dark forest with pistols drawn or hanged from gallows as a warning to all. Samuel Pepys described in his diary, on 11 April 1661, how 'Mrs. Anne and I rode under the man that hangs upon Shooter's Hill, and a filthy sight it was to see how his flesh is shrunk to his bones.' The hill is associated, if more in fiction than in fact, with the most famous highwayman of all, Dick Turpin and his horse Black Bess.

Carry On Dick is set in 1750 and tells of attempts by the newly established proto-police force the Bow Street Runners, led by Roger Daley (Bernard Bresslaw) and Captain Fancey (Kenneth Williams), to capture the notorious highwayman 'Big Dick' Turpin (Sid James). Much of the action takes place at the Old Cock Inn, between the villages of Upper Dencher and Lower Dencher. The locations are fictitious but, as they are described as being a night's ride from the capital on the London Road and they were filmed in Buckinghamshire, we can imagine they are on the north Buckinghamshire stretch of Watling Street.

Big Dick had been terrorising the London Road and taking the clothes of travellers at gunpoint. No one knew his true identity was that of a local parson named Reverend Flasher. The only clue Captain Fancey had to Big Dick's identity was that he was known to have 'a funny birth mark on his diddler'. Much of the film, therefore, recounts Fancey's attempts to get men's breeches down to look for this private birth mark.

Carry On Dick and 'The Miller's Tale' are undeniably similar in tone. They are both representative of a crude, bawdy, juvenile form of slapstick which is, and has always been, present in British comedy. We find it on the saucy seaside postcards of the 1950s, in the pages of *Viz* comic or in television comedies from *The Benny Hill Show* to *Little Britain*. It is a world of sexually predatory women and simpleton men, of frequent accidental undressing and innuendo, and of dirty laughs at the expense of establishment figures.

In both *Carry On Dick* and 'The Miller's Tale' the miscreants, be they thieves or adulterers, get away unharmed at the end while disaster falls on the authority figures. They are stories designed to prick pomposity and mock the self-righteous. They are wilfully unsophisticated and deliberately taboo-breaking, with the humour of the common man denying the authority of their social superiors. The way in which the drunk miller interrupted his social betters to lower the tone and insist on telling his preferred story is typical of this. This type of humour is also globally recognised as being distinctly British. You couldn't imagine India or Spain, for example, producing stories like 'The Miller's Tale' or *Carry On Dick*.

Nearly 600 years separate the two stories. In that time, Britain went from being a backward medieval country to a modern networked international state. An empire came and went, land was enclosed, and villagers were moved to cities to become first workers and then consumers. The rest of the world was encountered, learned from and absorbed. Population expanded massively, from about 1.5 million people recorded in the Domesday Book to about 65 million now. Britain became literate, and then media-literate. Our lives are now totally different to those of our medieval predecessors, and so is our culture. And yet this strain of humour remains unchanged. It is impervious to the social evolution of passing centuries and changes only in the details, like the spelling of the word 'ers' taking 600 years to mutate into 'arse'. It is almost as if it bubbles up from the land itself, contaminating anyone who happens to live here.

Stories tell us things about our ancestors that archaeology never can. They show us that people on this island, regardless of the century, always snigger at a socially inappropriate naked bum.

From Rochester, Watling Street passes Gravesend and the Bluewater Shopping Centre, dips underneath the M25, and continues through Dartford and Bexleyheath to reach Shooter's Hill. It was at Shooter's Hill that I had hoped to find my next guide on this journey, but it was not to be.

After people who live alone die, their homes undergo an inevitable and regular pattern. For the first weeks, and usually months, they are dark and quiet, as if in mourning. Then there is a sudden flurry of activity and a run of visits which climax with men loading the houses' contents into a large van. The contents depart the homes and are scattered wide, landing in relatives' houses, auction houses, charity collections, eBay listings and municipal tips. They are replaced by signs outside the houses, and perhaps a lick of paint inside. Then new people arrive, with new contents and new ideas. Curtains, gardens and cars change. The houses are no longer dark in the evenings, or silent at the weekends. They are different, but they are alive again.

Such is the fate of the house of Steve Moore, a writer who lived his whole life in a semi-detached 1930s house on top of Shooter's Hill, less than a hundred yards from Watling Street. His house was not far enough away to avoid the river of fiction washing along that road, and you can see it in the graphic novel *V for Vendetta* (1988–9) by Alan Moore and David Lloyd, where it models for the childhood home of the character Evey Hammond.

Steve was going to be my guide to Shooter's Hill. We had agreed on a day for him to show me round. As that date approached our plans became more detailed, but his emails also contained increasingly common references to his health and to angina. A few days before my visit, when I was thinking that he was taking an uncharacteristic-ally long time to reply to an email, our mutual friend Alistair Fruish telephoned to say that he had died.

Steve was born in 1949 in the same house he died in. He had a long career in comics and publishing which brought him respect and satisfaction rather than fame or wealth. But his impact on our culture, should you look for it, is considerable. He co-organised the first British comics convention, for example, quietly setting in motion the geek culture that has propelled the world of superheroes into their current position as the reigning kings of the zeitgeist. He taught his closest friend, Alan Moore (no relation), how to write comics, and he was also one of the founders of *Fortean Times* magazine, bringing all sorts of strange and unexplained ideas into the light.

Steve was not one to trumpet his own achievements, or thrust himself into the limelight, and this gave him something of a reputation as a recluse. A lengthy interview about his career by the Irish comics journalist Pádraig Ó Méalóid, for example, was entitled 'The Hermit of Shooter's Hill'. I found Steve perfectly sociable, but he was more interested in his inner world than he was in promoting himself in the outer one. Just before he died a big Hollywood adaptation of his *Hercules* comic book was due to be released, staring Dwayne 'The Rock' Johnson. 'Don't go and see it,' he told me, 'it'll be shit.'

The first work of Steve's that I read was his novel *Somnium* (2011). It told the story of a writer holed up in a Shooter's Hill inn in 1803, attempting to write a novel set in the Elizabethan era while being plagued by visions of a writer in the same location in the early twenty-first century. The novel warns us that mortal man should not fall in love with gods, because man exists in time and gods are timeless. To fall in love with a goddess, as the shepherd Endymion did with the Greek moon-goddess Selene, can only lead to madness or death, because these are the only ways in which the mortal and the eternal can be together. But this, the book suggests, may be a price worth paying. For Steve, the moon goddess represented the exquisite blazing realms of the imagination, a place whose beauty far overshadowed the wonders of the physical, material world. *Somnium* was a book written on the edge of sanity and is entirely devoid of cynicism. Until I read it I never really understood the concept of devotion.

Steve Moore's regular suburban house might look an unlikely place to find a moon worshipper, but then the spiritual lives of those inside similar houses are only rarely what you imagine. In the vivid world of his imagination, the goddess Selene became transformed from a dusty myth into a living presence. She became a companion to him, a voice in his ear, sharing his life in his otherwise empty hilltop home. At times he could see her, and on very rare occasions others claim to have seen her as well. As he remarked in a 2011 interview, 'I was born at the full moon atop a crescent-shaped hill, the main mineral found here being selenite, and I have a slightly rough-edged crescent birthmark on my left forearm, so I was obviously destined to be either a werewolf or a lunatic.'

Psychologists might classify Steve as someone who was experiencing a syndrome they call self-willed therapeutic schizophrenia. In the schizophrenic family of illnesses, the complex web of neurons that make up a human brain doesn't just generate one mind or personality, but it can also create voices and other hallucinations. With a more extreme syndrome such as Dissociative Identity Disorder, the brain doesn't just produce voices. It makes a coherent second personality, and sometimes more. It would be simple if we could say that these other personalities weren't 'real' and dismiss them. But if a character that emerges from connections between neurons isn't real, then what does that say about our own identity?

Classical schizophrenia is usually understood as unwelcome and frightening, at least in the West. According to research from Stanford University, hallucinated voices in India and Africa tend to be more playful and benign compared to voices heard in the United States, which are often harsh and threatening. Here in the West, the other voice or voices in your head are defined as illness, and you are trapped with them, unable to escape. But the 'self-willed' aspect of self-willed therapeutic schizophrenia means that the process is voluntary and intentional, and that the extra voices or personality is welcome, like an imaginary childhood friend for adults. Although many secondary personalities emerge spontaneously, people can also train their minds, through visualisation and meditational practices, in order to generate or strengthen this sense of a living, independent entity. On the internet, the process is known as tulpamancy. There are forums and support groups where people from around the world share tips on how they create and sustain their separate mental entities. Tulpamancy is not considered to be Dissociative Identity Disorder because the tulpamancer is not usually distressed by the brain's other personalities.

An early study on self-willed therapeutic schizophrenia reported positive increases in numerous mental-health markers, with 93.7 per cent of those who reported some form of mental illness or disorder claiming that their practice 'made their condition better'. This is the reason for including the word 'therapeutic' in the name self-willed therapeutic schizophrenia. The EU referendum shows us that we are living in a schizophrenic country, one which has become divided into two different voices or personalities. Perhaps, if tulpamancers are correct, this doesn't have to be seen as an illness.

Tulpamancers believe that if an area of the noosphere becomes sufficiently complex, vivid and unpredictable, it can for all intents and purposes be considered to be a living thing. The entities tulpamancers create are strange and varied, but they are often based on Japanese manga characters, or creatures from the My Little Pony toy range. There are not many who, like Steve, had a goddess living in their heads.

Steve died instantly, or so we were told. He was in his office in the upstairs box room of the house, working at his computer. On his desk was a printout of the latest draft of an academic book about Selene that he had been working on for many years and a half-eaten KitKat. The draft was about 99 per cent finished, with a helpful hand-written list of the work that still remained to be done placed on top of it. From the way his body lay when he was found, it was thought that he was dead before he hit the ground. He appeared in the dreams of many of his friends in the weeks after he died, including the comedian Andrew O'Neill. In his dream, which occurred before Andrew knew the circumstances about how Steve was found, Andrew asked him what dying was like. Steve told him, 'I just fell through the floor and kept going.'

From the evidence found in the house, it appeared that he died on Friday, 14 March 2014. He last checked his email on the Friday morning, for example, and he would typically check it multiple times a day. Both his diary and his dream journal, which he usually kept meticulously updated, also point to a death on Friday. Yet two separate neighbours claim they saw him in the cul-de-sac on Sunday, 16 March, which was the day of a full moon. They say he waved and appeared cheerful and normal.

In his journal, for the night of 12–13 March, Steve recorded a dream in which a man attempted to gain entry into his house via the upstairs box-room window. 'I went to the front door, which had already been opened outward somehow, and stepped outside,' he wrote. 'The man was up a ladder by the front door and seemed to be plastering all over the upstairs windowsill to seal it up somehow.' In the following week, after Steve's friends became concerned they were unable to contact him, a community police officer checked on the house. Unable to get an answer from the door bell, and conscious of the unopened post on the hallway floor, the officer borrowed a ladder from a neighbour and climbed up to the box-room window. Seeing Steve's body on the floor, the officer gained entrance to the house through that same window.

All but one of the pre-Roman burial mounds that had sat on top of the hill for centuries were bulldozed in the twentieth century to make way for housing. Shooter's Hill's last remaining Iron Age barrow is at Brinklow Crescent, and it was here that Steve's ashes were scattered underneath the August full moon. This pagan mound on top of the hill is said to be the same height as the cross on top of Saint Paul's Cathedral, but perhaps the extra few microns that this moon-worshipper's ashes added to the height were enough to make it taller. Brinklow Crescent is named after the Warwickshire village of Brinklow, which lies further up Watling Street. The name is thought to derive from the Old English *Brincehláw*, which means 'burial mound on top of a hill'. So the name couldn't be more apt, and the addition of the 'crescent' is perfect for a moon-worshipper such as Steve.

The Brinklow Crescent burial mound plays a significant role in *Unearthing*, an account of Steve Moore's life written by his friend Alan Moore. This began life as a contribution to *London: City of*

Disappearances (2006), a book edited by Iain Sinclair, and then spent the following decade mutating into an audiobook, live performance, photo essay and film.

Unearthing is the story of Shooter's Hill, the Moore family, and Steve's life and work, all of which builds to a study of Steve's relationship with Selene and what it means for a mortal man to spend his life in a devotional relationship with an immortal idea, not as a myth or a legend from the past but now, in twenty-first-century London. Towards the end, Alan Moore's account of Steve's life shifts from the past and begins describing first the present and then the future. It describes the morning when Steve receives the *Unearthing* manuscript in the post, spends the morning reading it and then goes out for a walk. 'He skims through these final pages, on to the conclusion,' it says, 'noting with increasing irritation and amusement that the narrative recounts how he concludes his reading, then goes out to take his morning constitutional along a route described precisely in the text that will deliver him to some lame and post-modern *trompe l'oeil* excuse for an ending, by the Brinklow Crescent burial mound.'

By writing this, Alan Moore was forcing Steve Moore to enact it. Steve's fastidious nature and his love of literature would not allow the ending of his biography to be inaccurate. He owed it to the written word to comply, which he did in every detail. 'Grudgingly he thuds downstairs and gets his jacket,' the text continued, 'calls from the back door to [his brother] Chris down in the greenhouse, explains away with some difficulty the complex and metaphysical necessity for his excursion, only halfway through remembering that this was mentioned in the story, in the manuscript. He stands on the rear doorstep and looks down the hillside's terraced slopes towards the wire-wool-coloured cumulus approaching over London from the north, deciding that he'd better take along his rolled umbrella, then recalls that this was mentioned too.'

The text compelled Steve to follow a prescribed route through the suburban streets towards Brinklow Crescent, where he intended to have his ashes scattered. It then described him vanishing, fading into the memory of the hill. Yet it was not so much the hill that he disappeared into at that point but the text. Steve is gone now, and memories fade. The memory of an average person typically lasts for the duration of the lives of their grandchildren, they being the youngest people sufficiently emotionally invested to form lasting impressions. After that we are gone, existing only as an unread random name in a forgotten ledger, our true selves lost for ever. But the text of *Unearthing* will last. It is both brutally honest and compassionate, and those who read it will know Steve more vividly and truthfully than some living people they might live or work with.

An odd thing about fictional descriptions of journeys along Watling Street is how often those journeys are set at night. In Thomas Hughes's *Tom Brown's Schooldays*, for example, the schoolboy hero first travels to his new school on a night coach from London to Rugby, which would have run along Watling Street. 'It had its pleasures, the old dark ride,' Hughes tells us, describing 'the music of the rattling harness, and the ring of the horses' feet on the hard road, and the glare of the two bright lamps through the steaming hoar-frost, over the leaders' ears, into the darkness.' In Arnold Bennett's 1904 crime novel *Teresa of Watling Street*, the hero first encounters the heroine on a moonlit night on that road when she is, a little unexpectedly, being attacked by circus elephants. On a later night they travel along the 'the twelve miles of lonely and straight Watling Street that separate St Albans from Dunstable. On this interminable and monotonous stretch of road [...] mile succeeds mile with a sort of dogged persistency, and the nocturnal traveller becomes, as it were, hypnotised by the ribbon-like highway that stretches eternally in front of him and behind him.' Bill Naughton's *Late Night on Watling Street* (1970) tells of nocturnal lorry drivers and an act of revenge against a speed cop who would use the dark to help catch speeding trucks. As the narrator describes a 2 a.m. drive, 'I was going at a fair lick, because you can see better on a dark night, since your headlights carve out the road for you, and you don't get those dicey shadows the moon makes.'

The immaterial idea of Britain has grown considerably since our hypothetical first man, our mythical Puck, first ignited it. Those first notes on the Albion songline have built into a symphony. In that noosphere, when imagination turns to look at Watling Street, it thinks of it as moonlit. For Steve Moore, moonlight symbolised imagination in all its seductive other-worldly wonder. He was born and lived a few yards from this road, and he spent his life in service of that human imagination. It was divine and worthy of adoration. He lives in that imagination now, typed into it by his friend, another story to emerge from these islands.

Like Miss Havisham in her faded wedding gown, Steve is now in the pages of a book. He was a real person while Miss Havisham wasn't, but that distinction might become uncertain in time. Who can say now whether the lodger Nicholas who received a red-hot poker up the *ers* was once a flesh-and-blood person? It seems unlikely, but we can't say for sure. The boundary between fact and fiction, which should be neat and simple in theory, is woozy and shifting in practice. Perhaps, with Steve, it is not important. What matters is that in the immaterial country of the mind, a moon-struck hermit on a hilltop is in the presence of his goddess and will remain so always.

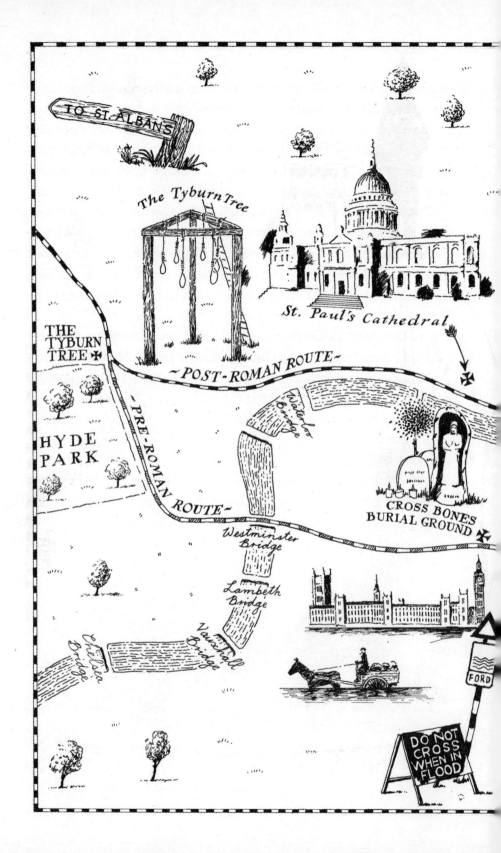

TO ST. ALBANS

The Tyburn Tree

St. Paul's Cathedral

THE
TYBURN
TREE ✠

~POST-ROMAN ROUTE~

HYDE
PARK

~PRE-ROMAN ROUTE~

Waterloo Bridge

CROSS BONES
BURIAL GROUND ✠

Westminster Bridge

Lambeth Bridge

Vauxhall Bridge

Chelsea Bridge

FORD

DO NOT
CROSS
WHEN IN
FLOOD

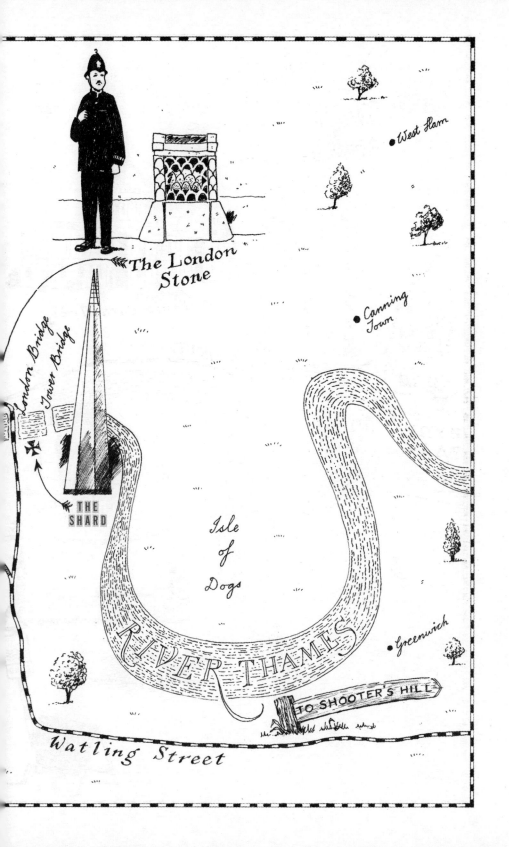

The London Stone

West Ham

Canning Town

London Bridge

Tower Bridge

THE SHARD

Isle of Dogs

RIVER THAMES

Greenwich

TO SHOOTER'S HILL

Watling Street

5.

CROSS BONES

The blessing of the Winchester Geese

In the mid-1990s, deep underneath Southwark, there was a tremor.

Southwark is the oldest of the London boroughs. It faced the medieval City of London from the south bank of the Thames, linked to it by London Bridge, but with its manors classed as 'Liberties', places outside of London's laws. It was the outlaw borough, the home of theatres and taverns, prisons and bear pits, pleasure and riots. It stands on old dirt, trampled down by thousands of years of continual occupation.

In Clink Street, near the Clink Prison that gave jails a nickname, are the remains of the Bishop of Winchester's early medieval palace. In 1107 the bishop was granted sole authority over the Liberty of the Clink, which made him the protector of the area's long-established brothels, or 'stews'. In 1161 these were regulated through a series of ordinances 'according to the old customs that have been used and accustomed there out of time of mind'. These granted prostitutes licence to go about their business in a relatively controlled and orderly way, but they also allowed the bishop to make a little profit from the application of fines. One ordinance, for example, designed to limit aggressive soliciting, warns that 'if any woman of the bordello [. . .] draw any man by his gown or by his hood or by any other thing she shall make a fine to the lord of twenty shillings'.

These ordinances were signed into law by our friend Thomas Becket, in the days before he clashed with the king. The sex workers of Southwark were licensed by a saint.

Because of their licence from the bishop, these women were known as 'Winchester Geese'. But even with this religious sanction, they were not deemed worthy of Christian burial. Being sex workers, they could not be buried in the consecrated ground of St Mary Overie, their local parish church.

'St Mary Overie' is an interesting name in this context. Its origins are unlikely to be related to ovaries or female sexual organs but are probably a corruption of 'over the river'. This makes St Mary Overie a name given to the south-bank church by those in the City of London. It defines it as 'other'. The obvious contenders for the identity of the 'St Mary' in the name are the Virgin Mary and the biblical prostitute Mary Magdalene, although a tradition first recorded in the sixteenth century claimed that Mary was the local ferryman's daughter. Her father, one telling of the legend informs us, was John Overs. He was a proto-Scrooge, a miserable London miser who hoarded his money. Overs faked his own death in the hope that his family and servants would fast during the mourning period and save him the expense of feeding them. Instead, they broke open his wine cellars and held a great party. When Overs returned and confronted them, the terrified party-goers believed he was a foul spirit, or the devil himself, and clubbed him to death. Mary inherited his fortune, and used it to found a nunnery on the site of a Roman temple. This was in the early seventh century and, over time, the nunnery became first an Augustinian Priory and then the parish church of St Mary Overie.

Given the work of the Winchester Geese, the name 'St Mary Overie' is almost too perfect. But it was too Catholic for the post-Reformation years and so it became St Saviour's, the name it is referred to by in Charles Dickens's *The Uncommercial Traveller*. It is now known as The

Cathedral and Collegiate Church of St Saviour and St Mary Overie, or, more commonly, as Southwark Cathedral.

The bones of the Winchester Geese that had not been laid to rest at St Mary Overie had to go somewhere. They were placed in unconsecrated ground, in a burial site that became known as Cross Bones. Here the bodies accumulated, over years, decades and centuries, with their names mostly forgotten and unrecorded. In time the site became established as a pauper's burial ground. According to our best estimates, Cross Bones was in use for around 500 years and holds the remains of 15,000 souls.

They were silent, those forgotten bones, over the long centuries. They were held unmoving in compacted, polluted earth. Then in the 1990s there came a vibration, which grew into a rumble, which became a tremor. The giant tunnelling machines of Transport for London made their awesome, violent progress through the ancient soil, cutting out deep tunnels for the London Underground Jubilee Line extension. The earth was churned as if drawn into a giant plughole, and the long-dormant geese, the resting unwanted, were disturbed.

On the night of 23 November 1996, a local poet named John Constable was wandering the streets of Southwark, his mind wide open and his feet drawing him randomly along the dark roads. Chance brought him to Cross Bones, and here he experienced something he later described as being 'jumped by the Goose'. The Goose was a spirit who represented all the Winchester Geese, and she gave the poet her story.

When Constable woke the next day, he discovered a lengthy, complete poem in his own handwriting channelled from the spirit of a forgotten medieval prostitute. He is still trying to come to terms with this.

It is Hallowe'en, 31 October 2015. I am heading to a vigil at the Cross Bones Garden of Remembrance in order to remember the forgotten.

I start in Borough Market, where there are some truly extraordinary pumpkins. They are stacked up in a chaotic hill, all shapes and sizes, piled high and loose. The largest looks too heavy to carry. It bulges like an over-inflated beach ball that should have burst weeks ago, had it not been so stubborn. It looks as if it would be great to sit on.

Back in the mid-1990s, when the Goose jumped the poet, Borough Market was no different to any other London wholesale vegetable market. Since then the prices of houses in this area have doubled, and then doubled again. The re-created Shakespeare's Globe theatre opened on the river front in 1997, the Jubilee Line extension was completed in 1999 and the Tate Modern gallery opened in 2000. The area has come up in the world. Borough Market, in response, has become a cathedral of gentrification.

The trappings of old London remain. The market still takes place under the same green and gold flowing Victorian ironwork and is nestled among dark brick railway arches. Yet the produce, the prices, the stallholders and the shoppers have changed beyond recognition. Signs now advertise poultry and game, wild Highland venison burgers, and classic ports and gins. Champagne is available by the glass or, if that's too extravagant for a trip down the market, you can settle for prosecco. Borough Market has become a food-lovers' paradise. When it stocks pumpkins, it stocks extraordinary pumpkins.

Many people complain about pumpkins and the modern British Hallowe'en in general. They are accused of being an unwelcome American intrusion, like Black Friday and climate-change denial. Personally, I'm all for them. Pumpkins are simultaneously fun and eerie. They are easy to draw, and easy to draw on, which are qualities that children like very much. I can still recall struggling to carve faces into turnips at Hallowe'en when I was a kid growing up in North Wales. A pumpkin is a vegetable far more suited to carving.

The origins of Hallowe'en, and hence the reasons that brought this pumpkin pile to Borough Market, are incredibly old. Hallowe'en was once considered to be the start of the New Year. This wasn't quite a 'new year' as we understand the term today, because the old calendar was more about the flow of the seasons than a linear progression of dates. The old Celtic calendar comes from an era when life did not change rapidly, and the world of your grandchildren could be trusted to be more or less the same as that of your grandparents. It was a calendar for a people who did not have to contend with the scale of changes that could wash over a single market in just twenty years.

If you're filling out a tax return or applying for a mortgage, then the Celtic calendar is not going to be much use. But there is still something appealing about the old calendar, and it is still useful. It divides time up into chunks of about six weeks, each separated by a party, which is an agreeably human way to think about your life. It tells you that things more than six weeks away are things which you don't need to worry about yet. At the same time, it encourages you not to focus solely on the present day, but to see the larger picture as the seasons unfurl. It puts the focus on the patterns and rhythms of life, rather than the passing of the years. The Celtic calendar doesn't come with quite the same level of stress and anxiety as the Gregorian one.

Here's how it works: the Celtic calendar describes the yearly recurring cycle of the seasons. It is also known as the Wheel of the Year, so think of one year as a wheel or a clock face. We can mark on that wheel two specific dates in that period of time, six months apart and therefore opposite each other on the wheel of the year. These are the shortest day, roughly 21 December in the northern hemisphere, and the longest day, usually around 21 June. These are placed at the twelve o'clock and six o'clock positions on the wheel.

One thing you notice, if you spend enough time out of doors, is that the place where the sun rises on the eastern horizon changes over the course of the year. It is further north in the winter and further south during the longer days of the summer. Its northernmost and southernmost positions are the shortest and longest days of the year, the twelve o'clock and six o'clock positions marked on our wheel.

Although the sunrise normally moves from day to day, when the sun is at its northern and southern limits it appears to rise in pretty much the same position over a three-day period. This idea that the sun 'stands still' is what gives us the word 'solstice'. We still mark the solstices with festivals today. The summer solstice, the point where our story began, is celebrated most famously by the Glastonbury Festival, which is deliberately held on the weekend closest to the summer solstice. The winter solstice was traditionally celebrated after the end of the sun's three-day period of standing still, when the days were once again growing longer and we were, in the words of Steven Moffat, 'halfway out of the dark'. That festival used to be called Yule, but we now call it Christmas. The early Christian church lacked a date for the birth of Jesus and the festival of Yule, associated as it was with the return of the light and the birth of the sun, seemed the most suitable festival to co-opt.

Marking these two festivals, then, splits the wheel of the year into two halves. The next step is to further divide those two halves and split the year into quarters. This is done by marking the dates when day and night are of equal length, the spring and autumn 'equinoxes', which are typically around 21 March and 21 September. Our wheel of the year has now been divided into four three-month-long quarters.

Now we add some more festivals. We divide our wheel one last time, turning the year into eight sections of around six weeks each. These last four divisions are called the cross-quarter days, and you are probably more familiar with them than you might think.

Beltane, for example, is the festival that falls midway between the spring equinox and the summer solstice. This is more commonly called May Day. It is associated with fertility and the celebration of the natural world returning to life after winter. It was also called Robin Hood's day, a time of feasting, laughter and good humour. It gives us traditions that survive to this day, from crowning a young girl as the Queen of May to Morris dancing around a maypole. May Eve was a time for the young to pair up and disappear into the woods, their 'Greenwood marriages' blessed not by the church but by the spirit of the woodland, the Green Man. The offspring of these unions were considered to be especially blessed. They were known as 'Merrybegots'.

More recently, this people's day has gained political overtones. It is now associated with International Workers' Day and anti-capitalist demonstrations. May Day has always provoked the anger of establishment figures, and there have been constant attempts to ban it. Even when these have been successful, such as during the Puritan Commonwealth after the English Civil War, May Day has always returned. It is a festival celebrating fertility and the inevitability of life. I cannot see it ever dying.

But we are six months away from May Day, at the opposite side of the year. Hallowe'en is the cross-quarter day originally known as Samhain. This is the midpoint between the autumn equinox and the winter solstice. While May Day was about life, Hallowe'en is about death. More specifically, it is about the living and the dead coexisting. Samhain marked the point when the dark winter had arrived, but larders were still full from the last harvest. It is said that this was the time when the veil between the living and the dead was at its thinnest, and the night when the dead could walk among us. This is a night of bonfires, apple-bobbing, trick-or-treating and divination.

The name 'Hallowe'en' derives from its later Christian rebranding, All Hallows' Eve, the day before All Saints' Day. It was through this Christian adaption that the festival made its way to Mexico, carried by the Spanish. In Mexico, 31 October echoes its old Celtic symbolism and is the beginning of the three-day Dia de Los Muertos festival, known to the English as the Day of the Dead. In recent years, Dia de Los Muertos imagery has become increasingly adopted by British Hallowe'en. Such is the way that culture sloshes around the world and across the centuries.

I am admiring the pumpkins in Borough Market while waiting to meet my friend Anna. Our plan is to head out to the Cross Bones pauper's graveyard and witness a performance from the Goose-jumped poet himself, John Constable.

I heard tales of John Constable for many years. They were not the typical type of stories you find in south London. I heard about how he had been possessed by the spirit of a medieval prostitute disturbed by the tunnelling of the Jubilee Line extension. I had heard how the vision poem he received that night had formed the basis for a play called *The Southwark Mysteries*, a legendary performance of which began at Shakespeare's Globe, progressed through the streets of Southwark and ended in Southwark Cathedral. I was told that this kick-started a campaign for recognition of the Cross Bones burial site, in order to prevent the building of an office block on top of this valuable piece of real estate, and how, after twenty years of work, the campaigners had now secured the site as a memorial garden. I heard how the current Dean of Southwark Cathedral had attended a ceremony on the site and offered a profound and touching apology from the Church for the treatment of the women under the ground. As stories go, it was an unusual mix of the strange and taboo and the establishment.

The Hallowe'en memorial vigil at the Cross Bones burial ground seemed an ideal way to find out more. Hallowe'en was the perfect time of the year for a vigil. If there was any night when the dead might be aware that they are not forgotten, it would be 31 October.

There are people who when you ask them to accompany you to a consecrated burial ground for medieval prostitutes on Hallowe'en aren't that keen. Luckily, Anna is not one of those people. She is from Tyne and Wear, works for the Home Office and manages to somehow be a 'no-nonsense' type of person who is also always up for a bit of nonsense. She also lives a short walk from Cross Bones. It wasn't until this afternoon that I realised she lived at the very end of the A2 section of Watling Street. All these years I hadn't noticed that Anna was like a modern-day Chaucer, who lived in rooms over Aldgate like a sentinel guarding that entrance into the old City of London. The realisation of how perfect and unlikely the position of her flat is, given my current journey, causes the spookiness of Hallowe'en to suddenly seem a little less cartoon-like than usual.

Together with our friend Dom, Anna and I make our way to the Table Café on Southwark Street, where the evening's events are due to start. We are promised songs, poems and scenes from *The Southwark Mysteries*, as well as a procession from the café to Cross Bones. Dom has recently moved down from Liverpool, so for all she knows this is perfectly normal for a night out in London. We check our names at the door with a woman dressed in black carrying a clipboard and a fistful of long white ribbons. We are told that we will each be given a ribbon to wear around our wrists. Every ribbon has the name of a person buried at Cross Bones written on it, taken from what few records of paupers' burials still exist. We are warned not to lose our ribbon. The idea is that everyone present will be responsible for remembering one outcast soul.

The ribbon is tied around my wrist. It reads Eleanor Hawthorne, along with the date in the 1720s when she died. From the faceless fact of 15,000 forgotten bodies, the idea of a single woman emerges. I know nothing else about this person, but a name is a surprisingly potent thing, and it snags in my mind. Dom collects her ribbon, which gives her mind a little more to work on. 'Edward, son of Edward the painter', it reads. The majority of the bodies in Cross Bones are children.

A third ribbon is tied to Anna's wrist, and we enter the café. Chairs are placed in rows for a performance ahead of the procession to the burial site. We find some seats while we can, for the event is sold out, and Anna examines her ribbon.

It reads, simply, 'a child found dead in a ditch'.

A hundred different emotions register on her face. The words are so brutal and bleak that you almost have to laugh, yet having them tied around your wrist is far from funny. Anna sits in a state of mild hysteria, blinking back tears, aware that she has drawn the short straw and not knowing what to say. Considering that we are only just through the door, this is quite a start to the evening.

I head to the bar and realise that the ribbon from my wrist has gone. I am a bit at a loss to understand how I lost it so quickly and start to scan the floor, determined not to let Eleanor Hawthorne down. Someone spots me hunting and points out a ribbon on the floor, and I thank them and tie it to my wrist. It's only when I return to my seat that I notice that it is a different ribbon. This one reads '24 July 1833 – Mary Davis, Dead House, Age 23'. A Dead House was a building used for temporarily storing bodies. It was of particular use in the winter months when the ground was frozen too hard to dig. I find my Eleanor Hawthorne ribbon on the floor but am unable to find whoever has dropped the Mary Davis ribbon, so I tie them both to my wrist.

Anna's ribbon

Then John Constable arrives. Tall, thin and white-haired, he wears an ankle-length purple velvet coat with a long light-blue silk scarf that hangs down to his knees, like a louche future Doctor Who. Or rather, it is not Constable who has arrived but his creative alter-ego, John Crow, a trickster with grinning eyes and theatrical gestures. The elusive real-life Constable will not be joining us tonight; he has vanished somewhere underneath the John Crow persona.

Crow skips and leers and is joined by the actress Michelle Watson. She is playing the role of the Goose and announces herself:

I was born a Goose of Southwark
By the Grace of Mary Overie,
Whose Bishop gives me licence
To sin within the Liberty.
In Bankside stews and taverns
You can hear me honk right daintily,
As I unlock the hidden door,
Unveil the Secret History.
I will dunk you in the river,
And then reveal my Mystery.

Mad John Crow and the Goose bat rhymes back and forth, like a medieval rap battle themed around the sacred and the profane. The Goose keeps things earthy and lusty, while Crow can't ignore her divinity:

Then the crow on the gargoyle caw caw caw
And he draw John a map of infinity
Where God rejoices more in the brazen Whore
Than in the Wife in her pinch-faced Chastity.

If anyone was expecting a sombre evening of paying respect to those no longer with us, then the level of bawdiness in this performance will surprise. Michelle is embracing playing the spirit of a medieval tuppenny whore with evident delight.

You don't know me yet, dear.
You will, dear, I promise you.
I am a tricksy tart, dear.
My aim is to astonish you.

This could have been an earnest event in the manner of a BBC2 documentary, where the trade of the dead women was acknowledged but not dwelt upon. Instead, their sexuality is front and centre. One poem, 'The Book of the Honest John', runs through the more special-ised acts of consensual sexuality with evident relish, portraying them as a form of spiritual healing. John Crow is intent on celebrating the life of the Winchester Geese, rather than mourning their death. Nor does he shy from the class element of this story, or the hypocrisy of the rich and powerful from Westminster and the City condemning the Geese as sinners while north of river, but using them for their own pleasure when they took the ferry south.

It is time for the procession from the café to the burial ground. Eleanor Hawthorne's ribbon has fallen from my wrist again, so I make a point of tying it back on tightly. Mulling over the evening's themes of class exploitation, sex work and dead children, I wonder if Dom and Anna are going to be less eager to come along to events I suggest in the future. Still, the evening has only just begun. Next, we have Morris dancers.

The Morris troupe is called Wolfshead and Vixen. They are men and women from Kent, and they have also journeyed along Watling Street from Rochester to be here. Morris dancing brings to mind images of bearded men in white clothes, with bells on their knees and hankies in their hands, skipping around a maypole on May Day for tradition's sake. But we are at the opposite side of the wheel of the year here, and the Morris troupe who will escort us in procession to the burial ground are a dark inversion of that.

There are four dancers, all female and all dressed in long, flowing black dresses with leather boots and Camden Market Goth jewellery. They carry a hefty wooden stick in each hand, about ten inches long and an inch thick, which they whack together with great force as they whirl and skip. It is aggressive, like a punk version of Morris.

The dancers are Vixen, while Wolfshead are the band. They consist of a half-dozen or so people also dressed entirely in black, with dark sunglasses, feathered top hats and studded-leather fingerless gloves on their hands. Their instruments – drum, fiddle, flute and accordion – are all acoustic but capable of making a wild racket. They remind me of how the musician Julian Cope described his band Black Sheep: they sound like they come from a future where civilisation has collapsed but rumours about what rock 'n' roll sounded like still persist.

Wolfshead

A couple of members of Wolfshead have adhered to the ancient Border Morris tradition of blackface. Blacking up was once such an integral part of these dances that the name Morris is thought to be derived from Moorish. It dates to the time when masterless men were classed as beggars and vagabonds, so they would black their faces to avoid being recognised and jailed. Blackface, in this tradition, was the sign of an outlaw. Blacking up in the twenty-first century is inherently dodgy, of course, and other traditional Morris troupes choose masks, or use a non-black colour of face paint, to avoid being racially insensitive. Seeing this Goth Morris troupe in the flesh, their decision to black up is less troubling in practice than it might appear on paper. No one would look at members of Wolfshead and think that they were attempting to portray someone of African heritage.

With drums banging and sticks clashing, Wolfshead and Vixen lead us through the streets of Southwark, with the gleaming knife of the Shard building hanging in the night above. You have to give the residents of Southwark their due: when confronted by a procession of over a hundred people led by a nightmarish vision of Goth Morris, they don't bat an eyelid. Perhaps this sort of thing happens more than I know?

We arrive at Cross Bones without incident, our number swelled by a few curious and confused drunks. The bars of the red-iron gates to the old works site are all but hidden under a mass of ribbons, poems and mementos, both to the outcast dead of centuries gone and to more recently departed sex workers. The surrounding hoardings are plastered with anti-gentrification posters and a Cross Bones collage by the artist Jimmy Cauty. Together, the gates and the hoardings form an ever-evolving spontaneous mural.

John Crow calls on us all to transfer the ribbons around our wrists to the gates, calling out the names on them as we do so. I go to remove my ribbon and discover that Eleanor Hawthorne, who was so recently attached with care and thoroughness, has escaped me once more. I take the hint. Ms Hawthorne has other plans and has no desire to be honoured by the likes of me. So I reach into my coat pocket and pull out the Mary Davis ribbon. It is Mary Davis whose name I call out, and who I remember as I tie her memorial ribbon to the railings. Dom calls out Edward, son of Edward, and Anna gamely calls out the nameless child who, at some forgotten time, was found dead in a ditch in these Southwark streets and brought to this paupers' graveyard.

The entrance to the Cross Bones garden is a carved wooden walkway, curved like the ribcage of a whale. Looking closer, I realise that the roof is carved into a goose wing. When it rains, the water runs off the goose's wing like water from a duck's back. This is channelled through a series of wooden pipes until it emerges from the mouth of a nearby gargoyle, carved into the face of the medieval Bishop of Winchester. The words of a poem from *The Southwark Mysteries* are carved in the arches we walk under. It reads,

> Here lay your hearts, your flowers,
> Your Book of Hours,
> Your fingers, your thumbs,
> Your 'Miss You, Mums'.
> Here Hang your hopes, your dreams,
> Your Might-Have-Beens,
> Your locks, your keys,
> Your Mysteries.

We emerge into a space perhaps twenty by thirty metres that is half concrete wasteland and half garden of remembrance. To one side stands a rough pyramid, around a metre and a half tall, built from rubble and oyster shells. The oyster shells represent the medieval food

John Crow

of the poor. The pyramid is next to a triangular pond, which from where I stand shows a reflection of the Shard. Prayers are conducted and songs are sung, and we slowly pass in front of an area that acts as an altar. This is dominated by a statue of the Virgin Mary, the local saint for those women who worshipped at St Mary Overie. She is pointed out to the crowd in the most inclusive way possible: 'If you're Christian, she's the Virgin Mary. If you're pagan, she's the Goddess, and if you're an atheist, she's the pretty lady.'

Then Wolfshead and Vixen move to the centre of the garden. The band and dancers launch into their raucous tradition, clattering and stamping over the bodies below. This could seem disrespectful, but it doesn't. The crowd clap and stamp along with them.

I look across at Anna and Dom, and see that they both have huge grins on their faces. When I first met them both, over twenty-five years earlier when we were all eighteen, I thought that getting older was a bad thing. This view is unquestioned gospel for the young, because they hear older people talk about aches and pains, disappearing hair, and of sagging and bloating bodies. They never hear them talk about how valuable friends become, or about how rich relationships can be with people you've known for decades. That is all left unsaid, a surprise present tucked away in a cupboard somewhere, safe in the knowledge that it will be found eventually.

With looks of glee, the crowd dance and stomp on the graves of the forgotten. If this doesn't wake them up, I think, then nothing will. But looking at the faces around me, I realise that this is not what the night is about. We arrived with the intention of remembering the outcast dead. It was a plan that made us feel worthy and righteous. We made their names ring out down Bankside streets, in the present day as they had in the past, but in truth it is the dead who are bestowing a kindness on us. By their absence, they are reminding us that we are alive. We are above the concrete garden, not underneath it, with our hearts pounding and our feet stomping and our eyes darting around the grins of the crowd.

We dance on the dead because Hallowe'en is for the living.

*

Later, I head back to Anna's flat at the very end of the A2 stretch of Watling Street. The Shard dominates the view from the window of her spare room. I spend a few minutes looking out at it before going to sleep.

This is a view that has only existed for a very small period of history. I worked in an office nearby, in Bermondsey Street, at various times during the years 2007 to 2012. I regularly walked past the place where the Shard now stands on my way to and from London Bridge station. I saw the hospital building it has now replaced being slowly dismantled, shrinking down from a squat tower block into a gaping hole in the ground like a bomb crater. I glimpsed through square holes in the plywood walls surrounding the site the foundations of the Shard being laid, and I saw the building rising from that hole, a flowering of immense concrete pillars that sprouted upwards out of the earth like crude Minecraft bamboo. Gleaming glass walls chased the pillars up and up, and cranes hopped ever higher into more and more implausible positions. I recall looking upwards at it when the exterior construction had evolved into the building we see today, proudly described as the tallest building in the European Union, which is a boast it will soon have to remove from its CV.

'That'll look good when it's finished,' I thought.

A couple of years later I realised that the strange jagged top was intentional, and that the building had been complete for some time.

It is said that you can tell the dominant power in any town or city by looking at the tallest building. At various periods of history this may have been the castle of a powerful king or duke, or a cathedral or university building. It may be a skyscraper in a business district or, in a tourist town, an attraction like the Blackpool Tower or Brighton's i360. If we apply this crude rule of thumb to the Shard, then it tells us that the dominant power in contemporary London is foreign money.

The following morning, I open the curtains and look out again.

The view is as expected, except that the Shard is no longer there. I am looking at the view out of this window as it was seven years earlier.

After a moment I realise that fog has descended, thick enough to conceal the nearby building. The fog lasts for the next three days, clinging to the country like a hangover, causing flights from Gatwick and Heathrow to be cancelled. News starts to filter through about things that occurred during that Hallowe'en night, and all of it is strange. In Kingston, the police received numerous calls about 'Five men dressed as traffic cones, blocking the road like traffic cones'. NASA released a short video of a newly discovered asteroid which passed close to the Earth on Hallowe'en and which looked for all the world like a giant skull.

A little to the west of Cross Bones, in William Blake's Lambeth, riot police were pelted with a petrol bomb and other missiles. Fourteen officers were injured and multiple arrests were made after police spent six hours attempting to end the unrest. An illegal rave called Scumoween had turned ugly. Nearby, hundreds of bikers gathered and shut down streets, throwing fireworks and performing stunts. Reports of gangs on motorbikes 'riding antisocially' came from across south London, from Lambeth to Bromley.

As riots go, these events receive little press coverage. It was said that the media reaction would have been different if the rioters had not been white, and while I don't doubt this I think the date was also a factor. The riots and mobs were forgiven because they occurred on Hallowe'en, a cross-quarter day of the old calendar. Even now, in the twenty-first century, we somehow remember that different rules apply during these transitional points of the wheel of the year.

There is a strange mood to the country during these three days of fog. It feels almost as if the events of Hallowe'en went too far and the veil between worlds was ripped aside a little too roughly. On a whim I perform an internet search on 'Mary Davis Southwark 1833'. I discover that a woman named Mary Davis was tried by a Southwark court in January of that year. I find no record of what she was accused of, but she was found guilty and sentenced to seven years' exile in Australia. She was transported on a ship called *The Buffalo*, captained by a Commander F. W. N. Sadler, along with 177 other women convicts.

The Buffalo left England on 12 May 1833 and arrived five months later, on 5 October. The convict Mary Davis would have been in the middle of the voyage on 24 July of that year, when the Mary Davis on my ribbon was being taken from the Dead House for an unmarked burial in the paupers' graveyard. Rationally this points to two different Mary Davises coming undone in Southwark in 1833, but we look at history through a fog, and fog can deceive. The records we have from the early nineteenth century are far from complete or accurate, especially when they regard the poor. Could the record of the burial of the woman from the Dead House be mistaken?

When I arrived at Cross Bones on Hallowe'en I believed it contained Mary Davis's twenty-three-year-old body. Now the possibility exists that she escaped that fate, and went on to live a full and long life in Australia. The atmosphere triggered by this strange fog obscures hard certainties. It seduces me into thinking that maybe the dead did rise that night.

The fog dissipates in early November. Transport returns to normal and the world seems solid and fixed once again. But memories of Hallowe'en linger with me. When I first heard about John Constable, I was told that he was an urban shaman, a man in communication with spirits. That seemed difficult to reconcile with a playwright working with those pillars of the Bankside establishment, the Globe theatre and Southwark Cathedral, or with someone who started the local Friends of Cross Bones campaign to persuade Transport for London not to develop such a valuable piece of central London real estate. Seeing a performance by this 'John Crow' character was interesting, but it raised more questions than it answered.

It is time to track him down.

*

'John Crow goes a long way back in my life,' says John Constable over a cup of intense black coffee. We are sitting in his attic flat, a stone's throw from the end of the A2 section of Watling Street. It is a couple of weeks later, and I am visiting him in a Georgian building overlooking an impressive sandstone church. He is immediately welcoming and open, with the air of a man at peace with the decisions he's made.

'All this is linked to Watling Street, funnily enough,' he continues. 'I was born in Much Wenlock, Shropshire, and I moved to Ellesmere, where I lived from the age of five to ten. That period is very vivid for me in terms of the lakes and the wilderness and the incredible beauty. I still find it the most beautiful part of the country, just where the Shropshire plain meets the Welsh hills. Then we moved to Oswestry because I got a scholarship to Oswestry School. Oswestry is three miles from the A5, and the A5 is Watling Street for a lot of the way. That was crucial to me in so many ways. I was a scholarship boy at a public school and by the age of seventeen I was all set to go to Cambridge. But by then a lot else had happened to me, not least my discovery of LSD – and hitch-hiking!

'When I was growing up, hitch-hiking was the way out of a small town in the sticks. One way along Watling Street went up through North Wales to Anglesey, and the other way led down to London and then on to the Continent and the rest of the world. When I was seventeen to eighteen I went three times to Rome, each time hitch-hiking the whole way and having these fantastic adventures and realising, Wow, there's a world out here! That's so important when you're from a small town, and back then Oswestry was a very small town, a repressed and repressive place, a place of twitching curtains.

'But back to John Crow. My friends had a cottage near Mold, in North Wales. It was there that I first did acid and had my first full-on experience of eternity, as I understand it, in those Welsh hills. I quote it in my solo show *I Was an Alien Sex God*, this "single moment complete in itself" and in *The Southwark Mysteries*, "one moment in Eternity". I think Blake influenced my perception of eternity, not as an enormous aggregate of all time, but as an infinitesimally small moment.

'On the next trip, we built this breezeblock altar in the garden. I don't know what we were playing at. It was a night trip, and in the middle of the night a friend and I got up on it, on a broomstick, and I was just larking, absolutely larking and . . . I turned into a crow.

'I saw it all happening but felt detached from it, then something shifts and I'm actually flying, looking down on our cottage and the fire in the garden, and my friends all sitting round the fire, and I'm looking down and at that point it occurs to me, this is really happening, I am a bird. It was not like I was in the vision world, I was in the "real" physical world and everything was as it should be. For instance, I could hear my friends talking, and it was exactly how you'd have heard their voices if you were flying thirty feet above them.

'Afterwards, I didn't really know how to deal with what had happened. Soon after I came down to London, I'd be tripping in squats in much more political and violent environments, and then in Berlin, which was so much more confrontational than expanding my mind up in the Welsh hills. I even found myself tripped out of my skull by the Berlin Wall. I used to use acid for writing, but I started to feel the price was too high, it was affecting my mental health. By the time I was twenty-three I was quite fragile. So I quit, and I didn't take acid again until the 1990s.

'After that I'd hear the name John Crow in strange circumstances. When I was in Trinidad in 1982 everybody wanted to tell me the story of Anansi, or Anancy, the Trickster spider, who is very big over there. They'd look at me and tell me stories about Anansi and Drop-Leg Goat and Half-Faced Pig – and Broken-Winged John Crow. That was a very intense time. You know how when you travel magic can really creep up on you? Trinidad was one of those times, definitely.

'So he's lingered with me over the years, this notion of a character called John Crow, who appears in some of my early plays, and over time it's become clearer who he is. John Crow isn't as nice or polite as me. He's rougher, harder, and he's seen a lot worse than me. I see him as an old Puritan priest who was sickened by a witch trial or a burning or a hanging, and went native with the witches. There's that idea of the lapsed Puritan in him, and there is a touch of the Puritan in me. John Crow is more like a vulture in Jamaica. Carrion crow, picking the dead – those are still links to Cross Bones. He's got puckish elements, but I do think he's got this sense of being somehow broken. A Puritan has a very strict idea of perfection and he'd fallen way below that into exile or excommunication, and from then on he was broken-winged John Crow.'

John Constable is a poet and playwright. He worked in street theatre in London at the start of his career and toured Europe from 1980 to 1984. He has written six or seven major plays for adults, including *Black Mas* and *Tulip Futures*, and many more for children. His stage adaptation of *Gormenghast* played two seasons in the Lyric Hammersmith and did three British Council world tours, and he also wrote and performed an autobiographical one-man show called *I Was an Alien Sex God*. But by the mid-nineties he was disenchanted with mainstream theatre and

John Constable

looking for something new. He began researching his local area and, having heard about the Winchester Geese, he thought that they could be the key to a new work. Their mix of the sacred and the profane seemed to him to somehow unlock the spirit of Southwark.

Constable was part of a writers' group that included the maverick theatre director Ken Campbell. He arranged a walk for the group around his local area. They started at The George, a seventeenth-century coaching inn off Borough High Street, and went to the site of the old Tabard Inn from *Canterbury Tales*, which was where Chaucer and his merry band of pilgrims set off for Canterbury. The walk continued to Southwark Cathedral, Mary Overie dock, Clink Street, the site of Winchester Palace and the Globe theatre. Constable then returned home. He was idly standing around at the back of his house when a voice in his head said, 'John Crow's back.'

'When I heard that voice in my head, I instinctively knew it was significant,' he tells me. 'And then as I was walking up the stairs, this other voice said, "Everywhere is special – if you know where to look," and I understood immediately what it meant. I'd been all over the world looking for magic, but it was right here in Southwark. I needed to find the magic, and John Crow was back to help. I saw that as a call to take acid again.

'A mutual friend, I won't mention who, happened to have a bottle of liquid acid and liberally sprinkled ten trips for me. I think it was ten, it might have been twenty. It depends how big the drops were. This was a few days after I heard that voice. I took the lot.

'I tell you this to be honest, but it's only this year that I've explicitly acknowledged the role of acid in the Goose vision. If you read *The Southwark Mysteries*, it's all there, there's no attempt to hide it. But if I'd stood up in 1997 and said that this piece of writing is the product of LSD, that would have made it impossible for the work to be accepted by the Globe or the cathedral. We wouldn't have been able to work with Transport for London or Bankside Open Spaces Trust, to get the

Cross Bones site saved and turned into a garden, if the work had been identified with psychedelics.

'I wasn't looking for a recreational-drug experience. I thought, I'll take a dose that makes sure I get through the doorway. And because I didn't know what was going to happen, I prepared in a way I'd never done before. I spent the whole day cleaning the house, cleaning myself. I did a lot of chanting. My message to myself was, I'm going to be empty. I'm not going to offer any resistance. Whatever comes, I'm going to let it do its dance, but I won't attach to it. So I'd prepared the ground but had no idea who or what was going to come and claim it.

'I started writing about seven in the evening. I was writing in the John Crow persona, and he was mostly ranting – very little of that made it into the final poem. Then, around eleven o'clock, it was as if the Goose did this...'

John gets up from the table he is sitting at, leaves the room and closes the door. Then he pushes the door open and barges into the room, heading directly for the table with two long, quick steps and looms behind the chair he had been sitting in.

'It was just whoosh, and she's here,' he continues. 'Not as in Miss Havisham in all the veils. It wasn't a visual hallucination. But she was here. And she was talking straight away – in verse! – just straight away, and I'm like... fucking hell, what is that. What is *that?!* I was just writing it down, and the rhymes kept leading me. Particularly this one, it was probably around midnight: 'You don't know me yet dear / You will dear, I promise you / I am a tricksy tart dear / My aim is to astonish you.' Fuck! I had never written verse before. I'd written poetry and songs but never verse. I did feel scared, and in quite primitive ways. I remember thinking, if the ancient adversary really wanted to ensnare me, would he appear in horns and tail, or as a temptress, a medieval sex worker?

'I'd effectively written half the poem by around two in the morning. It was like a dialogue between the Goose and John Crow. It was as if they were doing a dance, and the dance was the poem, and as they danced, in my mind, I went all the places in the poem. At the Tabard Inn I saw Chaucer! And by then the Goose had become very familiar. From the moment she appeared she'd spoken directly to John Crow. It was like they'd done this dance many times. Maybe they'd had a scene of some sort once, but they were beyond that at this point. They were here to work. I just happened to be the observer, really, the scribe. So that's what I did, I wrote it down.'

When John Constable talks about John Crow, he does so like an actor talking about a role they are learning, someone they have thought a lot about but are still trying to define. When he talks about the Goose he does so in a similar way to how Steve Moore talked about Selene, as someone whom they had met and who was just as real to them as you were. They both make a point of stating that they know their spirit is imaginary, and that they are not totally adrift from reality, but they seem to do so as an act of social politeness in order not to make others uncomfortable.

'A neuroscientist would say that these voices were the product of my own brain,' John adds. 'And they may well be right. But these characters knew things I didn't know, they knew each other in ways I didn't understand and they took me on a journey that night.

'At around two in the morning, it was like the Goose said, "Right, now we're going to walk it." So we went out, and we walked right up to the river and along it. It was the middle of the night. In those days, '96, this was a much more lairy area, but I didn't feel the least bit afraid. I remember seeing another crazy night-walker coming towards me, and the Goose said, "Don't worry, dear, we're the scariest thing out here tonight!" And he crossed the road! That was a brilliant moment. It has often supported me in a strange way because, even though I wouldn't wish ill on anyone, the sense that John Crow is quite scary can be a good protective feeling.

'Anyway, she took me to all those places, the Tabard, the cathedral, Mary Overie dock, the Clink, Winchester Palace, the Globe. And we somehow ended up at those Cross Bones gates, although I didn't know that was what it was at the time. It was just an old industrial site, a brutalised bit of land. I might have slightly embellished this unconsciously, as we do when we tell our own stories, but my memory is that when we got there, it was like... it was singing. It was just singing. There were lots of rattling cans and other creepy noises, but behind those sounds you could hear this singing. It was singing, "John Crow with a riddle and a madcap rhyme / Here to reveal my mystery..." That bit I didn't even write down until I got back, but it was like it had already been inscribed in me. Sometimes I say, "I'm not really the author. I'm the book. It got written in me."

'When I woke up the next morning, I'd written "The Book of the Goose", although it was three times as long as the finished thing which became the first poem of *The Southwark Mysteries*. I did polish it. Some people want to believe that I received it in a perfect, finished form, but I've never claimed that. Hopefully I've got a bit of craft! But it was complete, and it was so complete that when I read it the next day one of my fears, apart from that I'd gone mad, was that I'd somehow plagiarised it. It felt like it already existed. I thought, Did I read this when I was a kid? Have I just reiterated it?

' "For tonight in Hell / they are tolling the bell / for the Whore that lay at the Tabard, / And well we know / how the carrion crow / doth feast in our Cross Bones Graveyard." That was the first time I'd consciously seen the words "Cross Bones" written like that. My immediate thought was not, "Oh, I wonder where that is." I had this image of the Goose, with a little dagger in her garter. It was a piratical thing, and I'd thought I'd invented it. Where would she be buried? Cross Bones! A week later I was in the local library and I was thinking, "This is all back to front! I've already written the poem and now I'm researching it." I opened a book at random and there was John Stow's 1598 reference to the churchyard for medieval sex workers and a reference to another book. I went and found that book and opened it and there it was. The burial ground, it said, was later "called the Cross Bones". Fuck! Then I looked at the maps and I realised, Oh fuck, that was the street I was on.

'I went back and there were all these London Underground signs around the site. I mean "goosebumps" is obviously a bad joke – but for me, that's how it was. I just started shivering. The only thought I had was, "Fuck, they dug her up!" It was so obvious! They dug her up and she found me.

'One thing I have to say, because I'm not trying to mystify this experience, is that it could have been in the local papers, because from '92 to '96 they were building the Jubilee Line extension, and it had cut through the burial ground, so some rumour of what was happening there may have left an impression, though not consciously. Certainly I had no recollection of it. I reread my notebook to check, because there's seventy-odd pages of research in there, including the walk I did with Ken Campbell. There isn't a word about Cross Bones. And I checked with Ken and the other people on the walk, and no we didn't go there. Which obviously we didn't, because at the time I didn't even know about it.

'For two or three months after that night I was in shock, thinking that I'd pushed the boat out too far. This wasn't like anything I'd ever written, and I didn't even know if I had written it. I thought, "Don't trust the Goose. She's a trickster spirit and you'd be a fool to trust her." But I seemed to get daily affirmations of what I'd written, and I decided to act as if the vision was real, and soon after that I found myself thinking, "You know what, I'm going to serve her. I'm going to trust her and serve her unconditionally. I'm going to put myself in her service and let her decide what we're going to do." And when I did that, it was as if the Goose started opening doors...'

We leave John's flat and walk through Southwark streets towards Cross Bones to see the garden of remembrance in daylight.

'Friends of Cross Bones have always been people from the edge,' he tells me as we walk. 'We started with all the outsiders, so our first-ever reviews were in places like the anarchist press, the undertakers' in-trade magazine and sex workers' in-house stuff. Oh, and taxi drivers.

And I used to joke that with taxi drivers, whores and undertakers, we could probably reach most of society without needing to go above ground ever! I don't want this to become establishment. Our power has always been to represent the outsiders and, even now when we have access to the garden, whenever we meet for vigils, our place is on the street. We are the people of the street. We are the incarnate spirits of the streets come to honour our ancestors.'

I try to reconcile this approach, and the very personal acid vision that started it, with the pillars of the local establishment such as Southwark Cathedral and Shakespeare's Globe that have become part of the wider story. I ask John how this came to be.

'It turned out that the Dean of Southwark Cathedral was looking for a London cycle of medieval mystery plays,' he explains. 'We have a York cycle, as well as Wakefield and Chester and so on, but he couldn't find a London one. Somebody said to him, "There's this local playwright, John Constable, he's writing a new cycle of mystery plays." It was completely untrue at the time. I was writing a cycle of poems channelled by a sex worker spirit, the Goose. But as I had the title, *The Southwark Mysteries*, this seemed like a clear sign of what it should become.

'Colin, the dean, was a wonderful man, quite upright, and very progressive as a social liberal. The cathedral held a blessing of gay and lesbian Christians and a chapel for people living under the shadow of HIV and AIDS. But on theology he was an absolute stickler, and he had real issues with my use of the feminine in relation to God. He said to me, "So, it's a mystery play, it will include creation, Adam and Eve, the Fall, Noah's Ark, Cain and Abel and all that." And I'm like, "Yeah... we can work some of that in, but you have to understand, this is about the Goose."

'We could have had a complete communication breakdown, me and the dean, but the Goose, as Mary Magdalene, came to the rescue. It was obvious, really, the Goose is Mary Magdalene. She's been here for all eternity waiting for Jesus, and he's finally come back for her. When Colin realised that I hadn't conceived my mystery plays in the traditional way, we had some lively discussions! But once he decided to go with them, he supported them and staunchly defended them against the fundamentalist backlash which predictably followed. He's dead now, is Colin. I have nothing but love and respect for him.

'By now plans were moving for *The Southwark Mysteries* to go on in the cathedral. It was still two years away, but already this committee had formed around me. It was great, but there had been a discussion at the committee about whether having a prostitute, as they would say, as the lead character in a community drama was entirely appropriate. I thought, They're trying to cut the Goose out. I know there were exchanges of letters within the church. There were discussions about my "hidden agenda". And there really wasn't one! I did make a sincere effort to write a work that Christians would relate to. It just had to include the Goose.

'I was on one then, it has to be said. I was convinced that I was doing the work of the Goose. I was determined to put this play on at the cathedral *and* the Globe, as predicted in the poem. We were to do it on 23 April 2000, which was Shakespeare's birthday, St George's Day, and it happened to be Easter Sunday. The dean said, "Well, you need to talk to Mark Rylance," who was then the artistic director at the Globe. So I arranged to go and see him, and we had this absolutely bizarre meeting where I went and he didn't know what to make of me.

'I was quite messianic about it in the late nineties, and I took that attitude with Mark, telling him that it had to be on the twenty-third of April and so on. I honestly think that until I actually did the production he was never quite sure how mad I was. Sometimes in the *Mysteries* I wrote about John Crow and deliberately exaggerated this idea of him as a care-in-the-community character. Mark once said to me, "Was that really you, foaming at the mouth?" I said, "That was John Crow, he's a spirit!" Mark couldn't quite figure me out.

'Yet all the way through, I had this great confidence. Things seemed to work when I said, "I trust that the Goose is on the case here, and if

I'm doing her work I don't need to get too caught up in the politics." And what I found very interesting was that, when things were going against me, insiders would contact me. It was the same with Transport for London, just as it was with Shakespeare's Globe. It's not that we'd be going looking for them, but people who worked for these organisations would get in touch and offer to help.

'There was a woman called Jane Arrowsmith who ran the Globe bookshop and who took an interest. She said, "Mark's interested, but he's not sure. I'm going to keep on to him." I went to the bookshop and was looking at a book about Shakespeare when Jane came up to me and said, "What are we going to do with Mark?" or something like that. I said, "The Goose is on it", and at that point an entire bookcase collapsed. Literally – WHOOOMF! – every book fell down. And Jane, who was quite a remarkable woman, she didn't jump. She just looked at me and went, "Oh ho, Mister Crow!" And then I pointed at the book in my hand, at Robert Greene's reference to Shakespeare as "an upstart crow", and we laughed. It's little things like that that actually did the trick. I've always believed that. Mark had people at the Globe saying, "No, he's not crazy, he's driven."

'When we finally got to do it on the twenty-third of April 2000, everything was so charged. It was due to start at three p.m. and there was a thunderstorm at ten to three. But at three o'clock, it cleared, the sun came out and a rainbow appeared.

'We did the first part, roughly two-thirds of the play, in the Globe, where Roddy McDevitt, playing Jesus, did a great entry on his bike. This was a bit of business we put in the show because Roddy would sometimes arrive late for rehearsals, out of breath and carrying his bike. So we had Jesus arrive late, on his bike. He went up on stage, propped it up against a pillar and was about to walk away when he clocked the entire Southwark Cathedral clergy, all standing together in one area. And he gave them a really dirty look and locked his bike. It brought the house down.'

*

We walk past Little Dorrit Park, along Redcross Way and arrive at the memorial garden. In the daylight I realise it is next to an electricity substation. John unlocks the gates and shows me in.

Cross Bones looks larger now, when it is empty and in daylight. It feels quiet, although that's a daft thing to say with the rumble of rattling trains and south London traffic a constant presence. A pair of female police officers are paying attention to the ribbons on the railings, so John goes over to talk to them. They ask him about the Winchester Geese and the mementos for the more recently departed. They leave ten minutes later with an open invitation to the next monthly vigil.

I ask John about the church's blessing. He takes me to the centre of the garden and points to the position where the new dean of South-wark Cathedral stood when he blessed the dead a few months earlier.

'It was the dean's idea, the new dean,' he explains. 'We did *The Southwark Mysteries* again in 2010, and it was done entirely in the cathedral that time. Just before it went on I had a brief chat with the old dean and he said, "Is there anything more that we can do? If the bones were dug up, we could bless them when they are reburied." I said, "We're trying to stop them being dug up. Maybe you could do something at Cross Bones itself?"

'We agreed that a consecration might not be appropriate. A consecration might actually offend as many people as it would please, given all the history. Some of the more hardcore Friends of Cross Bones are quite uncomfortable about working with the church. But as I see it, it was the Goose's church, and her roots are medieval Christianity. That's a very different thing to modern Christianity, of course, but the point is that the Winchester Geese were excluded by the church. This ground is far from the parish church of St Mary Overie because they were in sin. So the church excluded them, and that's the wrong that needed to be addressed.

'Then Colin died, and is much missed, and I thought all this would lapse. But the new dean, Andrew Nunn, actually took it up. He said he would like to come and do something. It was Mary Magdalene's feast day, which is also my birthday. The dean was stood right there, with everyone around him, filling the whole graveyard. He spoke very simply, saying that at the moment lots of people are apologising for the wrongs of the past. And he said that for us to apologise would be a bit meaningless, because what was done was done. But we can do better. He called it "an act of regret, remembrance, and restoration." It was amazing, really, what he said was very beautiful and it really brought people in. He was expressing regret in a meaningful way, then actually honouring the women and performing an act of restoration. That was very powerful.

'I've always said you shouldn't believe or act on every thought that occurs to you on acid, but, as Jesus once said, "By their fruits ye shall know them."'

Listening to John talk, I am reminded once again of Steve Moore. If we were to take a psychologist's view of the voices in their heads, then we would say that the network of neurons that makes up their brains have somehow formed two distinct personalities instead of one. By this definition, their selves have become divided, just as the country has become divided. Yet while the country is full of angst and fear about its division, Steve Moore and John Constable seem enriched. Their divisions gave their lives direction, and purpose, and meaning. They led to the creation of work that inspired countless others. The splits in their minds may have been traumatic when they occurred but, in each case, they led to an emerging story, a new narrative that allowed each man to live as part of his own personal myth.

I look down at the urban concrete ground, imagining the 15,000 bodies below. We bury three types of things: seeds, treasure and the dead. The dead are expected to stay put, treasure is expected to stay buried until we come back for it, and seeds are expected to grow back into the light. Deep in the dirt, I wonder if these categories can get mixed up. If people as forgotten and marginalised as the Winchester Geese can be remembered, people so outcast that even the church wouldn't bury them, then who knows what else can return to us? Is there anything lost to the noosphere that could not potentially return?

I started this journey thinking of it as an excuse to look at our island's history, hoping that this might shed light on our current divisions. I assumed that what constituted 'our history' was pretty obvious. It consisted of well-known subjects such as Canterbury Cathedral or Chaucer's writing. A visit to Cross Bones has brought home not only how much richer and deeper our history really is, but how all that is seemingly lost can be brought back up into the light. If the history that we focus on fails to give us a coherent identity, then we can focus elsewhere. There's no shortage of raw material.

Perhaps our current division is a necessary stage in the emergence of a new national story? Other countries think we are crazy, of course, but haven't they always? It would be a small price to pay to find ourselves part of a new, living myth.

6.

LONDON

The forever stone and the nevergreen tree

In 2004 the graffiti artist Banksy painted two life-sized policemen kissing on the outside wall of the Prince Albert pub in Brighton.

I worked in an office in the same street for a number of years, so I walked past it every day. It was the location that made the graffiti work so well. It was on the side wall of the pub, on Frederick Terrace, which is an otherwise nondescript side street with a few bland office buildings and car-park entrances. Not many people have cause to walk down Frederick Terrace. Trafalgar Street, the road at the front of the pub, is much busier, not least because it leads down from the railway station. Most people would glimpse these kissing policemen if they turned their head while walking down Trafalgar Street. This gave the impression that the policemen had snuck down a quiet side street in order to make out.

Brighton may be the gay capital of the UK, but not everyone liked the painting. In 2006 a couple of men drove up in a plumber's van and covered it with black paint. They did so in front of a CCTV camera and were prosecuted, although damaging graffiti with graffiti might be something of a legal grey area. Much of the left policeman was destroyed but the barman from the pub did an impressive job of repainting him, and the graffiti was soon as good as new. It was then covered with a sheet of Perspex to protect it. Rain got behind the sheet and the image got distorted by damp, but it was at least safe from other attacks.

The wall began to attract more graffiti. The first to appear was a life-size image of the footballer George Best scratching his bum. Then a large portrait of the late DJ John Peel appeared above them both. In Belfast, where my partner Joanne is from, the tradition of end-of-row murals has historically tended towards the aggressive, the political and the intimidating, so we appreciate raising our kids in a town where end-of-row murals depict John Peel.

Before long, the whole wall became a mural. Around Best, Peel and the policemen, a couple of dozen dead musical icons appeared, including Kurt Cobain, Amy Winehouse, Jimi Hendrix and John Lennon. The overall result looks like a waltzers ride from a travelling fairground, which for a garish seaside town like Brighton feels appropriate. Pleasingly, the pantheon of dead rock gods includes Frank Sidebottom, the Timperley comedian who wore a large round papier-mâché head.

Watching the evolution of the wall over a decade has been fascinating. At the beginning, you saw occasional tourists photographing it. Within a few years, I found myself walking past entire tour groups on my way to work. The wall is now a common image on postcards and guidebooks. Banksy's kissing policemen have started to appear on other walls, where they are painted by more postmodern, less creative artists. When I first saw that funny black and white image on the wall down the side street I never guessed the extent to which it would grow into a vibrant, living, changing thing. By the portrait of John Lennon were written the words 'Bigger than Jesus'. At some point Banksy returned to the wall and added his own tag over the name 'Jesus', so it now reads 'Bigger than Banksy'. It sums up the wall nicely.

You might not realise it if you visit the Prince Albert now, but the kissing policemen graffiti was sold in 2014. A specialist restorer removed the paint from the wall and applied it to a canvas or board, which was sold at auction in Miami, to an anonymous buyer, for over half a million dollars. Much of that paint which was sold was the restoration work of the barman. An exact replica of the policemen was then painted in the position they had originally occupied, and a frame and Perspex cover were then placed over this copy, to protect it. This is what tour guides visit today, and what visitors photograph, underneath Banksy's cheeky signature.

As far as the art world is concerned, Banksy's *Kissing Coppers* (2004) is in a private collection. Its location is unknown but it is assumed to be stored in an American collection, quite possibly unobserved in a dark vault. It is an asset on a spreadsheet, a store of value that it is hoped will increase. As someone who has watched that painting over a decade, it seems to me that all that was sold in Miami was everything unimportant about it. Taking the paint off that wall was like taking a fish out of the sea: you get to walk away with the fish, but it is dead.

Where things are can be as important as what they are. The story of television is littered with famous presenters, such as Richard Madeley and Judy Finnigan, who were lured to other channels but were then unable to find an audience. They could only be successful in a certain time at a certain place. Likewise, the Parthenon marbles would have far greater impact in Athens than they do in the British museum gallery. In their current location they can't help but be mildly disappointing, like Keith Richards and Mick Jagger when they are not part of the Rolling Stones. Location and position can be an integral part of what makes some things valuable. Would the Mona Lisa be so revered if it wasn't at the heart of the Louvre?

It is 9 June 2016, and I am in the Museum of London. The object in front of me is making me think about Banksy's *Kissing Coppers*. It's called London Stone. It's just a stone, really. Or at best, a rock.

London Stone is a rough chunk of white limestone about twenty-one inches across, seventeen inches high and a foot deep. That's pretty much all you can say about its physical attributes, other than to remark upon how it shows sign of discoloration from years of exposure to London's smoke and smog. It is not obviously carved, and it does not seem to have been shaped for any particular purpose. The reason why the rock is in the Museum of London is that it has been called London Stone for a very, very long time.

London Stone is commonly said to be the oldest thing in London, but no one knows how old it is. It is mentioned in medieval documents going back to around the year 1100, where it is typically mentioned casually and in passing, as if the author expected everyone to be familiar with this famous landmark. It was originally taller than the fragment we have now, and was probably broken during the Great Fire of London in 1666. William Blake thought it was a Druid altar, while others claimed it was the stone from which King Arthur pulled Excalibur. More typically, it is said to be the omphalos of the City of London, the stone which marks its exact centre.

In 1450 the rebel leader Jack Cade brought an army of common men into the City to protest at the behaviour of Henry VI's government. He struck his sword on London Stone and proclaimed himself to be lord mayor of London. In *Henry VI Part 2*, Shakespeare mocked Cade by having him sit on London Stone as if it were a throne, while proclaiming wild declarations such as 'of the city's cost, the pissing-conduit run nothing but claret wine this first year of our reign'. The implication is that London Stone was thought to have the ability to grant political or royal authority in a similar way to the Stone of Scone near Perth, or the Anglo-Saxon coronation stone that gave Kingston upon Thames its name.

The stone is associated with London's founding myth. According to *History of the Kings of England*, a chronicle written around 1136 by Geoffrey of Monmouth, the pre-Roman founder of London was Brutus of Troy. Brutus had been banished from his homeland, and after a number of adventures he arrived on a deserted island where he discovered the remains of a temple to the Moon goddess Diana.

Sleeping there after performing a ritual in honour of the goddess, he received a vision of the land he would settle. This was an island in the western ocean which was almost uninhabited, apart from a few giants.

Brutus and his followers set sail for this land and after several more adventures, including a narrow escape from the Sirens, he landed at Totnes in Devon. He then defeated the giants of Albion, declared himself king and named the island Britain after himself. On the north bank of the Thames, he established the town of New Troy, or *Troia Nova*, which was said to be the origin of the later name *Trinovantum*. From this, London Stone acquired the alternative name of the Brutus Stone. It was said that 'so long as the Stone of Brutus is safe, so long shall London flourish'.

Modern historians, needless to say, don't believe a word of this.

I first visited London Stone in March 2009. It was housed in a metal cage and glazed alcove set into the front wall of 111 Cannon Street, underneath the window, which was then a branch of the Bank of China. The stone looked a sorry thing then, trapped in its iron cage and ignored by the stream of City workers passing by. I went with my friend, the late Beat artist Brian Barritt, who felt so sorry for this forlorn lump of rock that he decided to steal it and set it free. He began working out the logistics of cutting through the bars of its cages and winching the rock onto the back of a waiting truck. I'm not 100 per cent sure about this, but I think he was joking.

In the years since that visit, the Bank of China closed this office. 111 Cannon Street became first a sports shop, then a branch of WH Smith. The stone's glass alcove became no longer visible from the interior of the building, because a magazine rack was placed in front of it.

The building is now being demolished, so London Stone has temporarily been taken in by the museum until it can return to its old position in a new Cannon Street development. This isn't the first time that the stone has outlived the building that housed it. It was originally positioned on the opposite side of the road, where the entrance to Cannon Street tube now stands. When London's streets became busier it became a hazard to traffic, so in 1742 it was moved across the road and placed by the doorway of St Swithin's Church. The exact centre of London, clearly, is a woozy omphalos. It was moved around the church a couple of times over the following centuries, until it ended up where I found it in 2009. St Swithin's was destroyed in the Blitz, but a small section around the stone survived, just as it had survived the Great Fire of London. Number 111 Cannon Street was built around this surviving rock.

The Museum of London is just a fifteen-minute walk from Cannon Street, so London Stone has not moved far. It is now housed in a glass case on a bright pink angular plinth, with a stylish pink backdrop that has its name spelt out across the top in raised, all capital letters. A TV screen to its right runs a short, specially made documentary about the stone's history on a loop, and an information panel in front explains its links to Shakespeare. White lettering on the pink backdrop reads, 'This piece of limestone is reputed to be the stone that marks the centre of London. Usually at 111 Cannon Street, it has been moved here during

London Stone

building works. Stories have grown up around the stone and now in the 21st century it sends tweets to its followers.' I pull out my phone to see what @londonstone is saying, hoping for some gossip about Brutus or Jack Cade. Its most recent tweet reads, 'Some of my limestone cousins are in your toothpaste. This is rather strange so let's never talk of this again.' I put my phone away.

Like a Banksy in a Miami vault, London Stone looks dead in a museum. Physically, it is just an unremarkable rock. Its importance is almost entirely immaterial. As Roy Stephenson, the head of archaeological collections at the museum, said after they attempted to work out an insurance value for the rock, London Stone's value 'could be anywhere between £19.99, what it would cost to buy a slab of stone down the garden centre, and £19 trillion, the turnover of the City of London'.

With its striking plinth and video, the Museum of London has done all it can to treat the stone with the respect such a significant object deserves. The problem is that London Stone is not supposed to be in a museum. Even when it was at its most neglected, hidden behind a WH Smith magazine rack, as forgotten and ignored as the Winchester Geese, London Stone was still a thing of wonder. It had the stoic reliability of a member of the Queen's Guards on duty outside a London palace who remains unmoving while tourists take selfies around him. Celebrated or forgotten, London Stone was always there, a constant witness as centuries turned into millennia.

Myth, story and history have accumulated around London Stone and turned it into something more than its physical reality. Perhaps that shouldn't be too surprising. Although the street where it stood is now called Cannon Street, and was previously known as Candlewick Street, late-medieval maps show that the road originally flowed uninterrupted into the last remaining section of London's Watling Street to still keep that name.

London Stone is a reminder that the immaterial often needs something to form around, although it does not have to be something as long-lasting as stone. Both the murder of Becket and the moving of London Stone tell the same story: the noosphere is ultimately grounded in the geosphere. It flourishes when it is rooted in place.

I am sat in the window of Ye Olde Watling, a seventeenth-century pub on the stretch of Watling Street that runs through the City. Ye Olde Watling, the food menu reminds us, is 'famous for being Sir Christopher Wren's drawing office during the rebuild of St Paul's Cathedral'. Like the original medieval cathedral, all buildings along this stretch of Watling Street were destroyed in the Great Fire of 1666. If you're planning to build a cathedral, it's a good idea to build a pub first.

St Paul's

It is midday. A long queue of City workers emerges out of the door of a butcher's shop opposite and snakes down the street. The butcher's shop is selling vaguely named 'meat sandwiches', which have proven popular with a patient and entirely male lunchtime crowd. City workers, I notice, still favour grey or dark blue single-breasted suits and light blue shirts, but they have stopped wearing ties and now sport large amounts of hair product.

Change is constant in London, and things get forgotten. The original path of Watling Street is an example of this. You'll recall that, long before this city existed or the Thames was bridged, the road was aimed straight at a point where the Thames was easy to ford, roughly where the Houses of Parliament now stand. I'm tempted to follow this original route, because it would take us past such historically important places as Shakespeare's Globe and Westminster Abbey. Yet after the Romans bridged the Thames further east, around the point of the modern London Bridge, those travelling along Watling Street abandoned the original route in order to take advantage of this new easier alternative. After 2,000 years of change, the route of this detour has largely been obliterated but, against the odds, this short section of modern London has retained the name Watling Street, so this is where I head.

The survival of the name allows us to make an informed guess at the route of the detour. Having crossed the bridge travellers would have turned west around modern-day Cannon Street, which flowed into the surviving stretch of Watling Street, which in turn leads to St Paul's Cathedral. The route becomes speculative from St Paul's to Marble Arch, where we next have definite proof of Watling Street's route.

In Roman times a traveller would have crossed the bridge, turned left and passed first London Stone and then the Mithraeum, which was a temple to the Roman god Mithras. Mithraism was a visionary cult that favoured underground temples and was popular with legionnaires. The god Mithras was born from a rock, which perhaps makes his temple's position next to London Stone appropriate. In the fourth century his temple was rededicated to a new god, most likely Bacchus, the Roman god of wine, drunkenness, ritual madness, religious ecstasy and theatre. This god sounds far more appropriate for London. The Mithraeum may have reflected the original interests of Roman soldiers stationed at newly founded London, but the rededication suggests that slowly those legions were infected with the city's true spirit.

Antiquarians used to claim that a temple to the Moon Goddess Diana stood just past the Mithraeum, on the site of the present St Paul's Cathedral. Historians now treat this claim, which was based on accounts by the Elizabethan historian William Camden, with scepticism because they have been unable to find further evidence to support it. The boundary between myth and history, as we have noted, is a shifting, porous thing. A surprise discovery by archaeologists can promote legend to the category of history, such as the city of Troy, and a lack of supporting evidence can eject previously accepted history into the wasteland of myth. In the seventeenth century, for example, it was believed that Shakespeare wrote a play called *The Widow of Watling Street*, which was also known as *The Puritan* or *The Puritan Widow*. The play was included in the Third Folio of Shakespeare's collected works. Scholarly consensus now declares it to be the work of a different writer, and a once-accepted fact has been relegated to a historical myth.

Established history is like our memories: imperfect but incredibly convincing. We don't know the chain of events that led to Camden believing there had been a temple of Diana, so we can't judge the quality of his evidence. It may have been some now lost written source, or a surviving oral tradition, or a blatant lie sincerely retold. Assumptions, mistakes, ignorance, mischief, prejudice and propaganda have all played a role in forging what we think of as history and what we think of as myth. The safeguards of academia do the hard work of policing the boundary, but they do not claim to be perfect. Logically we know that some of our myths and legends will have their origins in fact, and a certain percentage of our history must be untruth credibly told. Some parts of our established history will be as false as my memory of reading C. J. Stone's *Fierce Dancing* before it was published, but who can say which parts?

The idea of the Temple of Diana could perhaps have been suggested by the stories of Brutus of Troy, who founded London after encountering Diana in a dream. If someone wished to elaborate on that story, they might include Brutus founding a temple to this goddess in New

Troy. Whatever the reasons for Camden's belief, it is a pleasing syn-
chronicity that St Paul's is now probably best known as the location of
the wedding of Princess Diana. The young Diana Spencer entered the
cathedral and was transformed into a royal princess or possibly, given
her unique position in the nation's pantheon, someone more than a
princess. Her story ended further up Watling Street, at the Althorp
Estate in Northamptonshire, where she is said to have been buried.
To the British people she became more important, and certainly more
loved, than the religion the cathedral was built to honour.

There may not have been a temple of Diana on that site in Roman
times, but in one sense there is now. Camden's account may no longer
pass muster as history, but it might work as prophecy.

I enter St Paul's Underground station and head down into the under-
city. Two slow-moving escalators descend through a long, steeply
angled tunnel, and a line of countless rectangular advertisements
runs along each wall. The air warms as I go deeper, becoming damp
and sticky, while the advertisements keep up their visual shouts and
screams, demanding attention and energy. The clangs of construction and the grumble of traffic from the surface are left behind and
gradually replaced by the noise of underground machinery and trains.
The artificial lighting down here is harsh and hungover. I fall into the
rhythm of the grey-faced shuffling mob as we make our way towards
the westbound platform.

There is no record of a road named or considered to be Watling
Street between St Paul's and Marble Arch. It is the only gap of its
kind along the road's route, the victim of the constant change and
reinvention of the centre of London. The road is known only by its
absence, like dark matter. It exists as a logical deduction, suggested by
the way that the north and south legs of Watling Street have always
been thought of as the same road. It has been consumed by the years,
not even surviving as myth or rumour. Because it has descended into
the underworld it is fitting that this is how we journey along it, on

the underground, where St Paul's and Marble Arch are linked by the Central Line.

This gap in Watling Street jumps from just beyond the end of the A2 to the start of the A5. Those names, the A2 and the A5, date back to a 1920s attempt to unify the country through a rational, French-style road network. Nearly a century later, during which time the road network has expanded massively and chaotically, you might not think British roads are numbered in a systematic or sensible way. But our numbering system began with good intentions.

The logic behind our road numbers was focused on the 'A' roads radiating out of the capital cities of London and Edinburgh. These radial roads were numbered in the manner of a clock, clockwise from the north or twelve o'clock position. The road running directly north from London was called the A1, Watling Street to the south-east became the A2, the road to Portsmouth in the south-west was the A3, the A4 ran to the west, Watling Street to the north-west was called the A5 and the A6 ran up to Bedford, close to the A1. In a similar way, the roads radiating out of Edinburgh were called the A7, A8 and A9.

The major roads encountered when you drove away from London or Edinburgh on these radial roads gained an extra digit, which increased the further away you got from the capital. If you drove along the A4 from London you would pass the A40, A41, A42 and so on, and if you turned off onto the A41, say, you would then pass the A411, A412 and A413. After a century of new roads and expansion, this logical system has dissolved into a very British mess thanks to endless fudges and practical necessity. But this well-intentioned system is why the ancient route of Watling Street was split into the A2 and the A5.

The Central Line I'm travelling on now was opened in 1900, when it was known as the Central London Railway. Both Mark Twain and the Prince of Wales, who would later become King Edward VII, were passengers on its inaugural journey. It originally ran between Shepherd's Bush and Bank, in white-painted tunnels between sixty and 110 feet underground, which twisted and turned to follow the course of the medieval streets above. It cost a flat fare of 2d a journey and became popularly known as the 'Twopenny Tube'. From this we get our modern name for the entire London Underground system, the Tube.

Inside my train, two rows of seats run along the length of the carriages so that passengers face each other. I take a seat. The six people opposite me look blank, while a strip of advertisements above their heads shows six healthy, vibrant, attractive faces who dazzle me with their unnatural teeth and glossy hair. It is as if the imagined dream-selves of Londoners are visible, hovering above their normal mundane selves. Visitors to London often comment on how unfriendly people seem on the Tube, but Londoners have learnt that a smiling face probably wants money.

'The next station is Holborn. Change for the Piccadilly Line,' a reassuring female voice informs the carriage. From St Paul's, the red Central Line stops at Chancery Lane, Holborn, Tottenham Court Road, Oxford Circus, Bond Street and Marble Arch. These names are ingrained into Londoners, like incantations. The Central Line is one of the busiest train lines in the country.

This trip west was also the final journey for at least 50,000 people, over the course of 600 years, between the twelfth century and 1783. It is the route from Newgate prison, by St Paul's, to the site of the Tyburn gallows, which is where Marble Arch now stands. Up on the surface, this was the road to the underworld for the condemned. The bell would toll and they would 'go west', a phrase that had a bleak meaning before it was reimagined during the California gold rush and, later, by the Village People. Prisoners were pulled through the jeering crowds on a cart, along with their own coffin, on the last day that they would see. Their journey to meet the hangman matches the absent section of Watling Street.

Executions took place at Tyburn since at least 1196, and probably earlier. The area was named after the River Tyburn, which is now buried underneath London but originally emerged as a spring in the Lyndhurst Road area of Hampstead. Its path to the Thames is uncertain, but we know it was a nuisance to the builders of the Twopenny Tube in 1900, as water kept flooding into their works. 'Tyburn' is a Saxon name, and 'burn' means a stream or brook. The meaning of the 'Ty' part of the name is disputed, but it is possible that it comes from the old one-handed god Tiw, whom the day 'Tuesday' is named after. If this was the case, it is appropriate, for Tiw was a god of law.

Condemned men and women were originally hanged from a prominent group of elm trees, which probably stood at a crossroads. To the Normans, elms were associated with justice, and to the Greeks they were associated with death. Smithfield, London's other major site of executions, was also originally referred to as 'The Elms', so the choice of tree seems deliberate. Tyburn was a rural area, sufficiently distant from the city so that the smell of bodies left to rot in hanging gibbets would not trouble the townsfolk. In 1222, Henry III ordered the building of permanent gallows on the site, and these gallows became, as William Blake puts it in 'Jerusalem', 'London's fatal tree'.

The gallows were rebuilt in a distinctive triangular shape in Elizabethan times, with three upright wooden posts, 18 feet tall, linked at the top by a triangle of lintels. It was from these top posts that multiple nooses would hang. The maximum number of people hanged on the 'Triple Tree' at the same time was twenty-four, or eight on each side, which occurred on 23 June 1649. It is this triangular shape that explains the reference to Tyburn in Shakespeare's comedy *Love's Labour's Lost*. When the lovesick courtier Longaville wonders if he is the first person to be lied to, Lord Berowne explains to him that he is the third:

> I could put thee in comfort. Not by two that I know:
> Thou makest the triumviry, the corner-cap of society,
> The shape of Love's Tyburn that hangs up simplicity.

Most of those hanged at Tyburn were petty thieves whose names were not thought worthy of recording, although famous criminals such as Jack Shepherd, a thief who escaped from four prisons, had their life stories told in sensationalised pamphlets that were written and printed in time to be sold at their execution. The nobility were generally spared the indignity of being hanged, drawn and quartered in front of a thrill-seeking mob. As a privilege of rank, they were usually neatly beheaded at the Tower of London. Witches were hanged at Tyburn, particularly after the 1563 Witchcraft Act, and a great number of Catholics were also hanged in Tudor times. The authorities insisted that they were being executed as traitors rather than heretics, but that did not stop their fellow Catholics viewing them as martyrs. As a result, the site of the gallows became sacred ground that the devout would pilgrimage to and pray at.

The site, naturally, attracted supernatural stories. In 1678, the gallows were discovered one morning uprooted and smashed into pieces on the ground. Witnesses claimed they had seen screeching ghosts sitting on top of the gallows before they were demolished. The story was told in a printed broadsheet entitled *The Tyburn-Ghost: Or, The Strange Downfall of the GALLOWS, a most true revelation how the famous Triple-Tree Neer Paddinton was on Tuesday-night last (the third of this instant September) wonderfully pluckt up by the Roots, and demolish by certain EVIL-SPIRITS.* A nearby building called Tyburn House was, according to the Swiss-born Elizabethan diarist Thomas Platter, 'haunted by such monsters as no one can live in it'.

The Tyburn Tree was a 'short-drop' gallows. The prisoner would stand on a cart underneath with the noose around their neck and the cart would be driven away. Unlike gallows designed to give the prisoner a long drop, this fall would usually be insufficient to break their necks and kill them instantly. Their bodies would jerk as they struggled, and spectators would say that they were 'dancing the Tyburn jig' or that they 'dance the Paddington frisk'. It was common for people to evacuate their bowels while being hanged, which gave rise to the saying 'a man will piss when he cannot whistle'. If the hangman was sufficiently kind-hearted, he might allow the prisoner's relatives to pull down on the hanged person's feet, in order to shorten their suffering.

Typically, they would die slowly of asphyxiation, or be cut down while still alive and disembowelled.

Occasionally, dead people would be hanged to make a point. The newly crowned Charles II, fresh from his stay at Restoration House, gave orders for Oliver Cromwell's body to be exhumed from its resting place in Westminster Abbey and hanged in chains at Tyburn. It was then thrown into a pit and his severed head was displayed on a spike. Charles II was known as the Merry Monarch, but his good humour did not extend to those who beheaded his dad.

Superstitions about objects associated with execution meant that the rope, shroud and prisoner's clothes could be sold by the hangman, and they commanded a premium price. Strands from the rope, it was thought, could cure toothache. For particularly notorious criminals, the hangman could sell the rope by the inch. From this practice we get the phrase 'money for old rope'.

The prisoner's clothes would frequently be taken before the execution, to prevent family members or the general crowd descending on the body as it was cut down and claiming their own souvenirs. Prisoners were often hanged in just a shroud or their undershirt, with a bag or hood over their head. In the case of James Fenn, who was hanged as a Catholic traitor for his part in a plot against Queen Elizabeth, his shirt was ripped away when the cart was pulled out from underneath him, leaving him hanging naked, 'whereat the people muttered greatly'. A young Irish prisoner named Hannah Dagoe threw her clothes into the crowd as she was brought to Tyburn, in order to prevent the hangman from getting his spoils. When he tried to prevent her from giving away her last garments, she kicked him in the groin, and as soon as the noose was around her neck she threw herself out of the cart, choosing to hang herself rather than be hanged. As far as the crowd was concerned, this was as good as it gets. In 1447, a reprieve arrived for five men being prepared for hanging and dismemberment after the hangman had already taken their clothes. They attempted to reclaim their clothes from the hangman, but he insisted that they were rightfully his. After much arguing, the reprieved men went home naked.

Hanging days attracted large crowds, who would come from London for the free entertainment. The crowd would in turn attract prostitutes, pickpockets, orange-sellers and hawkers of sensational broadsheets. The wealthy could avoid the crush by paying for a seat in a specially built grandstand. There were constant complaints about price-gouging, for the cost of a seat would vary depending on the fame of the prisoner. In 1758, when a prisoner received a last-minute reprieve after delivering a lengthy and boring final speech, the frustrated crowd rioted and demolished the viewing stands.

Given the number of pickpockets who worked the crowd, there is little evidence that public executions worked as a deterrent. The Tyburn Gallows was intended as a warning to law-abiding citizens and an expression of royal power, yet the crowds and prisoners subverted this. The crowd came for a good show, and many prisoners were prepared to give them one. The condemned were able to get the crowd onside by laughing at their predicament and mocking the authorities. The procession from Newgate to Tyburn was only about three miles, but it could take up to three hours, especially if a popular prisoner was enjoying the attention of the crowds and stopping off at the inns along the way for a drink, as was their right. Disliked prisoners, on the other hand, travelled much faster, pelted as they were with rocks, vegetables and excrement.

Prisoners who arrived numb with terror were considered boring, while religious heretics who expressed stoicism or sometimes joy at their fate were admired. But what the crowd liked best of all was the gallows-humour of an unrepentant, outrageous, ruling-class-mocking highwayman. Hangings were intended as a form of theatre in which the royal court displayed its authority over subjects, yet the crowd responded with an alternative, opposite theatre, one in which they refused to be afraid or intimidated.

Those last moments at the centre of the laughter and approval of the crowd were, for some prisoners, the high point of their life. They held the same attraction as an appearance on a modern reality-TV programme. The prize was a brief moment of attention and fame in a life that knew neither, before inevitable oblivion arrived.

The British public, perhaps, have not changed a great deal. I suspect ex-contestants of *Big Brother* or *The X Factor* would understand how, when the cry of 'Hats off! Hats off!' rang out across the crowd before the moment of execution, it was not intended as a mark of respect. It was to allow those at the back to get a better view.

Tyburn Gallows does not await when the escalator carries me up from the underworld and deposits me outside Marble Arch tube station, at the western end of Oxford Street. All that remains now is a round stone and metal plaque in the ground, on a pedestrian island at the southern end of Edgware Road, which reads 'The Site of Tyburn Tree'. Looking around, it is almost impossible to imagine this noisy, traffic-filled junction as the rural execution site of past centuries. Where once

Site of Tyburn Tree

stood Tyburn House, 'haunted by such monsters as no one can live in it', there now stands an Odeon cinema. It was recently closed down and boarded up, and is awaiting demolition.

No one calls this area Tyburn any more. A medieval church near here was called St Mary's by the Bourne, which in time became St Marylebone. Marylebone had far nicer connotations than Tyburn, so you can see how historic estate agents would have preferred it. This specific part of Marylebone is now called Marble Arch, after the unwanted imperial archway on the south side of the road. The arch was built to grace the entrance to Buckingham Palace but was soon deemed surplus to requirements. In 1847 it was moved to what was the north-east corner of Hyde Park, which is now a traffic island. This is not an unusual fate for an imperial arch, but at least the Arc de Triomphe in Paris is placed on a traffic roundabout at the junction of long, wide boulevards, giving the impression that traffic did once travel through the arch. The current siting of the Marble Arch gives the impression that they had to dump it somewhere, and there's not a lot of places a 269-foot-tall marble-clad archway can go in the centre of London. Marble Arch is the city equivalent of an expensive jet ski that seemed a great idea when bought late one drunken night on eBay but which now clutters up the back garden.

Despite its impressive size and skilled, intricate carvings, I am struck by how uninspiring Marble Arch is in comparison to the other lump of white rock we have just seen. Physically, London Stone is as far away from Marble Arch as a rock can get. It boasts none of its size or workmanship. But Marble Arch announces the imperial majesty of King George IV, while London Stone speaks simply of the permanence of place. London Stone, I think, has the better story. As any auctioneer or art dealer will tell you, it is by immaterial associations that we value material things.

South of Marble Arch is the corner of Hyde Park known as Speakers' Corner. Here anyone can proclaim their thoughts and beliefs to the general public, provided they are thick-skinned enough to brave the resulting heckles. Speakers' Corner came about after protests and demonstrations in the mid-nineteenth century led to the 1872 Parks Regulation Act, which recognised the right of assembly. Next to the gallows where once the condemned were free to give their final words, the right of everyone to speak openly became recognised.

Marble Arch

Speakers' Corner became globally famous. When Angela Merkel addressed both British Houses of Parliament in February 2014 she recalled how, on a visit to London in 1990, 'We walked through Hyde Park looking for Speakers' Corner, which – especially for us as East Germans – was legendary, the very symbol of free speech.' But Speakers' Corner has effectively died over recent years. It was damaged by a redesign of the park, and it became irrelevant to speakers who reach a far larger audience on Facebook or Twitter. Today, the area is entirely empty, as it was on my previous visit, with no speakers and no one for them to talk to. I watch the empty ground for a while. Occasional joggers do run across the tarmac, but I doubt they would stop and listen if I stood up and began declaring my opinions. It may return on weekends during the tourist season, but for now Speakers' Corner is just the name of an expensive park food kiosk, another unmourned aspect of our past that withered away when its time came. It is not just prisoners who die here.

I head back to the plaque marking the site of London's 'nevergreen tree' and start to walk up Edgware Road. This is the beginning of the northern leg of Watling Street. Here the road has a strong Middle Eastern flavour, with Arabic text displayed across shop fronts and groups of men sitting outside Lebanese restaurants, absent-mindedly puffing on elaborate hookah pipes while watching the never-ending traffic. This has long been an area associated with immigrants. In the eighteenth century it was a destination for persecuted French Huguenots, along with sizeable Greek and Jewish populations, and Arab migrants began arriving in the nineteenth century. Edgware Road was a portal through which foreign influences settled, to be absorbed by the wider British identity. The first Indian restaurant, for example, opened near here in

Edgware Road

1810. Given the road's origins as a pre-Roman Celtic trackway through the ancient Great Middlesex Forest, it is doubtful that any area of the country can claim to have experienced such constant change.

This part of Edgware Road represents the side of the country that was rejected by the majority of the English and Welsh population in the EU referendum. Theirs was a vote against endless change, foreign influence and urban tolerance. It was a vote, to a large extent, against London itself. Geographically, almost all of England and Wales voted to leave the EU, with the exception of London and a few other large or prosperous cities. If anyone was making the case for the benefits areas like this provide to the wider country, it was not reported by our media.

London, in the eyes of the wider country, is not popular. It is viewed as a place of the self-obsessed and the privileged, where wealth erodes normal human decency and empathy is scarce. It is where people kept reading the *Sun* in public after Hillsborough and where drivers don't bother to indicate at roundabouts because, as they see it, what's in it for them? London is where the media talks about London to Londoners, with little thought for the wider country, and where the country's wealth and opportunities are jealously guarded. When I lived in the north, there was a constant, unquestioned level of anti-London sentiment. Thinking back, I recall it had a lot to do with Londoners using mobile phones and eating hummus. With hindsight this might not appear that damning, but in the 1990s it was a devastating takedown. For most of the country, London is simply Other. It does not feel like it is part of their own nation. The people are too different.

Those sucked into the metropolis from the country for work discover that the people are essentially the same. There is just an awful lot more of them. The population of this one city is more than the populations of Scotland and Wales combined, which is why it is so prominent in the island's media. What makes Londoners different to the rest of the country is not some innate quality of Southern shiteness that infects all those who live there, but the simple matter of population density.

Increasing population densities increase the number of connections between people, which in turn increases economic activity. Businesses can find customers, and artists can find audiences. There are more ideas in circulation, and more options. The culture it generates spreads out to the rest of the country and around the globe. The wealth that it generates is supposed to spread to the rest of the country as well, although in practice a large chunk of that does seem to find itself in offshore tax havens.

There is a downside to all this. Being surrounded by an uncountable sea of people whom you don't know and can't trust can be isolating. Londoners are sharp, active and cosmopolitan, but there is a weight on their shoulders. From the London perspective, the rest of the country should be grateful for all their energy. This one city generates 22 per cent of UK GDP and pays 30 per cent of UK taxes, thanks in part to its role as a global financial sector. As Londoners would see it, much of the resentment aimed at them is jealousy and ignorance.

This gulf between rural and urban England is particularly wide in the wake of the EU referendum. Like the Trump red states and Clinton blue states of American politics, two distinct cultures have evolved and there seems little indication that they will reconcile. Londoners wished to remain in the European Union, active and engaged in international trade and affairs, an international city in a globally interconnected age. But the rest of the country wanted none of this.

The implications of leaving the EU will only become clear in the long term, but the early indications for London are not good. Unless a remarkable deal is reached in negotiations between UK and the EU, London's financial centre will get much smaller when Euro-denominated services move to Frankfurt, Paris, Amsterdam or Dublin. A shrinking financial sector could cause a collapse in the overheated luxury housing market, which in turn would affect London's housing in general, and this would have a knock-on effect for the broader economy. While the full impact of leaving the EU on London is still unknown, few think it will be positive.

I recall the myths that surround London Stone, which claimed that the city would flourish for as long as the stone remains. In theory, its current move to the Museum of London should not have affected this, because the museum is within the current limits of the City of London. But the stone is far older than those modern limits, and the city boundary used to be much smaller. The stone's current location is in fact a matter of yards beyond the old Roman walls. This means that it is currently just outside of the original city boundary.

To hear some bank workers talk, the evacuation of London's financial district has already begun and a major collapse of the industry is under way. That the City of London should face such an unprecedented threat as soon as London Stone was removed from the old City shows that, even in the twenty-first century, myths play out their stories on this island whether we pay attention to them or not.

The Museum of London will return London Stone to its original position as soon as building work allows. Given the current uncertainties and fears gripping the financial city, we can be forgiven for hoping this occurs sooner rather than later. The stories are vague about what happens if London Stone is removed and then returned, but the logic of myth should at least give us hope.

Whenever riots break out in London, there is usually somebody from a more secure and comfortable part of the country who says, 'I don't understand why rioters are destroying their own neighbourhood.' The answer to this is, well, what else have they got to destroy? If you've reached the point where you feel that the only option open to you is to start trashing stuff, you are unlikely to be thinking through the longer-term implications of your actions. To many Londoners, this is what the EU referendum vote felt like: a decision to smash what we currently have without any thought of what would come later. After the referendum, London felt like the condemned prisoner in Newgate condemned to 'go west' and be hanged for the pleasure of the mob.

The reasons the rest of the country gave for voting 'leave' made no sense to London. But perhaps, deep down, city folk and country folk are not that different after all. Perhaps at our core we are all the same, even if population density makes us see things differently. Sometimes the British people, like the London mob, just want to smash things. Sometimes they want to watch people hang.

Bedford

ICKNIELD WAY

Hitchin

The Wicked Lady

St. Alban's Executioner's Eyes

Watling Street

St Albans Cathedral

Verulamium • ●St. Albans

PANASONIC

Watford ●

The Dark Side

LONDON

ELSTREE STUDIOS BOREHAMWOOD

7.

ST ALBANS

I never voted for Saint George

A Roman emperor, dressed in a laurel crown and a bedsheet toga, is looking down at St Albans' main shopping street from a balcony. Looking around, everything else appears reassuringly normal. Pedestrianised areas are packed with slow-moving families carrying white plastic carrier bags and pushing buggies. All the mandatory chain shops – Boots, Clarks, O2, Clintons, Marks & Spencer – are present and correct. It is a typical British high street, but one that just happens to be surveyed by a portly, laughing emperor.

It is 21 June 2014, the longest day of the year, and it is gloriously sunny. In a couple of days it will be St John's Eve, the date of Shakespeare's *A Midsummer Night's Dream*. We are in an archetypal midsummer, and legendary events are about to unfurl. Those events are going to be re-enacted through the medium of twelve-foot-high puppets, which is always a plus.

I am only twenty-three miles up Watling Street from Marble Arch, but London feels a long way from here. From the site of the Tyburn Tree, the road runs north-west in a straight line up to Kilburn, where it becomes known as Shoot Up Hill. The fact that Watling Street is called Shooters Hill as it enters London and Shoot Up Hill as it leaves is a gift to writers of cockney crime thrillers. The road continues through Edgware to the leafy village of Elstree, with its many film and television sound stages, and then passes underneath the M25. For a brief period on its way to St Albans its road numbering randomly becomes A5183 instead of A5, but a sign for 'Watling Street Caravan Park' assures you that you're still on the old road.

The emperor overlooks the shoppers from the balcony of an imposing white building, with a facade of Ionic columns topped by a triangular pediment. It looks as if this was originally an important civic building, such as a town hall or a guild centre, although it is now a coffee shop. I've come to St Albans to witness the Alban Pilgrimage, the key event in a yearly celebration called the Alban Weekend, which begins with a parade through the town centre. The emperor is waiting to play his part in this parade, held in honour of Saint Alban, the saint who gave this town its name. Traffic has been diverted away from the route. The empty road, usually hidden by a row of barely moving cars, is revealed as an endlessly repatched stretch of mismatched grey tarmac and faded road markings. It looks like a depressed harlequin.

I hear the parade long before it comes into view. It begins with brass bands, local dignitaries and mobs of schoolchildren. The shoppers crowd the edge of the parade route and applaud the slow-moving spectacle. The children's oversized costumes, which represent red roses and multicoloured stained-glass windows, turn them into waddling blobs of colour. Behind them come the first of the giant puppets. Enormous lions tower over the children, alongside impressive Roman chariots. They are accompanied by a host of angels, with magnificent psychedelic wings that point to the heavens and double the angels' height. They look inspired by the imagery of William Blake. They give the impression they were designed by somebody with first-hand knowledge of exactly what an angel looks like.

In the distance is puppet Saint Alban himself. He is dressed in a resplendent blue flowing robe and is accompanied by a pair of fierce-faced Roman centurions. The way the giant puppet's arms flap in front of him and the tiny legs of the human puppeteer underneath the costume give him an endearing comic quality. He ambles along like a cross between Godzilla and Mr Punch. His giant puppet face looks unexpectedly like Ian Brown from The Stone Roses.

Puppet Saint Alban

I have a confession to make: despite being English, I feel no connection to the English patron saint, Saint George. I assume this puts me in a minority, although when you compare how little the English celebrate St George's Day compared to the Irish celebrations of St Patrick's Day or the Welsh marking of St David's Day, I wonder if my minority is larger than is usually recognised.

Saint George was not the original patron saint of England. That honour went to Edmund the Martyr. Unfortunately Edmund, a ninth-century East Anglian King, was just too English for the Norman-descended Plantagenet kings, who viewed an Anglo-Saxon spiritually personifying the country as politically unwelcome. Poor Edmund was removed from the position during the reign of King Edward III in the fourteenth century, and Saint George was imposed on the country in his place. The Plantagenets were not going to adapt to English culture; the English were expected to adapt to them.

George was a soldier from Roman Palestine who never visited England or had any connection to the country. But this didn't trouble our Plantagenet kings, many of whom also had as little to do with the country they ruled as they possibly could. They were more interested in the Crusades. George was a military saint who, in the eyes of many crusaders, was something of a pin-up and a superhero. So large was his fan base that he was made the patron saint of dozens of countries and cities, including Ethiopia, Romania, Serbia, Moscow, Ukraine and Beirut. George is rather promiscuous as patron saints go, so it is apt that he is also the patron saint of syphilis.

In recent years in my hometown of Brighton, members of far-right groups take part in a St George's Day event called March For England. They are greeted by anti-fascist counter-demonstrations, and the situation often becomes violent. My partner, Joanne, had to take shelter in a nearby shop when members of the last March For England started hurling chairs and tables from outside a café at members of the public on the opposite side of the street. You can see how events like these would deter the English from embracing St George's Day.

Then there is the business with the dragon. The English are supposed to be animal lovers, so representing them with a man who killed an endangered species is an uneasy fit, especially when that animal was as brilliant as a dragon. Dragons may have had a bad press over the years, and they are often accused of kidnapping princesses and eating people. But we can say with certainty that the actual number of people hurt by dragons in all of history is precisely zero. You can't say that about crusading Roman mercenaries like George. If it was somehow possible to restage the fight between George and the Dragon, I suspect I would not be alone in rooting for the dragon.

This is not to deny that Saint George is an important figure for many people, not just the far right or rabid dragon haters. John Constable, for example, sees George as an important and meaningful figure. To John, George's un-English foreignness is a strength. He sees George's patronage of so many disparate nations, and his associations with the Green Man and with Al-Khidr in the Islamic tradition, as evidence that George can be a saint for everyone. This is a nuanced and thoughtful perspective on George but, ultimately, he shouldn't have stabbed that dragon.

Of course, saints are anachronistic these days. Saints come from a time when we still liked our stories to include wonderful concepts such as flying horses or magic hammers, but we were starting to prefer those stories to be about humans rather than gods. They are the midpoint between the gods of old and the celebrities of the modern day. Our weakness for stories about exceptional, talented humans who had tragic early deaths goes back a long way.

A patron saint of a country is not a particularly rational concept. The idea that one person can personify an entire nation over many centuries is an easy idea to be critical of. But then, we are not entirely rational beings. A great deal of the most treasured things in our culture, including weddings, the Olympic torch and the monarchy, are the products of magical thinking rather than rationality. Having a patron saint is the sort of crazy thing that humans do, and if we are to have one, we should at least have one who is qualified for the job. The foreign mercenary George was imposed on us from above for political reasons. In this, he was as much a puppet as the giant Ian Brown wobbling towards me. To be personified by such a person is to define the English as compliant quisling serfs, prepared to be whatever they are told to be. That, surely, can't be healthy.

When part of your personal identity is defined by the British no-osphere, what can you do if there is part of that geographic identity that you just don't relate to? What if the country has imposed something on you that, in your heart of hearts, you just don't think works? In those circumstances, it seems reasonable to look for an alternative. And the most promising candidate to succeed Saint George as patron saint of England is Saint Alban.

The parade is getting closer, stopping at certain points to re-enact elements of Alban's story. The Roman emperor above is waiting for Alban to arrive so that he can condemn him to death. But it is the end of the story that most interests me, so I skip ahead, leave the parade, and head to the cathedral.

Patron saints are not the only signifiers of geographic identity that have been imposed from above, and it is striking how many of these signifiers date back to times when our monarchs were culturally far removed from Britain. The early Plantagenets who imposed George on us did not even speak English, and neither did the early Hanoverian kings, from whose time songs like 'Rule Britannia' and 'God Save the King' come from. It is as if these cultural expressions of geographic identity compensate for a failure of the monarchy to adequately represent the people.

Flags are another such symbol. The English flag, the Cross of St George, and the Union Flag are common sights in England in the twenty-first century. I am of an age where this can still seem strange, because the far right managed to ruin these flags for many in the 1970s and 1980s. Even as late as 1992, Morrissey waving a Union Flag at a concert in London was considered scandalous in certain parts of the music press.

Flags are an emotive subject, and I would never intentionally denigrate the relationship anyone has with their national flag. However, if we look at the subject calmly and rationally, I think we will all conclude that one flag is better than all the others. I am of course speaking about the Welsh flag, and the reason why it is better is because it has a dragon on it. No other flag has anything nearly as cool. The flag of Mozambique, which has an AK-47 on it, comes nowhere close. The fact that I was raised in Wales, of course, has in no way affected my views on this subject.

The dragon stands on green grass under a white, overcast sky. This says a lot about the Welsh. When they had the option of depicting their dragon under a blue sky, they thought better of it. They weren't trying to fool anyone: no point in pretending otherwise, a Welsh sky is an overcast sky. Perhaps, though, a blue sky would have changed the flag's meaning. With a blue sky, the flag would find itself symbolising the entire United Kingdom. The green lower half would represent England, Blake's green and pleasant land. The top half would symbolise Scotland, being St Andrew's blue. The dragon would represent the Welsh, and the fact that the dragon is holding up its red fist to the top left-hand corner neatly represents Northern Ireland. I believe that if the United Kingdom experimented with using that flag for a year, no one would want to go back to the Union Flag. Who in Scotland, England and Northern Ireland would not want a flag with a dragon on?

Dragons are also associated with China and Japan, where they are viewed as both positive and awe-inspiring. In comparison, consider the story of the Dragon of Wantley, a Yorkshire legend once as well-known as the Robin Hood story. It tells of a local lord, More of More Hall, who set out to save his local peasants from a dragon. He first headed into Sheffield, where he was equipped with a suit of armour so spiky he was said to resemble a hedgehog. He then hid in a well, and when the dragon arrived he sneaked out behind it and kicked it in the arse with his spiky metal boot. The Dragon of Wantley's one weak spot was indeed its bottom, and it dutifully dropped down dead. In China, by contrast, dragons represent potent and auspicious powers with the ability to control the elements. They are said to symbolise the emperor or empress of China themselves. A Chinese dragon story would not end in the dragon being kicked to death, and certainly not kicked in the arse. Perhaps the imposition of Saint George on our island's story has relegated our dragons to the role of beasts to be killed in order to make powerful men look good?

My second favourite flag was designed by the Scottish artist Bill Drummond. It is the flag of the North Atlantic Archipelago. This is

Drummond's name for the British Isles in their pure, original state, where all tribal politics have been wiped away. The flag, a yellow chevron on a black background, was designed to look as unlike all other countries' flags as possible. To fly the 'Old Chevron' is, in the words of Drummond, 'to ignore the political State and celebrate the geological State'.

I am looking up at a St Albans flag, which is a yellow saltire on a blue background, as it flies above the western face of St Albans Cathedral. It might not have a dragon or Drummond's unique perspective, but it is a fine flag. The yellow on blue brings to mind a glorious summer sky, which is appropriate for the flag of a saint who is celebrated on the summer solstice.

The cathedral itself is something of a Frankenstein building, especially when viewed from the south. It has been extended and rebuilt many times over the centuries in contrasting styles. It now looks like the physical embodiment of an argument as to what a cathedral should look like.

A small boy in the crowd, aged around six, says to his parents, 'I'm bored. When do the eyes fall out?'

The boy's comments highlight why Alban's story is still celebrated, 1,700 years after his death. Of course the boy is bored. He's a six-year-old trapped in a huge crowd. The parade must, to his mind, appear pointless. But he knows that there's a good bit coming up, and that bit has captured his imagination. Just as the best children's films include things which appeal to parents, so Alban's story contains elements that appeal to all ages. I'm with that boy. The bit with the eyes is my favourite as well.

A commentator is narrating events over the public address system to the waiting crowd as the parade arrives at the cathedral and the actors take their places. He is providing useful facts and historical context. 'The lions are real,' he tells us as the giant puppet lions come into view. 'There really were lions in England in Alban's day.' He is concerned that the crowd, when faced by a display of lions and angels, might find the existence of lions fanciful.

There are a number of variations to the Alban story, as you would expect from a myth of such antiquity. The most credible account is the one recorded by the Venerable Bede in the eighth century, and this is the version we are witnessing here. Alban was a citizen of the busy Roman town of Verulamium, the remains of which are about half a mile to the south-west, on the opposite bank of the River Ver. Alban was a pagan who gave shelter to a Christian priest called Amphibalus, who was on the run from the authorities. These events most likely took place during Christian persecutions in the reign of the Emperor Diocletian.

If Bede is to be believed, Amphibalus was at Alban's house for a number of days before the Romans tracked him down. During this time he spent entire days and nights praying, which is perhaps understandable in the circumstances. Alban was so impressed by this that he experienced some form of revelation. He became a Christian himself, and as his first Christian act he disguised himself as the wanted priest and was arrested in his place. This gave Amphibalus time to escape. The Romans soon realised their mistake. As Alban said that he too was a Christian, they decided to execute him instead.

All this paints a conflicted picture of Amphibalus. On the one hand he was a charismatic figure who was able to convert pagan Alban solely by example. On the other, he scarpered knowing that the stranger who gave him shelter and protection would almost certainly be killed in his place. This is hardly a shining example of Christianity. According to some accounts, Amphibalus was eventually captured, possibly in Wales, and received the execution he was so eager to avoid.

Our commentator, meanwhile, is getting flustered. He had announced that the burial place of Alban was unknown, but a member of the clergy has stepped forward to tell him otherwise. He comes back on the public address system to apologise. 'We do know where he was buried,' he announces. 'Also, we have a bone!' He blames Wikipedia for his earlier error, more comfortable trusting the word of clergy with a dead person's bone than he is trusting Wikipedia. He announces that the execution of Alban produced three miracles and that 'miracles occur at the cathedral to this day'. I don't think he got that last bit from Wikipedia.

The three miracles he referred to occurred during Alban's journey from Verulamium to the site of his execution, which is where the cathedral now stands. In the first miracle, the waters of the River Ver parted to allow him to cross. The next miracle was not quite so grand, but welcome nonetheless. Alban was thirsty, so God caused a spring to appear at his feet, and he was able to quench his thirst. Earlier that day I was desirous of a parking space and one miraculously appeared before me, so I can relate to these miracles.

The third miracle is the best, in my opinion.

This miracle is represented in the procession by two boys, who each carry aloft a beach-ball-sized eye on a stick. It is the arrival of these giant eyes that really pushes the spectacle into gonzo psychedelic territory. According to the story, the moment that the Roman centurion sliced the head off the shoulders of Alban's kneeling body, both of the centurion's eyes fell out. They hit the ground at the same time as Alban's head.

By anyone's standards, this was unexpected. You can see why it captured the imagination of the six-year-old boy to my side. It's the sort of detail that an author like George R. R. Martin could build a career on. It is brilliantly inexplicable. A God sufficiently angered by the decapitation of his new convert would have been capable of stopping the execution but instead chose to make the executioner's eyes fall out. Truly, He moved in mysterious ways. A pagan like Alban may have been familiar with an oral tradition that evolved into the story of Odin, who gave an eye in order to gain wisdom, but I'm not aware of any mythic precedent for two eyes falling out at once.

The parade treats these details tastefully. The eyes don't pop out of the centurion's head; it is considered sufficient that they are represented in the parade. Alban's head doesn't go rolling down the hill towards the crowd, gushing blood as it goes. Instead, a man calmly removes it from the kneeling puppet and holds it aloft. The Venerable Bede was also not looking for cheap thrills when he wrote about the execution. His description tips into Orwellian doublespeak, but you have to admire his attempt to put a positive spin on things. He wrote, 'Here, therefore, this most valiant martyr, being beheaded, received the crown of life which God has promised to those who love him.' 'Receiving the crown of life' is not how most people would describe decapitation.

Behold the head of puppet Saint Alban

When Alban's head left his shoulders he became a cephalophore, which is the name given to saints who are depicted carrying their heads. Cephalophores have been something of a problem for religious artists over the years because of the tricky question of where to paint the halo. They can place the halo either around the bloodied stump of neck or over the head carried in the saint's armpit, but in both instances it looks like they are being sarcastic.

After Alban's head has been held aloft, the parade is over for another year. The assembled pilgrims and members of the church troop into the cathedral in order to receive the Eucharist. The people of St Albans return to the secular aspects of the weekend-long Alban festival, which will include bands, street parties and a hefty dose of Morris dancing.

That was Alban's death, but what do we know about his life? If we are looking at him as a potential new patron saint of England, it seems reasonable that a candidate for such a prestigious position should be properly vetted. The only thing historians can say with any confidence is that he was a pagan with a house in Verulamium. Perhaps walking in his footsteps will give further insight?

I head south-west across the cathedral grounds and follow an unsettlingly straight path over immaculately manicured grass down into the valley of the River Ver, on my way to visit the ghosts of Verulamium. To my surprise I quickly find myself in what looks like a fairy-tale English country lane. It is the sort of place where you might encounter a badger wearing a waistcoat and walking upright, who tips his hat as he wishes you good morning. I am still acclimatising to this sudden shift of environment so close to the centre of a city, when I unexpectedly stumble upon the oldest pub in Britain.

Ye Olde Fighting Cocks sits in a quiet lane, yards from an idyllic crook in the river. There are a number of pubs that claim to be the oldest in Britain, but this one boasts the support of *The Guinness Book of Records*, and that is good enough for me. It has been rebuilt a number of times over the years, and the lovely octagonal part of the current building was originally a medieval dovecote, but a pub has been on this site since 795 CE. It was a pub in the modern sense, as opposed to an inn or a tavern to house weary travellers. The main difference between then and now was that the entertainment was cock fighting rather than fruit machines.

Inside, it is dark. Large windows were not an option when this building was built. I should wait for my eyes to adjust to the gloom but instead stride in and bang my head on a 'mind your head' sign helpfully attached to the low ceiling beams. The puppets earlier had me subconsciously thinking of Alban as twelve feet tall, so this encounter with the low ceilings in Ye Olde Fighting Cocks is a reminder of how short the British used to be.

The gloom is enhanced by exposed wood beams, the colour of dark chocolate, and by blood-red walls covered with paintings and other historic imagery. This decor appears muted and tasteful, which is impressive when you realise that much of it is themed around cock fighting.

The original cock-fighting pit is still present, which you reach by going down a few steps. There is a sign outside saying 'Ye Cock Pit'. The clientele are taking pictures of this sign, rather than sniggering at it, which tells you a lot about who this pub attracts. This is a family-friendly gastro pub, rather than a locals' boozer. A sign asks you to keep prams out of the bar area. This is the same bar area where Oliver Cromwell once saddled his horse.

I order a pint and some seemingly overpriced gastro-sausages which turn out to be worth every penny. We have the British weather to thank for the fact that we can find welcoming safe havens like this whenever we arrive in a strange town or village. As it rained all the time, this left our Celtic and Anglo-Saxon ancestors at a loss as to how to spend their evenings. If they wanted to get out of the house, that realistically meant going into somebody else's house. For this reason, enterprising folk opened rooms in their homes to the public at large and sold drinks to make it worth their while. Visitors were welcome to enter certain rooms of these 'public houses', but they could not walk into the private part of the house. This boundary was called the 'bar', because they were barred from going beyond it.

As I settle down in the welcoming gloom, it occurs to me that I can thank Saint Alban for the fact that the pub exists and is serving me excellent sausages.

Alban reached the site of his execution when he was taken east from Verulamium, over the Ver and up the hill to where the cathedral now stands. When Roman persecution of Christianity ended during the reign of Emperor Constantine, a shrine or church was built in the place where Alban died. King Offa of Mercia arrived at that spot 500 years later, in the eighth century, and supposedly dug up Alban's bones, having been told in a dream where to find them. By dreaming of finding bones, Offa is perhaps not unlike the poet John Constable, who grew up near Offa's famous dyke. Offa founded an abbey at the place these bones were found, and this is the origin of the current cathedral. His intention was to create a major Mercian religious centre. Possession of the bones of a saint, which our friendly commentator was boasting about earlier, was the sort of thing that gave a Dark Ages abbey serious clout.

The original pub on this site was built at the same time Offa built his abbey. There were once underground tunnels which the monks used to pass between the pub and the cathedral. It was probably beneficial to the public image of the monastery that when the monks staggered about drunk, they did so underground. Just as Ye Olde Watling in London was built for the builders constructing St Paul's, this abbey also required supporting infrastructure in the shape of a pub. Monks get thirsty, after all. So there is a direct link between the existence of this pub and the location of Alban's death 1,700 years ago. The deep past still exerts its influence.

The place where Verulamium once stood is now mainly open parkland. This has been a gift for archaeologists. Most major Roman towns had cities built on top of them, including London, Chester and York. Verulamium has not, so archaeologists have a clear understanding of the original town's layout. As a result, I am able to find and walk the original path of a now vanished section of Watling Street.

I follow its route, over what are today football pitches, to where it entered the Roman town from the south. The route of Watling Street south of this gate is now a golf course. This seems a sad fate for such a historic route, but at least it means that people are still walking on it.

The remains of the city gate, where travellers from London gained access to the city, are still visible. Here, between two large guard towers, were two gates for vehicles and extra passages for pedestrians. It gives an indication of how busy this road must have been. The remains of the city wall are a couple of metres thick and make the site look like a fortress. They were built over 200 years after Boudica first burnt down the fledgling city in 61 CE, which implies that Verulamium continued to feel threatened by the tribes outside its walls. The Romans may have been in control of the country and safe in their walled cities, but venturing outside was still dangerous. Looking at the walls puts me in mind of US Army bases in Iraq.

If Bede is correct about his dating of Alban's death, then these walls would have been built in Alban's lifetime. He would have seen them rise up. They would have protected his home, which in turn protected Amphibalus.

The city was abandoned after the Romans left Britain. But as Verulamium declined, the town of St Albans grew in the shadow of the abbey, which did good business thanks to the attraction of Alban's bones. At some point the Roman road to fading Verulamium was diverted to this new, emerging city. Regular coach services to London began in the seventeenth century and the city prospered. By 1876 there were seventy-two coaches passing through St Albans a day. This westward shimmy from declining Verulamium to growing St Albans was the result of Alban's journey to his execution. If he had been beheaded in Verulamium itself, then the shrine, abbey and city would have been built there, and our understanding of the Roman town's layout would be significantly less. Few modern cities can be as confident that a mythic story is the reason for their founding.

If you followed Watling Street through the gate and into Verulamium in Alban's day, the first major building you would come across was the city's largest temple. We know that Alban was a pagan, so it seems reasonable to assume that he would have worshipped there at some point. It would have been a curious temple; thanks to the angle at which Watling Street cut across the otherwise regimented Roman city streets, it is the only known classical temple with a triangular floor plan. According to the nearby Verulamium Museum, it was dedicated to the goddess Cybele and her consort, Attis. Cybele was the goddess of cities, protection and human progress, while Attis was a vegetation god who represented death and rebirth.

Walking the football pitches and parkland that now cover Verulamium gives a sense of the size of the city. The surviving mosaics give a sense of its sophistication and the thickness of its walls helps you appreciate how threatened it felt. But none of this directly connects us to Alban the man. There seems to be only one way to address this: we need to visit him.

The Shrine of Saint Alban is in a quiet chapel in the more secluded eastern end of the cathedral.

The shrine itself is an elaborate stone pedestal, carved from Dorset marble. It is tall – over three metres in height – and topped with a red silk canopy that represents the blood of the martyr. Early Christians rarely shied away from the gory aspects of their stories. The shrine dates from the fourteenth century, but was smashed into pieces in the sixteenth during the dissolution of the monasteries. Its remains were found in 1872, and it was painstakingly rebuilt. There were over 2,000 marble pieces to assemble. Further restoration work was undertaken in 1992 and 1993, and to look at it now you would never guess that it had once been so thoroughly destroyed.

Next to the shrine stands an intricately carved wooden structure, resembling a two-storey oak shed. This is the only surviving medieval wooden watching loft in existence. For anyone unfamiliar with medieval watching lofts, they are as the name suggests. Monks climbed the stairs, looked out of the windows and spent their days watching the shrine below. It also has spy-holes in the side and back, should the monks have needed to watch things other than the shrine.

But what of Alban himself? His mortal remains were seemingly lost to history when his shrine was smashed. But in 2002, St Pantaleon Roman Catholic Church in Cologne gave the cathedral a relic of Saint Alban – a shoulder blade, to be precise – which is now housed inside the shrine. This is the bone which the commentator was so proud of. Given what we know about the trade in medieval relics, a little faith is required to accept the bone as genuine, but it is certainly possible that the relic within the marble shrine is the remains of Alban.

After his long centuries of absence and the trashing of his shrine in Tudor times, Alban is making a return. First, his marble shrine was found and rebuilt. Then his bone returned home. Now the newly established Alban Pilgrimage brings his story to life. As saints go, he is on the up. But could he keep rising and take the job of patron saint of England from the endangered animal-killer and syphilis apologist Saint George of Palestine?

As a candidate, Saint Alban's case looks strong. To the Christian community, he is the first English martyr. He pre-dates any splits in the church, and so can stand for all. He isn't famous for killing anyone, human or dragon, and was martyred because he was helping out a friend. Surely this is exactly the type of 'British value' a patron saint is supposed to embody? A person standing up for a mate makes a better mascot for this country than a warmongering stranger.

In the strange, echoing quiet of the chapel, that odd detail about the eyes finally makes some form of sense. Christian writers talk of Alban's conversion and his expression of faith in the face of death as a form of illumination. He gave his life in payment for the sins of another, which has obvious Christian symbolism. In return he was granted the 'Light of Heaven', and for the first time he could truly see. The executioner, on the other hand, was blind to what illuminated Alban. His actions cast him into darkness. Or, to rework that in a way that would interest a six-year-old, his eyes fell out.

As we noted earlier, church attendance plummeted in the twentieth century and we are now what the former Archbishop of Canterbury Rowan Williams calls a 'post-Christian country'. So can Alban appeal to non-Christians? He lived his life in pagan terms, never went to church, and only described himself as 'Christian' when asked by the authorities. This seems entirely in accord with the twenty-first-century British.

His execution took place at midsummer, which is a date we always celebrate. A few hours before the Alban Pilgrimage began, 37,000 people gathered at Stonehenge and greeted the rising sun on a cloudless summer solstice. For those who find Stonehenge a bit too heathen for their tastes, Alban gives a Christian excuse to join in the party. Alban, it seems to me, can appeal to Christians and non-Christians alike. As a bonus, none of his supporters have ever thrown chairs at any member of my family. From my perspective, the case for regarding him as patron saint of England seems unarguable.

Then I look at the red silk canopy of Alban's shrine and notice that it is fringed with a row of gold 'A's, each containing an individually embroidered flower. The chosen flowers are ones that bloom during midsummer. One, I notice, is a thistle. Thinking about this, it dawns on me that there is one good argument against him being the patron saint of England.

In his account of Alban's story, Bede quotes the priest Fortunatus, who wrote 'Albanum egregium fecunda Britannia profert' – 'Fruitful Britain holy Alban yields'. Saint Alban was something that emerged from Britain, rather than something that was imposed on it. But Fortunatus talks of Britain, rather than England, and this is how Alban would have identified himself. Concepts such as 'England' or 'Scotland' did not exist in his day. This is easy to forget when you look around St Albans, because it is so quintessentially English. It has been home to Benny Hill, Jimmy Hill and Stephen Hawking, and that is surely

English enough for anyone. Alban, however, understood himself to be British. With the exception of the Picts in the far north of what would later become Scotland, and the Roman ruling classes, so was everyone else on this island at that time.

Perhaps making Alban patron saint of England is too parochial? Are we looking at a patron saint of Britain? The Latinised name Alban comes from the linguistic root *Alba*, which also gave rise to Albion, the first name of this island. This name survived longer in the north. Scotland is called *Yr Alban* in Welsh and *Alba* in Scottish Gaelic, so we can be confident that Albion refers to the whole island and not just England.

Sitting at the shrine in this quiet chapel, I wonder how it would compare to the strange triangular temple that Alban himself would have attended. The deities worshipped there were Cybele and Attis, the goddess of cities and civilisation and a god of rebirth. It strikes me how appropriate this is.

What does the name 'St Alban' refer to? Originally it was just a man. After he was dead, that name was given to his shrine. The abbey that grew out of the shrine then took on the name, as did the city that grew around that abbey. 'St Alban' was first a man, then a shrine, then an abbey and finally a city. They all had the same name, and they all contained his bones. Such is the afterlife of a man who worshipped rebirth and cities.

If we're prepared to take a leap of faith and suppose that it really is his bone in this marble shrine, then we can take this idea further. Thanks to the linguistic link between Albion and Alban, this whole island has his name. It contains his bone. Alban didn't stop when he grew into a city.

I came to St Albans looking for a patron saint of England. As I light a candle in the quiet of this chapel, that role suddenly looks unnecessary. There is no need to pitch Alban versus George, or to try and strip George of his current status. Saint Alban, I declare, is the patron saint of Albion. Albion was the name of this island before modern boundaries or borders appeared, like Bill Drummond's Atlantic Archipelago. Albion is inclusive and everyone is welcome, and his day is this gloriously sunny midsummer. No dragons will get hurt. No chairs will be thrown. Alban allows everyone to celebrate the longest day, regardless of whether or not they're Christian. And, for the kids, there's a good bit where a Roman's eyes fall out.

I don't relate to Saint George and was hoping to find an alternative, but I wasn't expecting to find something larger and more inclusive. The British noosphere is deep, and we are taught only a tiny fraction of it. If the bits that are forced on us don't please, we can dive for others. There are many other stories in our past. Should we care to look, we will find ones that chime with us and which echo with our footsteps more truthfully.

We are not helpless consumers of identity. We are not trapped by history. We can choose the stories we tell.

The noosphere is immaterial, like smoke. There is nothing easier to change.

8.

DUNSTABLE

Stand and deliver

Dick Turpin, the most famous of all the highwaymen, was originally a butcher in the early eighteenth century. He became part of a gang of Essex thieves known as the Gregory Gang, who used to break into people's houses in order to steal their valuables. In February 1735, the gang broke into the house of an elderly widow, Mrs Shelley, who refused to tell them where her wealth was hidden. Turpin yelled at her, 'God damn your blood, you old bitch, if you won't tell us, I'll set your bare arse on the grate!' Widow Shelley was then tortured in that fashion until she revealed the location of her valuables. Three days later they broke into a second house, which was the home of Joseph Lawrence, a seventy-year-old farmer, and his servants. He was beaten about the head and body with pistols, pulled round the house by his hair and had a kettle of water emptied over him. He too was forced to sit bare-buttocked in the fire while the maid was raped.

Dick Turpin was a terrible person. Yet when we think of him now we imagine him sat astride his mare, Black Bess, on a moonlit common with twin flintlock pistols drawn. He is wearing a long coat, black tricorne hat and mask, with a single lock of long black hair brought forward and tied with a ribbon. He awaits the arrival of his prey on the road below, where he will be charming and daring and will steal a kiss from his female victims before galloping away with pockets full of gold and jewellery. We do not think of him as a brutal torturer, burning the naked behinds of the elderly. Such is the romance of highwaymen. They exist as a form of quantum superposition where they are both fact and fiction at the same time. In theory it should be possible to study them in a historically factual manner, but in practice the fiction is too strong.

An eleven-bedroom manor house called Markyate Cell sits on Watling Street between St Albans and Dunstable. In the seventeenth century this home belonged to the green-eyed, red-haired heiress Lady Katherine Ferrers, known to legend as 'the Wicked Lady'. Ferrers' story has been told in a number of novels and films, most famously in the 1945 film *The Wicked Lady*, which starred Margaret Lockwood in the title role. Lockwood portrayed Ferrers as a selfish, heartless woman with fantastic hair and an amazing wardrobe, who was drawn to the life of a highwaywoman for the sheer existential thrill of it. By day she was a respectable member of society. At night, she stepped through a secret door in her room into a hidden chamber with a secret staircase. Here she would dress in buckskin breeches and a black cloak and mask. She would then sneak out of the house and ride over to Nomansland Common in Wheathampstead, where she would take what she wanted from whomever she liked. She was said to drop out of trees ahead of oncoming coaches with both pistols drawn, just like Adam Ant in the video for his 1981 single 'Stand and Deliver'.

Ferrers worked with another highwayman, Ralph Chaplin, who was also her lover. In time, her crimes escalated to include burning houses, slaughtering livestock and murdering a constable. In the Margaret Lockwood portrayal, she also stole her girlfriend's fiancé and poisoned and suffocated a servant who discovered her secret. She then betrayed and arranged the capture of her lover, Chaplin, and went to watch him hang at the Tyburn Tree. Lady Katherine Ferrers, the film couldn't emphasise enough, was a very wicked lady. She lived outside the morality of society. Who wouldn't want to hear her story?

One moonlit night, she was shot while attempting a robbery. She managed to ride back from Nomansland Common to Markyate Cell, but she died in a pool of blood before she could reach the entrance to her secret staircase. Her body was found the following morning by her servants, still dressed in men's clothes. She was twenty-six years old.

That, at least, is her legend, although almost none of it can be verified from the patchy records we have of the turbulent Civil War era. But in the 1800s, when the house was extensively rebuilt, workmen found a secret chamber and a false wall next to a chimney, just like the one the stories described. The chamber was empty, but it was enough to reignite the legend. The story of the Wicked Lady came almost within touching distance of history.

In 2014 the house was sold at auction, with a reserve price set at £4.25 million. Disappointingly, there was no secret chamber mentioned in the estate agent's description, and none was apparent on the floor plans. It seems that remodelling of the house at some point during the last couple of centuries has reclaimed this mysterious space. Even this one factual link between history and story has evaporated, becoming a part of the legend it once promised to prove. With highwaymen, legend always trumps truth.

When you rummage through history as we are doing, you quickly notice that the great majority of the stories you find are about men. This is particularly striking when you are used to exploring more recent history where the gender bias, while still present, is less extreme. The problem is one of agency: there are plenty of women in the history books, but unless they were a queen they were unlikely to have had the option of becoming an active protagonist who could generate the type of story we are looking for. In these circumstances, characters like Katherine Ferrers and highwaywomen in general seem ideal candidates for redressing this balance. But because of the transgressive nature of highwaymen, the gender aspect of these stories is not that simple.

One of the most prominent parts of the iconography of highwaymen, at least in the years after the Second World War, is cross-dressing. In *Blackadder the Third* (1987), a squirrel-hating highwayman called the Shadow is revealed to be the heiress Amy Hardwood, who is dressed as a man and speaks in a deep voice. The highwayman in a 2015 episode of *Doctor Who* turns out to be an immortal Viking girl, played by Maisie Williams, with a similar ability to disguise her voice. *Carry On Dick* (1974) includes both a young woman dressed as a male highwayman and a highwayman dressed as a woman. There may not have been any cross-dressing in the video for 'Stand and Deliver' by Adam and the Ants, but the 'dandy highwayman' was certainly in touch with his feminine side.

There is a reasonable amount of historical basis for the modern idea of gender-swapped highwaymen. The Wicked Lady was not the only female thief to dress as a knight of the road. Mary Frith, better known as Moll Cutpurse, was a highwaywoman who died three years after Ferrers, in 1663, at the age of seventy-four. Moll dressed in men's clothing from an early age and always smoked a pipe. It is said that she made no attempts to appear feminine or attract men, although she did marry. A play written about her in 1610 had the wonderful title of *The Madde Pranckes of Mery Mall of the Bankside*, but, sadly, this has since been lost. Most of Moll's career was spent as a pickpocket and fence, but she took up highway robbery during the Civil War, when she was approaching the age of sixty. Being an ardent Royalist, she only held up Parliamentarians.

Tom Rowland, in contrast, was a highwayman from Hertfordshire who always dressed in women's clothes. He rode side-saddle and only sat astride his horse when he had to make a quick getaway. Rowland was a bricklayer's apprentice who stole a horse from the Duke of Beaufort and went on to an exceptionally lengthy career as a highwayman, in that he lasted an impressive eighteen years before he was hanged at Tyburn in 1699.

Rowland's cross-dressing has been explained as a disguise that helped him avoid capture for so long, but from a twenty-first-century perspective it seems more likely that people like Rowland and Moll Cutpurse were transgender, and that living outside the law and outside society was their only option for being their true selves in that Puritan age.

A significant number of highwaymen would now be labelled as addicts. They stole in order to buy alcohol or, more frequently, to fund gambling habits. Their stories are ultimately nihilistic. They turned their backs on society and chose instead a life where their pleasures could be indulged, knowing that the cost would be that life cut short by the Tyburn Tree. Perhaps this is why highwaymen had such a reputation for bravado at the gallows, where they were expected to laugh in the face of death and joke with the crowds who had come to see them swing. It may be that death was not something they feared but a price they always expected to pay.

Highwaymen were active during the seventeenth and eighteenth centuries and only really disappeared when the arrival of railways displaced much of the coach travel. Yet despite this long span of activity, the highwaymen of fiction are most strongly linked with the Civil War era and its aftermath. This was a time of great chaos and confusion, when the social order was upturned. The common people had beheaded the king. The old ways were gone. What would follow was still uncertain, although it would not be what people had known before.

This was a time of revolutions in political and religious thought which gave rise to groups like the Diggers, the Levellers and the Ranters. The Ranters were a dissenting religious group who did not believe in personal property. They recognised the divine spark within themselves so had no need for churches or churchmen, and certainly no interest in a hierarchy of preachers or bishops standing between them and God. Being self-evidently holy they believed that they were incapable of sin, so they were free to get naked, drink heavily and have sex with whomever they pleased. The Ranters were a spark of the 1960s counterculture stranded 300 years too early.

It's not clear how numerous the Ranters were, or whether their numbers were exaggerated by their enemies, but it is easy to see why they horrified the establishment. The name 'Ranters' was not one that those in the movement gave themselves. It was an insult which, like 'punk' or 'impressionist', was used by the movement's enemies and which somehow stuck. They were using divine authority to argue for what we would now call a form of anarcho-communist revolution. As Abiezer Coppe wrote in a key Ranter tract, *A Fiery Flying Roll* (1649), 'Thus saith the Lord, I inform you that I overturn, overturn, overturn. And as the bishops, [King] Charles and the Lords have had their turn, overturn.'

Stepping outside society made more sense in those years of unease and uncertainty, when the old order had been overturned and the new order had yet to arrive. A popular ballad at the time was 'The World Turned Upside Down', the words to one version being:

If buttercups buzz'd after the bee,
If boats were on land, churches on sea,
If ponies rode men and if grass ate the cows,
And cats should be chased into holes by the mouse,
If the mamas sold their babies
To the gypsies for half a crown;
If summer were spring and the other way round,
Then all the world would be upside down.

Our use of the transgender iconography of highwaymen, where men dress as women or women dress as men and live free from the rules of society, is perhaps not just a quirk of modern culture but an indication that we are picking up on a larger truth about those days.

Highwaymen symbolise that era in a way that contemporary muggers or carjackers don't represent the modern world. The crimes committed by Dick Turpin and other highwaymen were shameful, cruel acts born of desperation and necessity and the legends and romance which grew from them are largely false, yet these legends still contain a truth about that transgressive period.

The Newgate Calendar, a popular compendium of executions from the eighteenth century, informs us that Moll Cutpurse specified in her will that she wished to be buried with her backside upwards, 'that she might be as preposterous in her death as she had been all along in her infamous life'. At a time when the world had indeed been turned upside down, what was more appropriate than that?

In the south-west tower of St Paul's Cathedral hangs Great Paul, the largest bell in Britain until the twenty-three-tonne Olympic Bell was cast for the 2012 Olympic Games. Great Paul is over sixteen tonnes in weight and rings a deep E-flat. It was cast in 1881 in Loughborough, Leicestershire, and the original plan was to transport it to London by train. But the railway companies refused to take it, fearing its weight would cause a derailment, so it had to travel along Watling Street. It was chained to a cart and pulled by two traction engines. The journey went reasonably smoothly until it got to Little Brickhill in Buckinghamshire, where the road collapsed under the weight. The rest of its journey was equally problematic and it frequently got stuck, blocking the road.

It was not just highwaymen that coach travellers had to be wary of. In the seventeenth and eighteenth centuries the roads themselves were frequently unpassable. Most roads were originally just compressed dirt and many were known as hollow ways, because they became lower in the centre as the earth under the path become flattened. In wet weather paths like these would often fill with water and become difficult to pass. This was why the Romans went to the trouble of building their famous roads.

Roman roads consisted of a number of layers of sand, cement or gravel, known as *agger*, topped with a layer of stones in a process called metalling. The thickness of the *agger* and metalling depended on the terrain underneath, with softer, marshier ground needing thicker surfacing. Roman roads were raised slightly in the centre and usually had ditches running along each side, so that rain ran off them. This not only made them passable in bad weather but protected the soil beneath the road from erosion, which helped keep the roads in good order.

After the Romans left, their roads held up pretty well for much of the next thousand years or so. The medieval British travelled either on foot or on horseback, and Roman roads could easily absorb the impact of a person or a horse. But the subsequent growth of coach travel caused great damage to roads.

The fashion for travelling in coaches dates back to the Tudor period, when Elizabeth I first used a coach to travel to the state opening of parliament. To the aristocracy, coach travel was an effective way to signal that you could afford your own coachmen, vehicle and horses. Laws were drawn up to limit the weight of vehicles, such as James I's 1621 proclamation that limited the weight of wagons to one tonne, but they were not enough to prevent British roads from falling into disrepair.

Road repairs were haphazard affairs, usually involving the dumping of more rocks and earth on top of areas that had been churned up by cart wheels. This was done more frequently in the busier parts of the street, such as the centre of a market town. Over time, these parts of the road became higher than others. They could also become higher than the buildings originally built alongside them, which at times become inundated with mud and gravel washed in from these elevated roads. Roads like this became known as the 'high street'.

I am in Dunstable High Street, about three miles further up Watling Street from the home of Lady Katherine Ferrers and twenty-three miles south of Little Brickhill. You can see evidence of the raising of the 'high street' at the front door of the Saracen's Head pub, which was originally a seventeenth-century coaching inn. Its front door is now a few inches below the level of the road and pavement. You now have to go down a step when you enter.

The high street is a central part of modern town life, but high-street stores have been closing at an alarming rate, especially since the 2008 recession. It seems as if only pound shops and charity shops are springing up to replace them. When the *Daily Mail* wanted a town to personify the collapse of the British high street, they chose Dunstable. 'Our disappearing High Streets: once thriving Dunstable now a ghost town with 43 boarded-up shops,' ran the headline of their 15 January 2015 article. It was accompanied by a relentless series of photographs of closed shops, grey metal shutters and charmless, decaying retail units. 'Property consultants warned that empty shops could create their own "downward spiral" for High Streets, where fewer shoppers led stores to close, which led to a further reduction in the numbers of potential customers,' it warned. In case this wasn't depressing enough, the online version of the story put a photograph of Dunstable town centre next to a photograph of a gravestone. 'Businesses near the town centre of Dunstable (left) are really struggling, although things at the graveyard (right) have been relatively unaffected by the struggles on the High Street,' it informed us.

The ugliest, most miserable photographs were of the Quadrant Shopping Arcade. What makes these particularly upsetting is the Quadrant's location. It is next to the crossroads at the heart of Dunstable, where Watling Street crosses what was once the Icknield Way.

The Icknield Way was one of the four medieval royal highways, along with Watling Street, the Fosse Way and Ermine Street. It ran for hundreds of miles from the south-west to East Anglia, and its name may derive from Boudica's Iceni tribe. Unlike Watling Street it was never paved by the Romans, so it retained more of the serpentine quality of prehistoric British pathways. The Watling Street and Icknield Way crossroads was an important location in the ancient world. It was the reason why Henry I established this town in 1109.

The names of the four streets leading from the crossroads, High Street North, West Street, High Street South and Church Street, help to give the town a sense of being a crossroads to the world. These roads divide the world into four quadrants, hence the Quadrant Shopping Arcade's name. For a country that took the French Napoleonic insult that it was 'a nation of shopkeepers' as a compliment, a shopping arcade at those crossroads should have been the heart of Dunstable. Its current state, in this context, becomes a symbol of the existential rot of small-town Britain.

The main reason for Dunstable's decline, the *Daily Mail* believes, is online shopping. 'The changes are being driven by a switch to buying on the internet,' it tells us, 'with British families spending more online per person than in any other nation.' The reader comments underneath the online version of the article predominantly blame a different target, the local council. Even when these commentators give contradictory reasons for the town's decline, such as the amount of traffic or attempts to reduce the amount of traffic, they still agree that it is all the council's fault. Those comments paint a picture of the town even bleaker than the photographs. The number of Dunstable residents, both past and present, who confirm the decline of the town far outnumbers the few who stick up for it.

In response, Central Bedfordshire Council produced a short film entitled *Dunstable – The Next Chapter*, which can be watched on YouTube, about plans to regenerate the town. It highlights positive changes to the town, such as the new Grove Theatre complex that has tempted BBC Three Counties radio to relocate there. It focuses on two new bypasses, the M1 link and the Woodside link, which are intended to reduce congestion, and it remembers the positive attributes of the town, not least its position to the north-east of the Chiltern Hills and the beautiful views from the Dunstable Downs. The video makes a case that Dunstable has a bright future. This is undercut somewhat by the top YouTube comment directly underneath, which simply reads 'Shit hole'. This is even harsher than the *Daily Mail* comments. The rudest they got was 'Dumpstable'.

For all these reasons, I travelled to Dunstable with low expectations. I arrive on a beautifully sunny Monday in May. It is twenty degrees Celsius, the sky is a vivid blue, and there is only the occasional suggestion of wind. As I drove here along Watling Street from St Albans, past Markyate Cell, the verges were a jungle of green leaves, with bushes fat and trees heavy with blossom. It is the type of day, in other words, when things never look as bad as the *Daily Mail* claims. It is true that I see a lot of empty shops and 'This unit for let' signs, but there are open shops as well which somehow failed to make it into the article.

Quadrant shopping arcade

The Quadrant, unfortunately, does not give a good first impression. Its 1960s design now looks tatty, with a closed-down shop facing a Poundland at the entrance. But inside there are outlets such as Boots, Greggs, New Look and Carphone Warehouse. They may not be upmarket shops, but they are valued by the people using them. It can't compete with Milton Keynes or Luton as a shopping destination, but for a local high street it does what you would expect. The initial impression I get walking around Dunstable is that, ultimately, there are worse places. I know this for a fact because I was raised in one of those worse places. As a result, I tend to view anywhere that has a WH Smith as pretty cosmopolitan.

There is an established etiquette for talking about horrible places in Britain. When you have lived in one of those places you are allowed to call it a shit hole, but it is not socially acceptable for visitors to call it that. Oddly, that rule breaks down when it comes to Buckley in Flintshire, where I lived from the age of three to eighteen. I have lost count of the number of visitors to the place who openly exclaim, 'My God, what a shit hole!' when they arrive. 'I can't believe how horrible this place is!' they add. This is extremely rude, not least because it robs those who've had to live there of the pleasure of moaning about it themselves. The ghost-hunting TV programme *Most Haunted* filmed an episode, broadcast in 2015, at Buckley's nightclub, the Tivoli. It included only one brief exterior shot of Buckley, yet somehow this was enough for Twitter to fill with people proclaiming, 'Look at that shithole! #mosthaunted'.

Yet when I think back to Buckley, I think of it as a fundamentally good place. This is primarily because of the Tivoli, where I used to work when I was sixteen or seventeen. The Tivoli was a bog-standard night club on most nights, but on Thursdays it was a heavy-metal club that had somehow got itself on to the international touring circuit. It was not uncommon to see credible American rock bands wandering around the street of Buckley after a sound check, with a look of absolute horror on their faces. Tivoli rock night might not appeal to everyone, of course, but it was *something*. It was a genuine community based around a living, thriving creative-arts scene, and not everywhere has something like that. A place with a scene like that is ultimately a good place, despite everything, because it gives you something to look forward to.

Watling Street curves around Birmingham, the birthplace of heavy metal and home to bands like Black Sabbath and Judas Priest. Metal is an example of an excluded side of Britain, a thriving working-class folk music that is all but invisible to the wider media. It is music intended to empower the powerless, and as such it holds little appeal to those from a more comfortable background. You never see heavy metal bands on the Mercury Prize shortlist or on programmes like *Later... With Jools Holland*. Instead, metal has created its own record labels, magazines, clubs and festivals. It does not seek acceptance from the establishment, instead taking its validity from the grass roots. Perhaps this is why it is still so healthy after forty years, while more critically approved musical genres have withered away to nostalgia revivals. Metal is a reminder that just because something isn't culturally visible, that doesn't mean there's nothing there.

I keep this in mind as I explore Dunstable on this pleasant day. The equivalent of a music scene or something to look forward to could thrive in a place like this, but it would not be immediately apparent to visitors.

Dunstable may have seen better days, but there doesn't appear to be anything fundamental missing. It has pubs, schools and super-markets, as well as a theatre complex and a beautiful old priory. This is surrounded by well-tended parkland containing conifers, beech and sycamore trees, and is where the marriage of Henry VIII and his first wife, Catherine of Aragon, was pronounced null and void in 1533. If you're looking for a tattoo parlour, you have plenty of choice. There is no shortage of places to get a drink.

Yet after an afternoon here the suspicion takes hold that something is indeed missing, even if that something is ineffable and immater-ial. I am trying to be positive, but the town keeps presenting images of absence. Next to the tourist information office, there is a large black-framed information board which features the words 'Welcome to Dunstable' in large golden letters over the top. The notice board underneath is completely empty. On the front of the priory there are alcoves for statues. They contain a pedestal, but those pedestals have no statues on them.

Dunstable Priory is said to be the 'wellspring of English theatre'. At the beginning of the twelfth century a Norman scholar called Geoffrey de Gorham wrote a mystery play about Saint Catherine. Catherine was a fourth-century martyr who was tortured and condemned to death on a spiked breaking wheel, which is where the Catherine Wheel firework gets its name. Geoffrey staged his mystery play at Dunstable Priory, and this is a strong candidate to be the first-known play ever seen in England. Remembering this, I walk over to the new Grove Theatre complex at the opposite side of the Quadrant arcade to see what current Dunstable theatre is like. Although it is still May, the front of the theatre is covered with a wall-sized advertisement for *Aladdin*, the forthcoming Christmas pantomime. It will star, the advert promises, a children's presenter from CBBC, someone from *Coronation Street* and two contestants from *Britain's Got Talent*.

The closed-down shops cause me to think of 'Ghost Town', that strange and brilliant single by The Specials. It is not the appropriateness of that song that troubles me, but the lack of a modern equivalent. In 1981, kids like Jerry Dammers and Neville Staple could take the economic depression and nihilism of the age they found themselves in and turn it into something magnificent. Theirs was not some niche statement from a musical sub-genre, for 'Ghost Town' went to number one and was fully recognised by the broader national culture. Where, I wonder, is the modern equivalent?

I begrudgingly begin to admit that there is something disquieting about the empty shops in Dunstable High Street. I do not want to pick on Dunstable, because this applies equally to all high streets where businesses are closed, shops are empty, and only pound shops and charity stores thrive. In the second half of the twentieth century we went from being viewed as workers to being thought of as consumers, and shopping centres sat at the hearts of our towns. This current era of inequality and austerity, when we can no longer afford to support our high-street shops, changes all of this. But if we are no longer consumers, then what are we?

The idea when I was growing up was that you'd work hard, buy a house and fill it with nice things for you and your family. It may not have been the most imaginative or inspiring plan, but at least it was a plan. The noosphere offered a map to follow and experiment with. For the Millennial generation, those who reached adulthood around the turn of the twenty-first century, the gnawing insecurity caused by zero-hours contracts, student debt and unaffordable housing means that dream has been abandoned by all but the most privileged. More than 7 million workers in this country are in positions classed as 'precarious', meaning they could lose their job without warning. The number of people classified as living in poverty despite being part of a working family is also 7 million, more than the number of people in poverty from non-working households. The idea of 'jobs for life' is becoming a thing of the past, and life in the perilous 'gig economy' is increasingly common. The writer and anthropologist David Graeber has coined the phrase 'bullshit jobs' to describe the general meaninglessness of the jobs created to replace the fast-disappearing middle-class work of earlier generations. What noosphere map do the Millennial generation have to guide them through this life of constant uncertainty?

Work is about much more than economics and GDP statistics. It is one of the key narratives around which our lives are structured. It is the framework through which we assess just what it is that we are doing with our lives. As that narrative collapses, we are left with a gaping void instead of a plan for the future. Looking at these empty retail units, this feels less like a world turned upside down and more like a world that has spluttered to a halt, unable to remember where it was going.

On one level, this is all crazy. It's no secret as to what makes life worth living. It is the love of family and friends, and community, and having interests to pursue. None of these things have disappeared. They all remain available to us. But the mood of the country does not seem to value these things, and the new jobs being created actively seem to fight against them.

Back in Edgware Road, the idea that Britain voted to leave the

European Union felt like economic madness. In places like Dunstable, it makes far more sense. The system that had been in place since the late 1970s only worked for a few. What other option did people have to change things? When you are watching television and the programme is terrible and you can't watch it any longer, you change the channel. You don't know what is on the other side, or whether it will be better or worse. All you know is that it will be something different, so that's what you choose. It's either that, or turn the TV off.

Of all the highwaymen and thieves in the long history of Dunstable, the most important was the one whom the town was named after, Thomas Dun. Dun was, in the words of the Newgate Calendar, a 'person of very mean extraction'. At the start of the twelfth century, when the crossroads of Watling Street and Icknield Way were still surrounded by thick woodland, Dun and his gang preyed on travellers before disappearing into the woods and caves to avoid capture. They were known for their outrageous outlaw daring. One story recounts how Dun and his men, wearing captured Norman livery, rode up to a castle and demanded entrance in the name of the king in order to search the castle for the outlaw Dun. Once inside, they proceeded to steal everything of value.

King Henry I, the fourth son of William the Conqueror, sent men to capture Dun. A folk poem, published in 1821 but possibly older, recalls how the king's men discovered Dun's hideout.

> With flaming torch, and glittering arms,
> The cavern they drew near;
> But slowly moved with trembling steps,
> Dreading some danger there.
> In armour bright the chief advanced,
> His Lancers cover'd close;
> And great was their surprise to find
> Within the cave a horse.

Having captured Dun's horse from the cave where it was stabled, but not the outlaw himself, Henry gave orders for the woods to be felled and a town to be built at 'Dun's stable'. The cave would probably have been in the chalk escarpment just to the north of the present town but, what with the logic of stories being what it is, it is sometimes said that Dun's secret cave is underneath the crossroads itself.

Henry then laid a trap for Dun. He attached his own gold ring to the iron ring that Dun's horse was tied to. The rings were placed on a pillar outside the cave and were heavily guarded. The king believed Dun would not be able to resist stealing his royal gold ring. It would tempt him out of hiding, at which point he would be captured. But Henry did not reckon with the rules of folk legends. Dun and his men managed to kill all the guards, escape the trap and take the king's ring, which now appears as part of the town's coat of arms. This story appears to be an earlier version of a better-known Robin Hood legend, in which Prince John and the Sheriff of Nottingham drew Robin out of hiding with an archery competition with the prize of a solid gold arrow.

When Dun was eventually captured, the king reacted in typical Norman style and was not merciful. According to the Newgate Calendar, he was taken without trial to the scaffold, where 'the executioners chopped off his hands at the wrists, then cut off his arms at the elbows, and all above next, within an inch or two of his shoulders; next his feet were cut off beneath the ankles, his legs chopped off at the knees, and his thighs cut off about five inches from his trunk, which, after severing his head from it, was burnt to ashes. So after a long struggle with death, as dying by piecemeal, he put a period to his wicked and abominable life; and the several members cut off from his body, being twelve in all, besides his head, were fixed up in the principal places in Bedfordshire, to be a terror to such villains as survived him.'

The extent to which the king of England concerned himself with a common thief might seem unusual, but it needs to be seen in the context of an unsettled and rebellious country still coming to terms with Norman rule. Dun rejected Norman laws and authority, and while he may have been an apolitical thief happy to take from Norman and Saxon alike, other challengers to the king were actively trying to overthrow the new order. The most important of these was Hereward the Wake, who led a guerrilla campaign against William the Conqueror a few decades earlier, in the years that followed the Battle of Hastings.

Hereward was born in Lincolnshire, and he was always trouble. He was exiled for disobedience before the Norman invasion and stories tell of how he fought giant bears and rescued princesses during those years. He returned after the conquest and found his family's lands taken and his brother's head on a spike outside his ancestral home. He responded by revenge killing a group of fifteen Normans single-handedly before embarking on a lengthy campaign to liberate his fellow Saxons from the invaders. If Hollywood were to make a Hereward movie, they would cast Liam Neeson.

Hereward's campaign ranged across much of eastern England but was centred on the marshy fenlands of the Isle of Ely in modern Cambridgeshire. Traversing that landscape was difficult before the fens were drained in the seventeenth century, and lacking the local knowledge of the Saxons the Normans had trouble pursuing Hereward or his men across that territory. Unable to find the safe routes through the marshes to the Isle of Ely, the Normans built a tower and put a witch on top. The witch's job was to shout curses across the fenland in order to demoralise Hereward and his men. But witch-towers did not prove to be an effective medieval military weapon, it was soon discovered, because they were easy to burn down.

No one knows exactly what happened to Hereward. There are a number of contradictory stories, but none of them can be corroborated. He melted away and disappeared from the pages of history, like most of the Saxon nobility. He made a brief return to our national story in the nineteenth century, thanks to Charles Kingsley's 1866 novel *Hereward the Wake: Last of the English*, but since then he has sunk back into the marsh and fog. As with Thomas Dun, some of the stories about him became inspiration for tales of the outlaw Robin Hood.

Unlike Hereward or Dun, Robin Hood is almost certainly a fiction. His stories are set not in the fens of east England but the forests further north, although he does still appear in the story of Watling Street. One of the oldest surviving Robin Hood stories is *A Lyttell Geste of Robyn Hode*, which was written in Middle English probably around the late fifteenth century. In the story, Robin wishes to entertain a guest for dinner in the greenwood. He sends his Merry Men down to Watling Street in order to kidnap somebody.

'Take thy good bow,' said Robin Hood,
'Let Much wend with thee,
And so shall William Scathèlock,
And no man abide with me;

'And walk ye up unto the Sayles,
And so to Watling Street,
And wait after some uncouth guest;
Upchance ye may them meet.

'Be he an earl, or any baron,
Abbot, or any knight,
Bring ye him to lodge with me;
His dinner shall be dight.'

The Merry Men return with a knight whose son has recently been killed. Touched by this sorrowful knight's story, Robin resolves to help him. This sets in motion a number of Robin's best-known adventures, including the story of the king's archery competition.

Robin Hood represents a lost England, an ideal that is more fiction than reality but which calls to us regardless. A frontispiece to a 1952 children's annual captures his appeal. 'Come to the Greenwood!' it declares. 'Robin Hood is calling you! – and his band of merry men join in welcoming you to the green-dappled shades of Sherwood. [...] Meet them and many others – outlaws and knights, Normans and Saxons, kings and jesters – all the glory and splendour of England when Robin Hood's tall, green-glad figure stalked the vastness of his beloved forest. Adventure, thrills and merriment you will find a-plenty. So why tarry? Come to the Greenwood!'

That call to the Greenwood was a call to reject authority, not in a nuanced or cautious way but as blatantly and provocatively as possible. This aspect of Robin was clear in the 1938 blockbuster movie *The Adventures of Robin Hood*, which starred Errol Flynn in the title role. An early scene takes place during a feast in the Great Hall of Nottingham Castle. Prince John (played by Claude Rains) and Sir Guy of Gisbourne (Basil Rathbone) are seated at the high table, discussing tax rises and laughing at the thought of 'a Saxon dangling from every gallows tree'. Talk turns to the rebellious Robin, a 'surly Saxon noble' whom Prince John calls for to be taken and hanged for poaching a deer in the king's forest.

At this point a disturbance is heard outside the hall. The giant oak doors are opened by none other than Robin Hood himself, with a huge dead stag across his shoulders and a longbow in one hand. Robin is dressed in a green so vivid that it possibly only existed in the over-enthusiastic early days of Technicolor. Prince John grants him entry and he responds by dumping the dead stag on the table in front of the prince, sitting down opposite him and openly laughing in his face.

Maid Marian, the prince's ward, is shocked by his behaviour. 'Why, you speak treason!' she exclaims. 'Frequently!' declares Robin without missing a beat, and he goes on to call Prince John a traitor to his face, along with 'every man here who offers you allegiance'. John calls for his capture, and Robin fights his way out from the heart of the castle, duelling with swords, climbing castle walls and killing scores of guards along the way. To walk into the lion's den in such an audacious way without fear or concern for his own safety, to risk his life just to deliver an insult to the unrighteous, was what made Robin Hood the stuff of legend. A clear conscience, good friends and an appetite for pleasure are what make life worthwhile, the stories assure us, and righteousness is the greatest power of all.

The fiction of Robin Hood evolved over the centuries, as the name of Hereward withered. Robin mutated from a wild spirit of the green-wood into something more politically acceptable. His pagan, trickster background and his associations with May Day, fertility and the Green Man of the wildwood were passed over, while the Christian-friendly aspect of his morality were brought to the foreground. His habit of robbing from the rich to give to the poor became emphasised because, as *A Lyttell Geste of Robyn Hode* made clear, it 'dyde pore men moch god'. This was perhaps inevitable when his stories jumped from the oral tradition into written ballads, because writing was a highly specialised skill utilised only by the church and nobility.

Thanks to the prejudices of the sections of society which had access to writing and printing, Robin is now thought of as a nobleman. He is often referred to as Sir Robin of Loxley or the Earl of Huntingdon. Because Robin Hood was a moral hero, establishment logic dictated that he could not be a commoner. A superior man had to be a member of the nobility. But the whole point of Robin Hood was that he wasn't a nobleman. He was an English everyman. Even though Robin's original status as a yeoman was the very heart of his character, it had to go.

Robin's troublesome attitude to authority then had to be addressed. The solution was to move his stories from the reign of Edward III, which is where most of the earliest surviving versions of the stories were set, to the earlier period when Prince John was manoeuvring to take the crown from his absent brother, Richard the Lionheart. In this setting, Robin now fought against an unjust prince and his corrupt officials, but he did not question the legitimacy of the Plantagenet dynasty and he bent his knee to 'good' King Richard. It was a neat solu-tion that made Robin more palatable than outlaws such as Hereward or Dun, even if the idea that John was 'bad' while Richard was 'good' is not one that medieval scholars have much time for.

Robin is far from the only British folk hero to have had his social status promoted. Hereward, in some accounts, was said to be the son of Lady Godiva, while a story called *The Real Hereward* in the 1985 *Doctor Who Annual* claimed that he was none other than King Harold, who had survived the arrow in the eye and continued his fight undercover. That story was written anonymously, but it is almost certainly the work of Steve Moore. Doctor Who himself was simply a mysterious traveller when he first appeared in 1963, but by 1969 the BBC had upgraded him to a Lord, and a Time Lord at that. James Bond, who was long assumed to have had a middle-class background, was revealed in the 2012 film *Skyfall* to have grown up on a large country estate in Scotland, complete with gamekeeper and other upper-class trappings. Just as hedonistic artists and rebels like Mick Jagger and Elton John are absorbed into the establishment when they accept knighthoods, so British folk heroes are claimed by the world they might otherwise threaten.

American folk heroes such as Bonnie and Clyde, Al Capone or Billy the Kid are noticeably different. They have no respect for any authority other than their own individual liberty, and rob, steal and cheat in order to get rich. This is a contrast to British folk heroes, who fight not for personal gain but for the greater good. They may still be headstrong individuals who play by their own rules, but ultimately they respect authority. James Bond may be a law unto himself who constantly goes rogue and disobeys orders, but he is always loyal to his country. Doctor Who is a wandering alien bohemian, but he works as a scientific adviser to the military organisation UNIT when they need him. Sherlock Holmes operates independently from Scotland Yard, but he helps them, and Her Majesty's Government, when he is called on to do so. In a similar way, Robin Hood is an outlaw who might rob from the rich to give to the poor, but his sword is pledged to Richard the Lionheart.

Hereward's inability to be co-opted in this way puts him in a strange position. His story of a doomed rebellion is similar to those of Boudica and King Arthur, who both ultimately failed to defeat the foreign armies that invaded Britain. Yet Hereward remains largely unknown while Boudica and Arthur have become part of the national heritage. This is perhaps because Arthur fought Saxons, who were themselves conquered by the Normans, and Boudica fought Romans, who left of their own accord a few hundred years later. Celebrating a brave but ultimately doomed attempt to overthrow Roman and Saxon authority is uncontroversial, because the Romans and Saxons no longer have any authority. But Hereward challenged the Normans, and modern British landowners are still the descendants of those same Normans. This leaves no way to retrofit Hereward into the role of an establishment-supporting character in a similar way to how Robin Hood was neutered. Like people such as David Bowie, Aldous Huxley and John Lennon, who all turned down or returned honours, Hereward can't be brought onside.

Thomas Dun has also largely been forgotten. Fighting the Normans, instead of the Saxons or Romans, has disqualified him from the pantheon of folk heroes. The early Norman period lacks the transgressive potential of the Civil War era, so he has not been assigned the romance of a highwayman. His exploits have been absorbed into the fiction of Robin Hood, where they have made more of an impact than Dun did in the world of myth and legend. This suggests that his deeds weren't the problem. It was Dun himself who lacked an acceptable purpose.

This 'missing purpose' is a recurring theme in Dunstable and, by extension, small-town Britain in general. Yet looking at the process in which the stories of Robin, Hereward and Dun evolved, the extent to which the small section of society who were literate defined what we think of as 'acceptable purpose' is striking. Our troublesome British folk heroes have been made to bend the knee to the establishment in a way that American folk heroes never have, and as a result they don't have anything to offer in a situation caused by the establishment's failings. They are like American oil-industry-funded politicians in the face of climate change. The pillars of narrative that surround careers and work have crumbled, and other narratives would normally be expected to compensate. But, instead, there is silence.

Perhaps we need new folk heroes? The noosphere is rich and deep, as we have seen, and in there somewhere will be stories that make sense of uncertain times. Or perhaps we just need to reclaim our original folk heroes and nullify any contracts that bind them. It was Robin Hood, after all, who taught us that a clear conscience, good friends and an appetite for pleasure are what make life worthwhile. This would be a fine start for redrafting the maps to our lives in the noosphere.

Dunstable, meanwhile, still has the crossroads. They caused the town to be built. Watling Street brought travellers and trade, as well as plague and crime. It brought coaches which allowed it to prosper and modern traffic which choked the town's centre. The *Daily Mail* blamed online shopping for hollowing out Dunstable High Street, but the town's traffic links also brought a new Amazon warehouse, which opened a kilometre from the crossroads in May 2015, creating 500 jobs. What the road will bring to Dunstable next is unknown, but it will bring something. Perhaps it will bring a sense of purpose which Thomas Dun can retroactively acquire, and come out of his cave into the warm sunlight.

9.

BLETCHLEY PARK

The 'what if?' game

'Guess what?' says my partner, Joanne, as our family sit around the dinner table. 'I've won a competition!'

I exchange glances with our two children. You never quite know what Joanne has been up to. This could be leading anywhere.

'I've won a family ticket to Bletchley Park,' she continues.

We are all impressed. This in itself is an achievement, for our children are aged twelve and sixteen and finding day trips of interest to the whole family is something of a challenge. There have been numerous family days out where the children have been unable to hide their desire to be back at home, or at least somewhere with Wi-Fi. The days when they would be happy with a slide and an ice-cream van are sadly behind us.

But everyone seems excited by Bletchley Park. The children know about it from the film *The Imitation Game*. Our daughter, Lia, was automatically on board, for the film contained both history and Benedict Cumberbatch. Our son, Isaac, climbed inside his computer a few years back and only really now surfaces if he's hungry, but he was interested in the early computer history of Bletchley Park. There is something about massive electromechanical machines which are unable to run a *Team Fortress 2* online gaming server that he finds very funny.

'What was this competition?' I ask.

'Ach, some ol' shite,' Joanne says, batting the question away. 'So are we all keen? When shall we go?'

We were all keen, so we climbed into the car and drove to the outskirts of Milton Keynes, where we entered Bletchley Park.

At 3 p.m. on 28 July 1937, Bletchley Park Estate was put up for auction. The sales brochure made the property sound highly appealing. The estate consisted of 581 acres, it explained, including 'The modern mansion, pleasure grounds & parklands', a farm, thirty cottages and 'Nearly a mile of frontage to the main Birmingham Road (Watling Street).'

Location and transport links were a key part of the estate's appeal. Its position on Watling Street made it accessible from the south and the Midlands, there were good roads to Oxford and Cambridge, and it was adjacent to a railway junction. Bletchley itself was a small, nondescript Buckinghamshire village, but it was only an hour away from London.

Certain details in the sales brochure indicate the social set that the property might appeal to. 'The Estate is exceptionally well placed in an important Hunting district,' it stressed. 'It is in the centre of the Whaddon Chase, whose Kennels are close by, and the Duke of Grafton's Bicester and Oakley Hunts are all within easy reach.' Other claims sound more contemporary, and relatable. The estate, the particulars promise, is 'within a few yards of the principal shops'.

It's possible that the mansion itself might have put off potential buyers. It dated back to the late 1870s and had been bought by the stockbroker Sir Herbert Leon in 1883. Leon's family hosted grand weekend parties at the estate throughout the early decades of the twentieth century. They also expanded and rebuilt the house, although not in any coherent style. The original Victorian Gothic, with dark panelling and faux stained glass, was supplemented with details like Italianate pillars and a copper dome. To those with refined architectural tastes, it was a strange and unappealing building.

Ultimately, the excellent location and transport links were sufficient to find an unexpected buyer: the Government Code and Cypher School (GC&CS). Established in 1919, the GC&CS was responsible for analysing encrypted foreign messages. It had been based close to Whitehall, in a building it shared with MI6 next to St James's Park. But in the late 1930s another war looked increasingly likely and GC&CS knew that it would need to both expand and move to somewhere less at risk from air raids. Bletchley Park Estate was an ideal solution. It was obscure enough to be overlooked, but not too remote to hinder recruitment or its daily work. The head of MI6, Admiral Sir Hugh Sinclair, feared that government bureaucracy would delay this vital purchase, so he simply paid for it himself.

In May 1938 the Post Office connected the house to Whitehall by dedicated cables. In the estate grounds construction began on a number of huts, built from wood and asbestos. The transformation of a sleepy country estate into a wartime secret base was under way.

Initial recruitment occurred on an informal 'friend of a friend' basis. A side effect of this was that Bletchley Park very quickly became strikingly upper class. An early draft of a recruitment document for 'Temporary Assistants of the executive type in a branch of the Foreign Office in a country district of Bucks', for work that was 'secret and particulars of its exact nature cannot be given', stated that work at the park would be suitable for people 'who because of their social position would find it difficult to settle down in an ordinary office. This difficulty should not arise in the present instance and, while it may appear to be snobbish to have regard to considerations of this kind, the fact must be faced that those already in post in the establishment in question belong to a certain social grade and people who move in the same circles would more easily fit themselves into the present organisation.' Commander Alastair Denniston, the operational head of GC&CS, had this section removed from the final document, but the prejudices it displayed reveal a lot about the social attitudes at Bletchley Park, particularly at the start of the war.

Admiral Sir Hugh Sinclair, for example, arranged for a chef from the Ritz to come and cook for the staff, and meals were initially provided with waitress service in the main house. This pleasant arrangement could not last long, especially in a war marked by serious food rationing. An MI6 agent, Hugh Trevor-Roper, meanwhile, recalled how he 'found it compatible with my conscience to make my visits to the Code and Cypher School at Bletchley Park coincide with my hunting days with the Whaddon'.

The majority of the staff at Bletchley Park were female and the senior codebreaker, Alfred 'Dilly' Knox, who worked in a building known as the Cottage, had a reputation for specifically recruiting attractive young debutantes. His staff were known as 'Dilly's fillies'. The social nature of initial recruitment was captured by the recollections of a codebreaker, Mavis Batey, who worked for Knox at the start of the war. 'The first two girls in the Cottage were the daughters of two chaps that Denniston played golf with at Ashtead,' she had said. 'Denniston knew the family, he knew that they were nice people and ... well, that their daughters wouldn't go around opening their mouths and saying what was going on.'

Bletchley's approach to staffing is evident in an anecdote about a visit by Vice-Admiral Lord Louis Mountbatten, Chief of Combined Operations, who arrived at the site accompanied by senior military staff. Mountbatten walked into the index room only to be greeted by a young codebreaker, who remarked in surprise, 'Uncle Dickie, what are you doing here?' That codebreaker, the Honourable Sarah Baring, would later recall one problem associated with recruiting her class. 'There were a lot of young girls at that time who were mad about going to Germany and thought that Hitler was really rather wonderful,' she recalled. 'Silly girls.'

The distinguished parliamentarian Roy (later Lord) Jenkins was another example of someone recruited for their social status and connections, rather than their skill as a codebreaker. In his memoirs, Jenkins recalled that he was drafted into Bletchley Park due to the involvement of Baron Lindsay of Birker in the recruitment process. Lindsay was Vice-Chancellor of Oxford University and Master of Balliol College, which Jenkins attended. Lindsay 'had decided that the traditional role of Masters of Balliol [...] of placing Balliol men in what they regarded as appropriate jobs outweighed any irritation with my poor philosophy mark,' Jenkins wrote. 'Why he thought I would be a better cryptographer than a philosopher I do not know, but the fact that he did appeared to be decisive.' Lord Jenkins may have been a man of many talents, but it was said by other Bletchley veterans that he 'was not the world's most talented codebreaker'.

These social attitudes almost prevented the recruitment of Bletchley's most famous codebreaker, Alan Turing. Although he was privately educated and had gained a first-class honours degree from King's College, Cambridge, Turing was still a mathematician, and mathematicians were seen by the wealthy as the 'wrong sort'. Latin and Greek were viewed as subjects of greater value than science or engineering, because practical subjects like those were associated with work and trade. When war broke out, eighteen out of the first twenty-one 'men of the professor type' that Denniston hired were humanists, typically linguists and classicists. Yet even Denniston could see that, if he wanted to crack Nazi encryptions, then it might be sensible to hire a mathematician or two to join his lecturers in Ancient Greek and professors of medieval German. As a result, in 1939, the brilliant, athletic, endearingly eccentric and possibly mildly autistic Alan Turing made his way to Buckinghamshire.

Turing has always been a well-known figure in computer circles. His 1936 paper 'On Computational Numbers' proved that machines capable of performing any calculation were theoretically possible. It is because of this paper that what we would now think of as a 'computer' was for a time called a Turing Universal Machine. His later work on artificial intelligence produced a benchmark test for defining AI, called the Turing Test. Those frustrating 'CAPTCHA' tests, familiar to anyone who has struggled to fill out online registrations, are rooted in this work. CAPTCHA is an acronym for Completely Automated Public Turing test to tell Computers and Humans Apart.

Turing statue

But, outside computer circles, Turing was an unknown figure until relatively recently. When he died of cyanide poisoning in 1954, two years after a conviction for gross indecency for his then-illegal homosexuality, his wartime work was still covered by the Official Secrets Act. It was only after the story of Bletchley Park came to light, from the 1980s onwards, that Turing rose to his current status of national hero.

His ascent was rapid. In 1999 *Time* magazine named him as one of the 100 most important people of the twentieth century, and in 2002 a poll for the BBC *100 Greatest Britons* programme placed him at number 21, behind Paul McCartney and Margaret Thatcher but ahead of Queen Elizabeth II and Stephen Hawking. In 2014 he was portrayed by Benedict Cumberbatch in the film *The Imitation Game*, and that year a musical version of his life story, written by the Pet Shop Boys, was performed at the Royal Albert Hall as part of BBC Proms. In 2009 the Prime Minister, Gordon Brown, made an official government apology for his treatment, and the Queen announced his pardon in 2014. These gestures of official regret were the result of complicated constitutional hoop-jumping, for Turing was guilty of what he was convicted of and there was legal and political resistance to setting a precedent for the pardoning of people convicted by unjust historic laws. Yet Turing's status was such that the Policing and Crime Act 2017 contained the 'Alan Turing Law', which pardoned all men convicted or cautioned under historic anti-homosexuality laws. Turing's current reputation is nicely demonstrated by a remark made by Apple's Steve Jobs, who was asked if it was true that his company's logo, an apple with a bite out of it, was a reference to the theory that Turing killed himself by eating a cyanide-coated apple. Jobs replied, 'God, we wish it were.'

Even after a story has been in the public eye as much as Turing's has this past decade, it can still be illuminating to return to. History is infinitely rich, and you always find new nuggets when you dig. This is certainly the case with the Bletchley Park story.

When he arrived at Bletchley, Turing and his fellow senior code-breaker Gordon Welchman, a charming Bristol-born Cambridge scholar, faced a seemingly insoluble problem. The German military were using a machine called Enigma to encrypt their communications. Enigma was a mass-produced machine that had been on the market since 1923, and had initially been used by banks. The British government considered them for military purposes in 1926 but took the view that the machines were too large and ungainly for use in the field.

By the time the Second World War broke out, Enigma machines had been refined to the point that they were capable of encrypting text in 159,000,000,000,000,000,000 different ways. If you did not possess the correct decryption setting, which the Nazis changed every day at midnight, then decoding Enigma-encrypted communications looked impossible. This is what Turing and Welchman, helped by access to earlier work by Polish Intelligence, set out to do.

Codebreaking was essentially a giant 'what if?' game. What if the letter 'g' represented the letter 't'? What if the letter 'x' represented the letter 'p'? The amount of possibilities was huge, and cracking the code would take some doing. Their approach was, essentially, inspired guesswork coupled with mechanical brute force.

First, they made a guess about what common phrase the German message might contain, such as 'Heil Hitler', 'nothing significant to report', or 'message number'. Welchman's work on traffic analysis was invaluable here, for it helped suggest what text the message might contain based on where it was sent from and to whom. The next stage required a large electromechanical machine, called the Bombe, which Turing and Welchman designed. The Bombe was built by the British Tabulating Machine Company in Letchworth and transported to Bletchley on the back of an open lorry, with no security or escort in order not to draw attention to it. The machine was programmed with the guessed text, which the codebreakers called their 'crib'. It then ran through all of the 159,000,000,000,000,000,000 possible combinations until it found one which successfully decrypted the message in a way that included this crib.

The success of Turing and Welchman's machine led to Bletchley Park expanding massively. It became a decryption factory, requiring thousands of employees working around the clock to decrypt the vast number of wartime Axis messages. By the end of the war there were nearly 10,000 people working at the park, the majority of whom were women. This expansion diluted Bletchley's status as an upper-class enclave but left its staff working in a strangely undefined atmosphere that was neither properly military nor civilian. Its oddness was captured in a poem by the Bletchley machine operator Bobby Hooper, who described it as:

This place called up at war's behest
And peopled by the strangely dressed.

Hooper went on to describe the different types of people who played their part in the codebreaking effort:

The Air Force types that never fly
soldiers who neither do nor die
landlubber navy, beards complete
civilians slim, long-haired, effete.

Among the regular visitors to the site was a young Ian Fleming, then a lieutenant-commander in Naval Intelligence. Fleming's experiences in Naval Intelligence form the roots of his James Bond character, and novels like *You Only Live Twice* (1964) and *From Russia with Love* (1957) feature codes and codebreaking as part of their plot. It is said that Bond's codename, '007', is a reference to the First World War German cipher code '0075'. The German High Command used 0075 to encode a message, the Zimmermann telegram, which proposed an alliance with Mexico in an attack on the United States. British Intelligence cracked this code, and the incident was a factor in the United States entering the First World War.

Bletchley's success required total secrecy. If the Germans realised that their messages were being listened to, they would have immediately changed their procedures. Numerous tricks were used to give the impression that German communications were secure. When Bletchley identified the location of German ships, such as the *Bismarck*, the Air Force sent out a lone patrol that would be spotted 'discovering' the boat before the navy attacked. Many people believe that Churchill knew in advance about the Coventry Blitz on November 1940, and that he did not order an evacuation in order to protect Bletchley's secret. There are also claims he knew about Pearl Harbor and didn't forewarn the Americans because he needed them to enter the war. Neither of these claims has been proved, but they do illustrate the awful responsibility of keeping Bletchley's secret. The codebreakers who signed the Official Secrets Act viewed it as a lifelong oath, and frequently went to their graves without telling their immediate family members what they did in the war. Many Bletchley staff never forgave Gordon Welchman for writing a book about cracking Enigma in 1982, *The Hut Six Story*, even though he did so more than thirty years after the end of the war.

It was not the case that after the arrival of the Bombe machine all Bletchley Park had to do was sit back and listen in to German messages for the rest of the war. German cryptography kept advancing and the Enigma machines became increasingly complicated and secure. A cryptographic arms race was in progress. The Bletchley codebreakers managed to keep up thanks to hard work, occasional moments of good fortune and help from the rest of the armed forces, such as the capture of a German codebook from the submarine *U-110*.

In late 1940, Allied radio listening stations across Europe began picking up German messages that were being encrypted by an entirely new, and completely unknown, machine. The British didn't even know the name of this encryption device, so they nicknamed it Tunny. It was soon clear, from traffic analysis, that it was being used for very high-level communication, including Hitler's orders to his generals on the battlefield. Due to the complexity of the code, it was going to need a machine far faster and more powerful than a Bombe to crack. A series of machines named Robinsons were designed, and the Dollis Hill communications research laboratory of the British Post Office was given the job of building them, but they proved unreliable and were prone to catching fire.

A Post Office engineer at Dollis Hill called Tommy Flowers thought that he could see the solution. Machines like the Bombe used mechanical switches, called relays, to turn circuits on and off. In the years before the war, the Post Office had been experimenting with valves instead of relays and found that valves could make telephone switchboards work thousands of times faster. The Robinson machines used some valves, but not enough to make a significant difference. What if, Flowers wondered, the entire processor was built with valves? Surely that would produce a computing device of sufficient power to crack the Tunny code?

Flowers showed his designs to Bletchley. What he was proposing was radical, massive and incredibly complicated. He estimated that it would take a year to build. They turned him down.

'Well,' thought Tommy Flowers, 'I'll build it anyway.' He told his boss, the director of Post Office laboratories, Gordon Radley, that what he was doing was necessary for Bletchley. Then he got to work, gambling that they'd be grateful for the machine in a year's time.

He assembled a team of about fifty engineers, technicians and scientists in a Birmingham factory. They worked twelve-hour days, six or six and a half days a week. Flowers covered the inevitable wartime financial shortfalls out of his own pocket. They worked, as Flowers later put it, until their 'eyes dropped out', and eleven months later they had their first computing machine. It was the size of a room and weighed about a tonne. When it was taken to Bletchley Park, the women who operated it named it Colossus.

Colossus was followed by the even more powerful Colossus II. This was installed at Bletchley days before the D-Day landings and quickly began breaking the Tunny cypher. One such decrypt was from Hitler to Field Marshal Rommel. The invasion of Normandy was imminent, Hitler told Rommel, but it was nothing more than a feint designed to draw troops away from the Channel ports. The real invasion would occur five days after the Normandy landings at those Channel ports, Hitler believed, so Rommel was ordered not to move any of his troops. A courier took this message direct to President Eisenhower, who was at the Supreme Headquarters Allied Expeditionary Force on the eve of the D-Day landings. Eisenhower read this message and, being unable to tell the assembled military what he had read or where it had come from, simply told them, 'We go tomorrow.'

By the end of the war, there were ten Colossus machines working around the clock at Bletchley Park. With the arrival of peacetime Churchill ordered that eight of these be destroyed, along with the

Bombes and all record of what had been achieved at Bletchley during the war. Machines were dismantled and records were dutifully burnt. Churchill was now focused on the war to come, the potential Cold War with Russia. He did not want Stalin to know what British Intelligence was capable of. Churchill did not realise that Stalin already knew. Moscow had a spy in Bletchley Park sending Tunny decrypts straight to Moscow. This was John Cairncross, the alleged 'fifth man' of the famous Cambridge Five spy ring, who passed more than 5,000 documents to the Soviets between 1941 and 1945.

Come peacetime, the thousands of people working at Bletchley dispersed. Most went back to civilian life, some to the military and others to academia, where a number played an important role in the development of computing at Manchester University. In 1946 GC&CS was renamed GCHQ and moved from Bletchley to Cheltenham. Gordon Welchman moved to America and worked on secure communications for the US Military. His work on traffic analysis, together with the work on decryption produced at GCHQ, led to a communications-monitoring programme called Five Eyes which allowed America, Canada, New Zealand, Australia and the UK to share intelligence from decrypted communications. Communications monitoring has continued to expand in the age of the internet, and the Bletchley Park work of listening to Nazis has grown to the point where now everyone is monitored. Following the passing of the UK Investigatory Powers Act 2016, every person in Britain has each website they visit recorded, along with every phone call and email. This information is available to authorities ranging from the taxman to immigration officers.

Tommy Flowers, however, did not play a part in all this. He was just an engineer at the Post Office. That's where he remained, forbidden by the Official Secrets Act from revealing anything about Colossus.

The class issue of Bletchley Park had been problematic for Flowers. He was the son of a bricklayer from the East End of London who taught himself engineering through night classes. He enjoyed a good relationship with Turing but was looked down upon by Welchman, who actively campaigned to prevent his access to technical resources. An example of his condescension can be seen in a memo Welchman wrote on 4 June 1943. Flowers 'is probably very good at his ordinary work', he wrote, 'and also very good at designing apparatus for a definite problem that he can understand, but I have found him slow at grasping the complications of our work and his mind seems altogether too inflexible'. Welchman's dislike of Flowers played a large factor in Bletchley rejecting the initial plans for Colossus, and for Flowers going ahead with it on his own initiative.

The first programmable computer was built by the German genius Konrad Zuse in the late 1930s, but this was strictly mechanical and not an electronic computer. The Colossus was the world's first large-scale electronic computer, many orders of magnitude more powerful than Zuse's machine and certainly the first computer that was actually of any use.

The list of British computing pioneers famous enough to be known to the general public is not long. It consists of Charles Babbage, Ada Lovelace, Alan Turing, Tim Berners-Lee and perhaps even Sir Clive Sinclair. Even though Tommy Flowers actually designed and built the world's first electronic computer, a phenomenal achievement of incalculable importance to human development, he is shamefully not on that list.

Flowers's inability to tell anyone about what he had created overshadowed his later life. He was granted an MBE in 1943 in recognition of his achievement, but his direct boss received a knighthood and he was overlooked in the Post Office reorganisation of 1947. After the war he attempted to get a loan from the Bank of England in order to build another computer, but the bank did not believe anyone was capable of building such a fantastic-sounding machine and turned him down. Theoretically, Flowers's achievement should have put him in a great position to make major advances in the telecommunications industry but, as he wrote shortly before he died in 1998, he had 'no power or opportunity to use the knowledge effectively. With no administrative or executive powers, I had to convince others, and they would not be convinced. I was the one-eyed in the kingdom of the blind. The thing that I lacked was prestige.'

Two of the ten Colossus computers were not destroyed at the end of the war and were instead taken to GCHQ in Cheltenham. When they were finally dismantled in 1960, Flowers was ordered to destroy all his records. As he later recalled, 'I took all the drawings and the plans and all the information about Colossus on paper and put it in the boiler fire. And I saw it burn.'

Tommy Flowers had no choice but to sit back and watch as the later American computer ENIAC was heralded around the world as the 'first electronic computer'. As he wrote about the enforced secrecy surrounding Colossus, 'I accepted the situation philosophically.'

On a sunny Sunday in late January 2016, Joanne, the kids and I arrive at Bletchley Park's visitors' centre, having somehow made it through Milton Keynes's bewildering system of roundabouts.

After the GC&CS became GCHQ and left for Cheltenham in 1946, the Bletchley Park Estate became a training school. It was used at first by the Allied Control Commission, which governed post-war Germany, and later as a teacher-training college. As the years rolled on, while the wooden codebreaking huts slowly rotted and Alan Moore (with some help) built the town of Milton Keynes over the surrounding countryside, the training centre continued to develop. It was used by the Civil Aviation Authority and then the GPO, which became British Telecom. After British Telecom left, with no use for the property apparent, the government looked into selling it off. It was surprised to discover that it didn't actually own it, as it had been personally bought by the head of the Secret Intelligence Service, the late Admiral Hugh Sinclair, at the end of the 1930s.

For a while it looked like the old house and all the huts would be bulldozed and the land used for a new housing development. This was not an uncommon fate for historic Second World War sites. The

Dollis Hill rooms where Tommy Flowers built the first Colossus, for example, are now apartments. Fortunately, in the early nineties, the Bletchley Park Trust was formed to preserve the site's infrastructure and turn it into a museum. This was a mammoth job, for the mansion was crumbling and the huts were riddled with asbestos and pigeon droppings. There were, contemporary press reports stress, an awful lot of pigeons roosting among the ruins of Bletchley Park. Thanks to the hard work of the Trust, the site is now a thriving museum with the huts and mansion restored to their wartime state.

Having made it through the visitors' centre, we find ourselves looking at the famous house across the lawns and the lake. Swans swim idly across the water. This lake figures heavily in the memories of those who worked here during the war. Codebreakers skated across it when it froze in winter, and swam in it in the warmth of summer. Less idyllically, it was also home to a great many frogs, which would be trodden on accidentally during blackouts.

'Those trees look like Donald Trump's wig,' Isaac points out, indicating a clump of trees in front of the mansion that do look something like Donald Trump's hair. Children always add a random element to proceedings. This is the joy of visiting anywhere as a family.

I am keen to see the reconstruction of Tommy Flowers's Colossus, which is located in Bletchley Park's wartime 'Block H'. But our family is a leaderless collective, capable of compromise and groupthink, which wanders about at random in whatever manner causes the least grief. In this instance we first go to look at Alan Turing's office, in Hut 8, which is reconstructed to look as it would have done in 1940. It includes Turing's mug still chained to the radiator, which he did to prevent people from hiding it. Shortly after we enter Hut 8, the kids discover a room within it containing a 'Pigeons in War' exhibition. After this the rest of the afternoon takes a decidedly pigeon-based turn.

The Pigeons in War exhibit is presented in association with the Royal Pigeon Racing Association. It includes a collection of memorabilia concerning the National Pigeon Service, a volunteer civilian organisation formed just before the outbreak of the Second World War, which provided homing pigeons for military communication. I pick up a leaflet in the exhibition in order to learn more. The leaflet has a black-and-white photograph of a pigeon on the front, onto which an infantry helmet and a row of medals have been Photoshopped. It begins, 'Sir Winston Churchill, Lord Montgomery of El Alamein, Douglas Bader, Mary of Exeter. All names of eponymous Second World War Heroes? Yes, but did you know that Mary was a pigeon?'

I confess I initially suspected this was over-egging Mary of Exeter's contribution to the war a little. But I then learn that Mary managed to find her way home despite being wounded three times, having part of her wing shot off and being badly injured by 'a German hawk'. Mary was just one of 250,000 pigeons used in the war effort. Often they would be parachuted behind enemy lines, to be used by Resistance fighters on the continent. The pigeons were placed in small wooden or cardboard boxes, which had a little hole at one end for their heads to stick out of. There is something about a surprised-looking pigeon's head sticking out of a small wooden box hung from a parachute that children, and indeed I, find remarkably funny.

Reading the exhibits, we discover that Bletchley had a few homing pigeons of its own. Whether these are connected to the many hundreds of later pigeons roosting in collapsed roofs, leaving decades' worth of waste for the Trust to deal with, is not clear. We learn that their keeper was always seeking more pigeons and more funding, and that he tirelessly campaigned to promote the use of pigeons in war. A place like Bletchley Park, on the cutting edge of computing and communications technology, must have been the absolute worst place to be for anyone hoping to promote the use of pigeon communication.

Military pigeon use is still a hot topic in the twenty-first century. In 2004, the Labour MP Tony Banks tabled an early day motion in parliament entitled 'Pigeon Bombs'. Banks was pro-pigeon and very much against pigeon bombs. His motion reads, 'This House is appalled, but barely surprised, at the revelations in MI5 files regarding the bizarre and inhumane proposals to use pigeons as flying bombs; recognises the important and life-saving role of carrier pigeons in two world wars and wonders at the lack of gratitude towards these gentle creatures;

Pigeon parachute

and believes that humans represent the most obscene, perverted, cruel, uncivilised and lethal species ever to inhabit the planet and looks forward to the day when the inevitable asteroid slams into the earth and wipes them out thus giving nature the opportunity to start again.' Banks's motion has the air of something written late at night while tired and emotional, and his desire to see humanity wiped out by an asteroid is, by anyone's standards, quite excessive. Nevertheless, the motion received two more signatures: Jeremy Corbyn and John McDonnell.

According to Professor Tim Guildford of Oxford University's Department of Zoology, pigeons navigate familiar journeys by following roads, to the extent of turning at junctions and banking around roundabouts. Bletchley's homing pigeons were likely to use Watling Street themselves, a reminder that this road is not just a human story. Crows are thought to follow roads as well, which is frustrating for anyone using the phrase 'as the crow flies'.

It is around this point that Joanne, Lia and Isaac develop a Bletchley Park sitcom.

'It would be like *The Big Bang Theory*,' Isaac suggests, 'although they would be nerds from history.'

'Historically there were more women than men working here,' points out Lia, 'but the nerds still wouldn't be able to get girlfriends because nerds couldn't in those days. They were not socially adept. The women would be harder for them to understand than the Nazi codes.'

'*Big Bang Theory* meets *Dad's Army*,' summarises Joanne, who has worked in TV development.

'Of course, the pigeon man would have to be in it,' Lia points out.

'Oh yes. Always trying to get the War Office to get him some more pigeons,' says Isaac.

'Whenever they would be inventing computers and stuff he would be at the back with a sad voice going, "but ... pigeons!" ' says Lia.

We continue exploring the park. We find a reconstructed working Bombe machine and a display of *The Imitation Game* props and costumes. We fail to find our way to the reconstructed Colossus, the route to which always seems to be blocked by fences. Yet for the rest of the afternoon the memory of the 'but ... pigeons!' man never leaves us. There is no corner of the park that isn't improved by the thought that he was going to appear and make the case for more pigeons.

This is the random element that comes from going somewhere as a family and especially with children. When people get together ideas spring up in the space between them that would never arise if they were alone. There is an unpredictable nature to groups, which is perhaps why we are so drawn to them. The sum is greater than the parts. It's a reminder that, although our films, novels and documentaries about Bletchley Park focus on men like Denniston, Turing and Welchman, Bletchley Park's achievements ultimately arose from the interactions of thousands of men and women, all of whom played their role. Those achievements bubbled up from the exchanges between them.

Our family day out at Bletchley Park is a great success. It is only after I get home that I realise I have not seen the reconstructed Colossus. An online search reveals that, while it was on display in Block H of the Bletchley site as I had thought, that building is operated by a separate organisation to the Bletchley Park Trust, and access from the main park had recently been blocked by a fence. According to a report in the *Daily Telegraph*, this fence was a 'Berlin Wall' across the Bletchley estate, and the product of tensions between differing Bletchley Park charities. Whatever the reasons are for this, it is undeniably a shame. The Bletchley Park story ceases to be properly told when parts are left out, and it feels horribly ironic that Tommy Flowers's contribution has been fenced off from the official story.

How important was Bletchley Park's codebreaking in terms of the Allies winning the Second World War?

President Eisenhower credited the efforts of Bletchley Park's staff with shortening the war by two years. Sir Harry Hinsley, who wrote the official account of British Intelligence during the war, thought that it shortened the war by up to four years. There's an interesting argument that Bletchley Park was even more important than this, a clear tipping point in history without which the Allies would have lost the Second World War. As the codebreaker Jack Good remarked, 'I won't say that what Turing did made us win the war, but I daresay we might have lost it without him.'

This argument is focused on the early years of the war, when the

Nazis had overrun much of Western Europe. As the national myth put it, Britain stood alone. The national myth downplays the support of the Commonwealth, but in other respects it was essentially accurate.

The first couple of years of the war went badly for Britain. There had been a series of defeats, such as the Dunkirk evacuations of the British Expeditionary Force, together with some courageous acts of defence, such as the Battle of Britain. Hitler had yet to declare war on the United States and Russia, the Nazi–Soviet non-aggression pact was still intact, and the Japanese had not yet attacked Pearl Harbor. Churchill was under no illusion: Britain could not defeat Nazi Germany. But even though he couldn't win, and even though many in Washington and elsewhere thought that Britain was about be defeated, Churchill refused to give up.

Churchill became Prime Minister in May 1940, eight months after the outbreak of war, at a time when the bleakness of the British situation was becoming apparent. It was during the summer months which followed that he made the speeches he is best known for. 'I have nothing to offer but blood, toil, tears and sweat,' he told the House of Commons on 13 May. On 4 June, after the Dunkirk disaster, he was weary but even more resolute. 'We shall go on to the end. We shall fight in France, we shall fight on the seas and oceans, we shall fight with growing confidence and growing strength in the air, we shall defend our island, whatever the cost may be. We shall fight on the beaches, we shall fight on the landing grounds, we shall fight in the fields and in the streets, we shall fight in the hills; we shall never surrender.' On 18 June he suggested that people in a thousand years would look back at this time and declare of the British, 'this was their finest hour'.

Churchill couldn't win, yet he refused to lose. In his favour he had the strength of the British Navy, which kept him in the war but could not defeat a largely land-locked country like Germany, and the hope that his attempts to persuade the Americans to enter the war would eventually come to fruition, which was far from certain. As valuable as a big navy and a transatlantic hope were, they didn't seem enough to sustain or justify his pig-headed determination.

This was why Bletchley Park was so important. Churchill had an ace up his sleeve, and it was one that no other nation knew about or even believed possible. Turing and Welchman's Bombe machine began decrypting Nazi Enigma communications in early 1940. The psychological value of this at such a pivotal point of history, before the Americans and the Russians joined the Allies and before the first real British land victory at El Alamein, must have been extraordinary. Churchill knew that the situation wasn't quite as desperate as it looked to everyone else. He knew this during the summer when he told the House of Commons that 'we will never surrender'. President Eisenhower and Harry Hinsley were correct when they said that Bletchley Park decrypts shortened the war, but they also brought hope at the darkest point, and that in many ways could have been more important. It is certainly possible to imagine ways that without Bletchley Churchill would have crumbled and Britain would have lost the Second World War.

This is a popular idea in the 'alternative-history' genre. Just as cryptography is essentially playing 'what if?' with substituted encrypted characters, so the alternative history genre plays 'what if?' with moments of history. Arguably the greatest example of this genre is *The Man in the High Castle* (1962) by the American science-fiction author Philip K. Dick.

The book is set fifteen years after a 1947 surrender of the Allies to the Axis Powers. Part of the reason why the book's history differs from ours is the attempted assassination of Franklin D. Roosevelt by Giuseppe 'Joe' Zangara in 1933, which was unsuccessful in our history but successful in the novel. But references to the European war make it clear that Dick's history of the war diverged from ours before the Americans became part of the conflict, in circumstances compatible with the idea that Enigma remained unbroken and that Churchill lacked the ace Bletchley gave him. The book's heroine, Juliana Frink, for example, says that 'if the Germans hadn't taken Malta, Churchill would have stayed in power and guided England to Victory'. Had Bletchley Park failed to employ Turing on the grounds that mathematicians were the 'wrong sort', then our history could have been far closer to Dick's.

The Man in the High Castle is set in an alternative history of the United States, where the Pacific states are under Japanese control and the eastern and Midwest states are part of the Greater German Reich. A neutral zone, which roughly matches the Rockies, separates the two. The fragile peace is in danger, and a change of leadership in the Third Reich has the potential to trigger a German nuclear attack on Japan. All this sounds like a set-up for a terrific thriller. But Dick wrote a very different book, and one far more interesting than that scenario suggests.

Dick's novel tells two different stories. The first is about Juliana Frink, a judo instructor in the Rocky Mountains neutral zone, and her journey to meet Hawthorne Abendsen, the writer of an alternative history in which the Allies won the war. In the second story her ex-husband, Frank Frink, is starting an artisan jewellery business in San Francisco. You might expect that these two strands will join up by the novel's end, and that Juliana and Frank will be reunited, but this is not to be. Both stories unfurl with a great sense of purpose but, unlike a traditional thriller, it is impossible to predict where the story is heading.

Chance plays a large part in this. The *I Ching* has a significant role in the book, particularly for characters who live in the Japanese-ruled Pacific states. The *I Ching* is a Chinese divination text which is probably around 2,500 years old. Unlike Western divinatory techniques such as astrology or tarot cards, it should not be thought of as a technique for telling the future. Instead, it is a method for better understanding the present moment, from which advice about the best course of action can be given. The tossing of coins or the throwing of stalks are used to generate random numbers, which are said to represent the wider unfurling cosmos at that point in time. These numbers are mapped to one of sixty-four different outcomes, called hexagrams, that are described in terms that echo the growth and decay of nature. Events in the larger world are constantly growing, decaying, being blocked or breaking free, and the hexagram offered up by the universe at any one moment is interpreted as a representation of how things are developing.

Dick used the *I Ching* himself while writing the book. 'I used [the *I Ching* as a plotting device] in *The Man in the High Castle* because a number of characters used it,' he told an interviewer in 1974. 'In each case when they asked a question, I threw the coins and wrote the hexagram lines they got. That governed the direction of the book. Like in the end, when Juliana Frink is deciding whether or not to tell Hawthorne Abendsen that he is the target of assassins, the answer indicated that she should. Now if it had said not to tell him, I would have had her not go there.' This helps explain why Dick's unfurling story remains so unpredictable and never settles into the expected thriller tropes. It also explains why Juliana's and Frank's stories never merge. It was entirely down to chance. It just wasn't meant to be.

Dick had a reason for using this technique for this story. A prominent theme of his novel is the contrast between the Eastern Japanese perspective and the Western Germanic world view. Eastern thought, as Dick saw it, was holistic, concerned with the wider picture and with understanding the present. Western thought, in contrast, was focused on linear progress and reaching a golden future. The Nazis in Dick's novel were already building rocket ships and travelling to Mars and Venus, because that is what the narrative logic of Hitler's Thousand-Year Reich demanded. They possessed technology far in advance of the Japanese, who were more concerned with correct behaviour and formal social standing. Dick takes these two extremes, those of dreaming the future and perfecting the present, and uses *The Man in the High Castle* to explore how they would impact on twentieth-century America.

The Man in the High Castle is often described as Dick's greatest work but, unlike many other novels by him, it has not been adapted into a film. This is perhaps because of its controversial vision of a Nazi eastern America or its lack of a cinema-friendly plot. But in 2015 it was adapted into a TV series for the Amazon Prime internet streaming video service. In the current golden age of long-form TV drama an internet TV service like Amazon can tackle controversial stories that traditional TV channels, concerned about the reaction of their advertisers, tend to shy away from.

Turning an experimental novel like this into a high-budget, potentially ongoing mainstream television drama must have been quite a challenge. The first job was to take the novel apart. The characters, settings and events were all separated out, cut free from the narrative that originally contained them. At this stage, much of the book was discarded. The idea that Nazi America had reintroduced slavery for African Americans, for example, was one idea that was dropped. Ideas like that may be acceptable to an audience who like experimental science-fiction novels, but could alienate the larger, more casual, audience Amazon Prime was seeking. And as the idea was dropped, so were Dick's reasons for including it. The TV series does not attempt to discuss America's attitude to race in the same way that the book did.

The characters were made more conventionally likeable. Juliana Frink is no longer a wife who has left her husband and is sleeping with other men. The couple are together at the start of the series and Juliana's relationship with a Nazi spy remains platonic, even while her husband's jealousy is exploited for dramatic tension. In the novel, Dick explores life as it is typically experienced in occupied countries, where people have no choice but to accept the political situation and remain focused on their day-to-day lives. The television adaptation, in contrast, adds an underground movement modelled on the French Resistance. This allows the series to portray its American characters as heroic underdogs rather than acquiescent quislings.

With these tonal and thematic changes made, the remaining dismembered characters and events were recombined to fit the requirements of an ongoing hourly drama. Events in the book were placed back in the series, at times occurring to different characters for different reasons. The iconography and mythology of the novel were amplified and reworked. The identity of the titular 'man in the high castle' was changed to refer to Hitler, a plot point simpler and neater than in the novel, and more dramatic. The novel's alternative-history book-within-a-book, which depicted the Allies winning the war, was changed to become reels of films. These are said to be able to alter history, and are hunted by both Nazis and members of the Resistance. The novel does not visit the Nazi-occupied eastern states so the television adaptation invented new characters based in this part of the world, most notably Rufus Sewell's all-American SS officer, Obergruppenführer John Smith. This gave the series the shocking visual images that worked so well in the trailer: Nazis behind white picket fences, swastikas and the 'Work will set you free' slogan in Times Square, a Nazi version of the Stars and Stripes flag.

The adaptation of *The Man in the High Castle* was a success. At the time of writing, a second series is in production. It is, however, a very different beast to the novel. But, curiously, the differences between the book and the TV series neatly echo the differences between Eastern and Western perspectives that the original story explored. Dick's writing was an individual artistic act of creation and discovery, while the series was a pre-planned, skilfully crafted, large-scale building project. His use of the *I Ching* to dictate events gave him a book that unfurled in the moment, in keeping with the Eastern world view of the Japanese, and in which the future was impossible to guess. The television adaptation, on the other hand, was linear and structured. The narrative obeyed the expected rules of its genre in order to bring its characters to the intended conclusion. In doing so it echoed the Western, Germanic perspective.

When we look back at the story of Bletchley Park, we do so already knowing the outcome of the Second World War. Because of this, we cannot help but automatically interpret it as part of that larger historical narrative, the positive outcome of which is inevitable. It is hard to think about wartime stories without the shadow of approaching victory colouring events. We look at it in much the same way as Dick's western Nazis viewed the world in his novel. Yet the codebreakers during the war years did not know what the future would be. They experienced events in a similar manner to Dick's Japanese characters. They could only focus on doing their very best in the present moment, because whether or not they managed to decrypt the Axis message in front of them could have significant implications for future events. The work they carried out could, potentially, change the outcome of the war. As the *I Ching* itself would advise, intense focus on the task at hand is what is important, not dramatic theories about historical inevitability.

In the alternative-history genre there is usually one moment when history pivots and a different future emerges. Alan Turing, undoubtedly, was one such real-life historical tipping point. Yet the more you look at a place like Bletchley Park, the more you realise how many similar moments there are. If Tommy Flowers had accepted Welchman's snobbery and not built Colossus regardless, how would that have affected the European endgame? What if the mansion had found a different buyer at auction in 1937? What if German spies in Moscow had gained access to Bletchley Park intelligence brought in by the spy John Cairncross?

After information about Colossus was made public, Flowers was approached by a German engineer and scientist. This engineer told him that he had attempted to interest Hitler in a similar codebreaking machine at the start of the war. Flowers believed this engineer had the technical knowledge needed to do what he himself had done but just needed the resources. Hitler asked him how long he needed, and the engineer estimated that building the computer would take two years. Hitler declined, believing that the war would be over and Germany would be victorious by then. Quite what the history of the war would have been if Hitler had granted the necessary resources, we can't say. Even seeing progress on such a machine would have revealed to Hitler that his communications might not be as secure as he believed.

What if Tommy Flowers had not been overlooked for being working class? What if he had played a central role in the development of computing after the Second World War? Would his head start and expertise have led to some of the great computer corporations being

British, rather than almost exclusively American and Japanese? Would Flowers himself have become a new type of role model for council-estate kids, an alternative to the footballers and musicians they are usually limited to?

Watching Lia and Isaac exploring this part of their past, and trash-talking pigeons, makes the 'what if?' game personal. It brings home how lucky we've been. If events hadn't brought me and Joanne together in Liverpool in the early 1990s, they would not be here. But, then, what were the chances of our own parents meeting? They were children in wartime and their stories could easily have been very different. And what about their parents, and their grandparents, and so on along the line of ancestors? All lives past were the product of uncountable decisions, any of which could have been pivotal to the present. How lucky have we been? The odds are unfathomable. They are not something that a Bombe or Colossus, or indeed the fastest modern supercomputer, could ever hope to calculate.

None of those 'what ifs' occurred. Our alternative histories remain inside fiction or in some of the more psychedelic corners of physics. What we have instead is *now*, the present unfurling moment, just as the *I Ching* stresses. Like the codebreakers of Bletchley Park, we don't know what the future holds, and can only focus on the task in hand. We can't know what the results of our actions will be, any more than the Leon family could have known what would result when they put their family mansion up for auction. We are like characters in Philip K. Dick's novel, not the characters in the TV adaptation.

Given the events of history, the odds of me and Joanne being able to watch our children joking by the Bletchley Park lake, living free on this unconquered island, are unfathomable. They are far higher than the 1 in 159,000,000,000,000,000,000 chance that you could correctly guess a particular Enigma code. And yet, here we all are. Uncountable disasters and apocalypses have been sidestepped, and the present continues to unfurl. The island's story is never-ending, but we improvise our roles as we go.

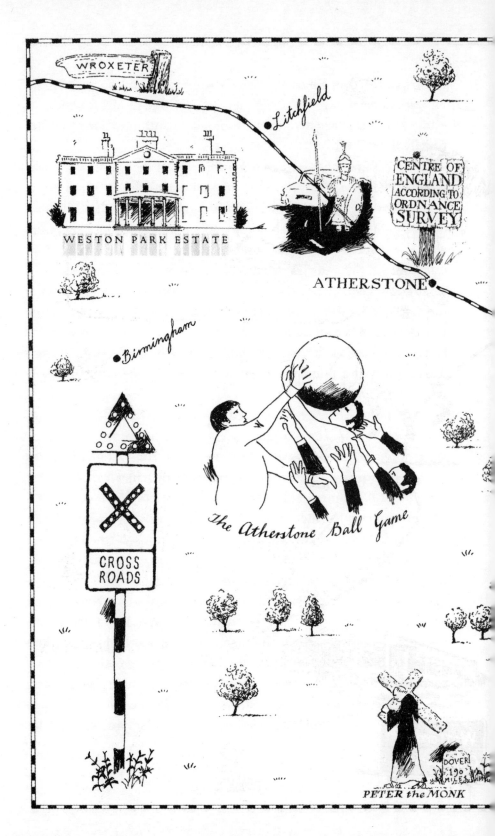

WROXETER

Litchfield

WESTON PARK ESTATE

CENTRE OF ENGLAND ACCORDING TO ORDNANCE SURVEY

ATHERSTONE

Birmingham

The Atherstone Ball Game

CROSS ROADS

DOVER 190 MILES

PETER the MONK

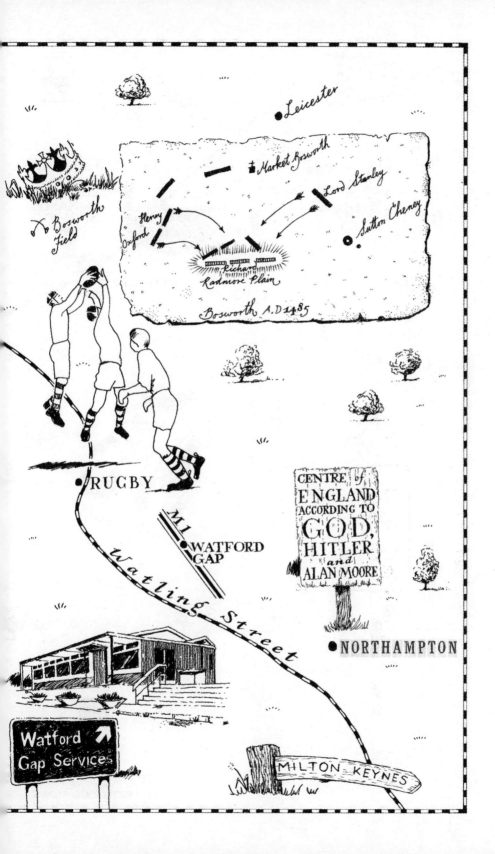

Leicester

Market Bosworth

Lord Stanley

Sutton Cheney

Henry
Oxford

Richard
Radmore Plain

Bosworth A.D 1485

To Bosworth
Field

RUGBY

M1

WATFORD
GAP

Watling Street

CENTRE of
ENGLAND
ACCORDING TO
GOD,
HITLER
and
ALAN MOORE

NORTHAMPTON

Watford
Gap Services

MILTON KEYNES

10.

NORTHAMPTON

In the centre of it all

I'm a little early for my rendezvous, so I pull off the M6 into Watford Gap Services to grab a coffee and kill some time. Watford Gap appears, at first glance, to be no different to all the other brand-filled motorway service stations up and down the country. It contains a Costa, a McDonald's, a WH Smith, some toilets, a cash machine which charges you to take out money and a booth selling all manner of covers for your telephone. But, to motorway aficionados, this is ground zero. Watford Gap dates back to 1959 and is the very first motorway service station in the UK.

It was known then as the Blue Boar, and it had a special place in the burgeoning British music scene. Artists such as The Rolling Stones, Pink Floyd, The Beatles and many other bands crossed paths here late at night, after gigs up and down the country. Pink Floyd's drummer, Nick Mason, recalled that at 2 a.m. on a Sunday morning the Blue Boar looked like a Ford Transit van rally, and that 'crushed velvet trousers outnumbered truckers' overalls'. Jimi Hendrix heard the name 'Blue Boar' mentioned so often that he assumed it was a hip nightclub.

The name 'Watford Gap' refers to the narrowest point of a ridge of limestone that runs across the country, just a little to the north of the services. Watling Street ran through this gap but the Victorian road that became the A5 was diverted away, for fear of quicksand. By the mid twentieth century construction techniques could compensate for the soft ground, so Watford Gap became the point where the M1 briefly swaps with the A5 to follow the old route of Watling Street.

Watford Gap also symbolises the dividing line between the north and the south. We speak about the country 'north of the Watford Gap' or about heading 'south of the Watford Gap'. Those with a shaky grasp on British geography can sometimes confuse Watford in Hertfordshire with Watford Gap in Northamptonshire, but this is the place that is the middle. This is highly apt; the reason we are going to Northampton is to visit the centre of the country. In all likelihood, we will also discover far more, because we are about to meet a most extraordinary guide. Like Watford Gap Services, he is an original, he is steeped in the 1960s counterculture and he is definitely at the centre of something. I grab a coffee, return to the car and drive into Northampton to meet Alan Moore.

In 1977 the twenty-three-year-old gas-board contractor Alan Moore quit his job. He was suffering from the youthful romantic notion that spending his allotted years doing a job he hated was a poor life choice. What he liked was writing, drawing and reading comics, and he dreamed of making his living in this uncertain way.

This was not one of those pie-in-the-sky dreams where someone turns their nose up at good honest work because they think they deserve to be a famous footballer, rock musician or film star. It was much worse than that. There was no money or fame in comics in the 1970s. There was no job security, and there certainly wasn't any social kudos. His was a dream that made sense to him alone. But he liked what he liked, and he was the one who had to live his life, so Alan went into the office and handed in his notice. He then went home, and his wife told him that she was pregnant.

His work colleagues were understanding. The resignation could be forgotten, they told him, and the job remained his if he wanted it. All rational analysis favoured this option. He would soon have a family to support, and the alternative was selfish and foolhardy. His potential futures hung suspended above his young head, staring down, curious as to which he would choose.

Alan Moore knew that if he did not quit his job at that point, he never would. Once the baby was in his arms, looking up at him with beautiful, helpless eyes, he would not be strong enough to make his fool's leap. If it was to be done, it had to be done then. This is always the way with fool's leaps. He jumped.

Back in the 1970s there was still a social safety net. He was able to resign from paid work and claim £42.50 a week from the state. It did not take long before he was drawing weekly comic strips for *Sounds* and the *Northants Post* and was able to sign off the dole and support his family with his comics work. His older friend Steve Moore, up on Shooter's Hill, taught him how to write scripts. He began to specialise as a writer, rather than an artist.

The comics industry was then, as it is now, dominated by two big companies: Marvel and DC. Alan found work for Marvel, writing short comic strips for *Doctor Who Weekly*. Steve Moore was also writing for this comic, but he quit following a disagreement about their plans for a character he had created. In a display of solidarity with his friend, all the more remarkable given the fledgling nature of his career, Alan quit too. With a couple of minor exceptions, he has not worked for Marvel ever since. This was the beginning of a pattern that would repeat itself throughout his life. Financial and career considerations would remain stubbornly secondary to questions of integrity. He was not a man who would bend or compromise for expediency's sake. He had the mind of a true artist and a terrible politician.

In the 1980s he wrote for DC comics, and the work he did for them casts a long shadow. A Batman story he wrote in 1988, for example, was still DC's bestselling graphic novel in 2015, twenty-eight years after it was first released. But it was the quality of the work, rather than its commercial success, that the comics industry is still trying to come to terms with. Before the 1980s, comics were a medium considered only really suitable for telling children's stories. Alan Moore was the most significant of a new wave of artists and writers who knew that the medium was capable of far more. His *Watchmen* (1986-7, art by Dave Gibbons) was included on *Time* magazine's 2005 list of the 100 best novels published since 1923, the only graphic novel to be included.

But DC's actions caused upset. They had been selling *Watchmen* badges, which they classified as promotional items, rather than merchandise, which meant they could avoid paying him royalties. The money involved was only a few thousand dollars but, as ever with Alan, it wasn't about the money. In a similar way to how he stopped working for Marvel, he now refused to do any more work for DC. He was like a top international footballer refusing to play in either the Premier League or the Championship, but opting to ply his trade in the smaller leagues on a point of principle.

In time Hollywood decided to adapt a number of his books, including *Watchmen* and *V for Vendetta*, which were legally owned by DC. Unable to prevent these adaptations, he took his name off the films and refused his share of the fees, which went to the books' artists. If Alan Moore had played the game, he could have become a millionaire many times over. But he was that rarest and most dangerous of beasts, a man without a price. He made enough money to keep writing, there were no compromises in his past that he was ashamed of and he had a clean conscience that allowed him to sleep at night. Wasn't that the ultimate goal of any artist? Wouldn't it be lunacy to want anything different?

In the years that followed, and as the extent to which his DC work had transformed the industry became apparent, Moore continued to embark on projects with zero regard for what his audience expected. He doggedly pursued his own muse wherever it took him, and he always spoke his mind when others held their tongues. To give one example, he speaks publicly about his disappointment over the stranglehold superhero films currently have over Hollywood. The most successful cultural products of the early twenty-first century are retellings of stories from the 1960s aimed at eight-year-old boys, and he had personally hoped for something more. Is it so unthinkable that such a creative industry could produce original and imaginative new stories? This is a point not usually expressed by a writer whose audience consists largely of comic-book fans.

It almost began to look like every project Alan undertook after splitting with DC, and every statement he made, was an attempt to sabotage his own following and credibility. He produced an elaborate, literate work of pornography, *Lost Girls*, with the American underground artist Melinda Gebbie. This took sixteen years to complete and led to the pair getting married. At his fortieth-birthday party in 1994 he announced that he intended to become a practising magician. He revealed he was a worshipper of Glycon, a second-century Greek snake god, which the satirist Lucian described as a hand puppet operated by a man called Alexander the False Prophet. With his long beard, his cane carved into a snake and the exotic collection of silver rings across his knuckles, he embodies the visual archetype of a powerful wizard every bit as much as Merlin or Gandalf. All of this could have been reason to dismiss Moore as little more than a curiosity or an eccentric, had it not been for the work he was producing.

From spoken-word performances such as *The Birth Caul* or the Steve Moore-focused *Unearthing* to *Promethea*, his kabbalah-based map of imagination, or *From Hell*, his psychogeographic exploration of Victorian London, Moore was always trying something new, always extending his ambition and always displaying intelligence, compassion and originality. Looking at his body of work, it is true to say that he had a commercial peak in the 1980s, but it cannot be said that he ever had an artistic one. His major achievements are just as likely to be found in his later work as they are in his early or middle period.

A book called *The Black Dossier* is a good example. This was a collection of background material for *The League of Extraordinary Gentlemen* comic series, which is an ambitious if borderline insane attempt to stitch together the entire history of fiction into one narrative. *The Black Dossier* should have been a throwaway offering, the equivalent of DVD extras of interest to diehard fans only. Yet Alan turned out an astonishingly dense work in which he wrote a 'lost' Shakespeare play, a Jack Kerouac homage, a spoof P. G. Wodehouse short story and many other wonders. Given the distinctiveness of Moore's own prose, his casual ability to disappear into the minds and voices of such different and distinct writers is extraordinary. There are writers with original voices and writers who can imitate, but few writers who can imitate in order to support their original voice. *The Black Dossier* reads like the work of a writer without peers looking to see if he can find his limits and discovering that he has none. And that was his approach to background material.

His ability to use different styles of writing as tools, utilised only at specific places for specific purposes, is perhaps most evident in his novel *Jerusalem*. *Jerusalem* is, in the words of Melinda Gebbie, a work of working-class genetic mythology. It is 615,000 words long, took ten years to write, and is probably the last thing his audience of superhero-loving comic-book fans wanted from him. It tells the story of his family going back generations, and of the Boroughs, the area of Northampton where he was born. The Boroughs have all but disappeared now, wiped off the map by post-war town planning. In *Jerusalem*, Moore uses the memory of this unloved, discarded and dirt-poor neighbourhood to invoke William Blake's eternal city. His intention, as he once put it, was to 'prove to the satisfaction of every reader the non-existence of death'. *Jerusalem* is a book that should trigger long dark nights of the soul for many novelists. Reading it is to be confronted by their own lack of ambition.

There has been a spring in Alan's step since he finished the book, as if a weight has gone from his shoulders. *Jerusalem* was the major work that all his previous projects had been leading up to. It achieves what he set out to do. He has lived up to his potential and he has honoured his talent; he knows this in his bones. External confirmation is irrelevant.

For my money, Alan Moore is England's greatest living writer. I base this not on awards or literary credibility, but on the scale, originality, daring, technical brilliance, humour and compassion of his body of work. I would love to be wrong about this, because it would mean discovering someone else with a back catalogue greater than his. That would be a joy indeed.

There are people who are frightened of Alan Moore. He is the Grudgekeeper General, a stubborn man with an intimidating mind and an understanding of the world far deeper and more occult than most. This is a man who beat the physicist Professor Brian Cox in an argument about physics on BBC Radio 4's *The Infinite Monkey Cage*, and, as the programme's co-host, Robin Ince, pointed out, there aren't many self-described wizards who can claim that.

Strange things happen around Alan Moore. For example, I had a box of hardback copies of my last book and gave one to him. I later found that one book in the box had become water-damaged, and I couldn't work out why. How could only one copy have got wet, I puzzled, while all the others stored in the same box were pristine? I then dreamt that water was coming in from the roof and running down my wall. Visiting Alan and Melinda a few days later, I discovered that water had come in through Alan's roof, run down a wall, and soaked the copy of my book that I had given him.

Alan's son-in-law, the Liverpool writer John Reppion, once told me how he had been walking up the stairs in Alan's house and, out of the corner of his eye, saw what looked like a cat crossing the upstairs landing and disappearing through a door. The door, however, was closed. He went downstairs and told Alan that he'd just seen something strange. 'Did it look like a cat?' Alan asked. John nodded. 'It wasn't a cat,' Alan said. The subject was dropped.

Or to give another example, our mutual friend Alistair Fruish met a new neighbour and learned he worked in a nuclear-power station.

Meeting Alan in the park later he said, 'You'll never guess what my neighbour does.' Alan shrugged, not knowing the neighbour, and said, 'I don't know, do they work in a nuclear-power station or something?' All of these stories can be explained away as coincidence, of course, but they are examples of the odd things that tend to happen in his orbit.

Alistair Fruish is a writer-in-residence who works in prisons. He runs a prison Shakespeare project, in which prisoners are encouraged to read and perform Shakespeare's works, and he has a strong dislike of conspiracy theories regarding the authorship of Shakespeare's plays. There are many of these, but in their most common form they boil down to a disbelief that one relatively uneducated merchant's son could produce a body of work whose brilliance eclipses the work of the country's best-educated writers. The real author of these plays, under this logic, must have been an aristocrat or, failing that, a team of aristocrats. To those who cannot accept that one working-class man was able to produce such a body of work, allowing for the normal level of collaboration you would expect from Tudor theatre, Alistair counters: go to Northampton, spend an afternoon with Alan Moore and see if that changes your mind.

This is exactly what we'll do now.

'John! Come on in, mate. That was good timing. I've just got the kettle on. Milk, no sugars, isn't it? Make yourself comfortable, I'll sort out the tea.'

Alan Moore's reputation is a bit like a hurricane: awe-inspiring from a distance, terrifying for those who get too close but entirely calm at the centre. In the eye of that hurricane Alan is revealed to be a welcoming, very funny man who's interested in how your kids are getting on and whose face lights up whenever his wife walks into the room. He is tall but not threatening, with long hair tied back and his beard grey, and his most striking features are his eyes. They call to mind the cartoon dog Droopy, had Droopy ever stared too long into the abyss Nietzsche warned us about.

Mugs of tea distributed, he settles into his regular armchair in the front room of his terraced house, surrounded by piles of books, papers and overflowing ashtrays. Behind him is an arched stained-glass window of the deepest blue, with orange stars arranged in the shape of the Kabbalah's Tree of Life. It is simultaneously a map of the soul and a map of the entire universe, and it hangs over his head as he talks. The walls of his front room are smoke-stained and wood-panelled, hung with relics from early-twentieth-century magical orders, and his ceiling is white with gold stars painted across it.

Alan Moore

We plan to take a walk with Alistair Fruish around what used to be the Boroughs, the territory explored, and to some extent now defined, by *Jerusalem*. But first he sits back, wreathed in ideas and smoke, his voice as slow and deep as history, and he tells me about Northampton.

'I have described Northampton in the past, perhaps unfairly, as an industrial running sore halfway between London and Birmingham,' he says. 'I've called it a black hole for similar reasons, but it's also like a black hole because there's a lot of people in Northampton who came here for a weekend and they're still wandering around, not entirely sure how they ended up here. They can never get out. You can't get up the escape velocity to get out beyond Northampton and if you try, inevitably you'll be sucked back in. It's a place where people end up, rather than where people go to. It's invisible to the light of the media. You can only really tell it's here by the devastation at its perimeter.

'It has that gravity and mass that I think you need at the centre of a country. It's a heavy place. Sometimes it could be seen as a miserable place. I don't think that's true, but I think that the people here probably will not make friends with you quickly. Jeremy Seabrook, who wrote the first important book on post-war English poverty, *The Unprivileged*, came from a Boroughs family. He was also my French teacher when I was eleven. He was asked what people in the Boroughs were generally like and he said, well, they were narrow, mean, as good as their word, bloody-minded, grudge-bearing and a lot of other things which, other than narrow and mean, do sound a lot like me. I get the sense with Northampton that there is a bottom line about its psychology. You can generally rely on people to be what they seem. That's not to say that they'll be good people, but they will be obviously what they are. I can handle that. I thought it important to write about these people because no one else seemed to want to. When most novelists write about the working class, they write them as either victims or scum, and nobody thinks of themselves as victims or scum. I'm thinking of books like Martin Amis's *Lionel Asbo*. No one deserves that.

'I think one of the things that caused me and Steve Moore to bond was that we felt very comfortable in the landscape that we were born into. As we often remarked, we were nothing like each other. We were completely different in temperament. He was introverted. I'm fairly extroverted. He was retiring middle class. I am loud working class. But we got on great, probably because we were complementary. We both saw ourselves as fixed points, I think. Steve more than me, because he stayed in the same house all his life. I have at least moved house a bit.

Although we did use to say, if people asked, that we lived just down the road from each other. Just because he was at one end of Watling Street, and I was pretty much on the way to the other.

'You know how your grandmother told you that if you got stung by stinging nettles, always look around because there would be dock leaves, somewhere, growing nearby? It's one of those marvellous things that nature does. Actually dock leaves don't really work, but it's a comforting idea. I think that me and Steve both had a sense that probably everything we needed, all the elements that you'd need for your life, are probably at hand. That if you understand your area deeply enough, then a deep understanding of a single place is probably more useful than a broad understanding of the world. It's good to have a broad understanding of the world as well, but you don't have to. It's probably all there in the microcosm, in the synecdoche. Self-similarity at different scales.'

I ask Alan why Northampton figures so heavily in his recent work, and he nods slowly as if to say, 'That's a big question, how long have you got?'

'There's a lot of history here,' he begins. 'We have Neolithic settlements, we have mammoth hunters, we have the remains of Bronze Age and Iron Age settlements, we have remnants of the Roman occupation. The Romans probably had a river fort down by the Nene. It was during the Roman occupation that we formed our unusual relationship with money. We were forging Roman coins, out at Duston, which was a crucifying offence back then. And immediately after the Romans pulled out, we started minting the first actual English coins, the first English gold coins. We were one of three or four mints around the country.

'Northampton is a place where you can look back at the Dark Ages and say, "Ah, those were the good old days!" Alfred the Great, who wasn't called "the Great" for nothing, said that Northamptonshire was "foremost amongst the shires", or, in effect, the capital. We were in the centre of Mercia, and Mercia was the most important of the English kingdoms at that time.

'When the lights went on after the Dark Ages, Northampton was revealed as a fully formed, very nice, functioning market town. This was largely because of King Offa, the man who had attempted to saw off Wales. He had his thorpe, a country retreat, at Kingsthorpe in Northampton. He needed a market town nearby to supply it, so we were providing everything. He established his sons at his palace in Marefair [in the Boroughs]. This would have been the equivalent of Clarence House, something like that. He had a chapel built across the road for them – this was St Peter's Church. So, it was going pretty well for Northampton during that period. It was a pretty little market town. It's all been downhill since.

'We are spoiled for choice in Northampton, if you want reasons for us being on the country's shitlist. We have got so many people who have offended the reigning authorities, it could have been the fault of any of them. You have to look back to the first one. So it wasn't just Diana Spencer. It wasn't just Charles Bradlaugh. He was the Victorian MP who refused to swear the parliamentary Oath of Allegiance that assumed all MPs were Christian, when he was an atheist, so they locked him in the Big Ben tower. It wasn't just the Civil War and Cromwell, although that can't have helped. It wasn't just the gunpowder plotters about fifty years before. It wasn't just the revolt of the rebel barons in the 1260s that got the town sacked and more or less burnt to the ground by Henry III. No, I think you have to go back to the eleventh century and Hereward the Wake. He's the man. He's the man who first marked Northampton out as trouble.'

'Look along the bank, see how straight it is?' says Alistair Fruish, pointing along a stretch of the River Nene. 'That's been artificially straightened.' Alistair, Alan and I are on a narrow stretch of path underneath a bridge, and the Towcester Road traffic rumbles over our heads. We have left Alan's home and gone on a walking tour of the locations in *Jerusalem*, and I have asked Alan to show me what he claims is the centre of England. But before we get there, Alistair has another location to show me.

'This is called a mill race. It's where they straightened the river to speed up the water flow, to give more power to a water wheel. So that means that pretty much right here, under this bridge – this is where Marvel's Mill would have stood.'

Alistair is dyslexic, a condition diagnosed only at the very end of his school career. As a boy in the 1970s he loved the TV programme *Doctor Who* and desperately wanted to know what was happening in the comic strips inside the pages of *Doctor Who Weekly*. The pictures looked thrilling, but to understand what was going on he had to decipher the dancing squiggles in the speech bubbles. Those words, in a neat coincidence, had been written by Steve Moore. It was Alistair's determined efforts to understand Doctor Who comics at that young age that forced him to read. Writing is still difficult for him, but he can do it with effort, and he has now written two novels, *Kiss My ASBO* and *The Sentence*. For that he credits the deceptively modest cultural footprint of Steve Moore.

'Marvel's Mill,' Alistair continues, 'was the first powered cotton mill in the world. The men behind it had built one powered by donkeys the year before, in 1741, but this was powered by water and so the first powered mill as we think of them now. So this was where it all started. "Jerusalem"'s dark, satanic mills. The Industrial Revolution. The modern world.'

'Adam Smith either came here to see it, or he heard about it. We haven't found out which,' says Alan, speaking about the Scottish economist. 'But he was hugely excited by it. He said it was marvellous, how the cotton mill was working all by itself like that. He said that it was as if it was being operated by some kind of "invisible hand". And a voice in the back of his head must have thought, Hey, that's a good metaphor, and filed it away so he could use it again someday. If that was the case, then you don't just get the industrial age being born on this spot, but the whole tottering edifice of neoliberal economics.'

'And you get climate change,' adds Alistair. 'The start of the Industrial Revolution was the start of man-made climate change. Regardless of what we do from now on in, what we've done to the climate since the Industrial Revolution will affect the planet's climate for at least 10,000 years. It has postponed the next ice age. You have a whole new geological era, the Anthropocene, which is an ecosystem change on a global scale, all starting here, at this exact point.'

I look around at this auspicious location. We're on a narrow muddy path, about five feet across, separated from the river by a low brick and concrete wall which someone has left a can of energy drink on. The roof of the bridge is a flat slab of dark concrete, scrawled with graffiti, only a few inches above our heads. The side wall is old, brick and damp, on which the letters SFK have been sprayed in a large blocky font. A single duvet patterned with a vivid 1980s abstract of cyan and purple is dumped on the ground, next to a single child's black school shoe. Reeds emerge from the shallow river alongside a large traffic cone, the mandatory shopping trolley and a wheelie bin with the number '34' painted on the side in large white figures.

Empty cans and drink bottles litter the dirt floor. I bend down to pick up the green plastic bottle closest to me. It is a flattened three-litre bottle of 3 Hammers cider, with an alcohol content of 7.5 per cent and a retail price of around £3.50. For that you get 22 units of alcohol, more than a man's weekly recommended limit. It is the name that strikes me – 3 Hammers, a name more brutally honest than perhaps any other brand of alcohol.

Here, then, is the birthplace of the modern industrial world, a location simultaneously horribly wrong and almost too perfect. Criticise the modern world all you want, but at least it offers you the comfort of staying dry while you blot it out.

I'm far from the first to remark that the membrane between Alan's fiction and reality seems worryingly porous. This is demonstrated most famously in the *V for Vendetta* Guy Fawkes mask, which made the jump from the book he wrote with David Lloyd to the frontlines of global political protest. His upcoming film *The Show* experiments with this idea as a form of reverse product placement; products in the fictional world such as Fuel Rods energy drink, the Electricomics digital comic platform and Tunguska Russian Vodka ('It'll flatten you') are potentially going to exist in the real world. The idea is not really to sell energy drinks, but to set a precedent. If products can be birthed from fiction, then perhaps so can social institutions and political ideas.

Standing here, under this bridge, I have a momentary suspicion that we've fallen through in the opposite direction and slipped out of reality into Alan's fiction. This setting seems too bleakly perfect to be the birthplace of the modern world. A name like 'Hammers' is exactly what he would invent for a brand of street cider. That this is just a short walk from Alan's house seems a little too convenient. Given his history with the comic industry, it's hard to discover that the original dark satanic mill was called Marvel's Mill and not see his fingerprints all over it.

But it is history, and not fiction, that is the troll under this bridge. This particular history troll is simultaneously terrifying and awe-inspiring and, like any good troll, it will extract its price or eat us up. I wonder how visible that troll would be, during a long evening under that bridge, huddled in that garish duvet for warmth, halfway through a bottle of 3 Hammers.

'Come on,' says Alan. 'Let's go to the centre of England. It isn't far.'

The idea that a point in Northampton is the centre of England explains the name sign on the front of Alan's terraced house. It reads 'Seaview'.

The name is a joke, of course. The sign was a present from Alistair. I noticed it earlier, when we left Alan's house, and it reminded me of a map I saw on Facebook a few days earlier. The map was titled The British Isles: July 2100. Wales, Cumbria, the north-east and much of Scotland looked more or less familiar, but rising sea level had reduced the Midlands and the south of England to little more than archipelagos of small islands. These are currently our most heavily populated areas, because they were the low-lying fertile farmland areas that so attracted the Saxons and Normans. On this map Northampton is on the new east coast, because most of the lower fenland to its east has been submerged.

The map didn't contain any information about the data the map-maker based his new sea level on. After a few back-of-the-envelope calculations, I realise this is a map of how our coastlines will look when all the polar ice is gone, and this assumes a much faster rate of glacier melt than that estimated by the Intergovernmental Panel on Climate Change. Based on this, I'd say that the map was just another piece of false information for the internet to spread, and that Northampton is unlikely to be a coastal town in 2100. But, if the house stands for long enough, the events that Marvel's Mill set in motion mean that it could have a sea view one day.

After we met Alistair and set out from Alan's house, on the way to this bridge, we took a walk around key locations in *Jerusalem*. The area which the Boroughs covered proved to be far smaller than I had realised from reading the book. Recent buildings that his novel had soaked with meaning and significance looked compressed and apologetic, as if they never wanted the attention. The old neighbourhood which these new buildings replaced, where generations of families huddled in rows of tiny houses living lives both beautiful and tragic, has been almost entirely wiped away. They would all be for ever invisible, had Alan Moore not trapped them in language and nailed them to the ground for all to see. Still, the occasional trace remains, as if to prove they can never really be entirely forgotten. After kicking around in a grass verge between Spring Lane and Scarletwell Street, we found a row of bricks that were part of the back wall of Alan's childhood house.

We pass a rail bridge over the River Nene, which Alan points out. 'I must show you this. It was the best hiding place when I played hide and seek as a lad. There's a gap that if you wedged yourself in, no one would ever find you. Oh, they've blocked it off.'

A fan-shaped row of grey railings now covers the gap where the brick wall meets the steel girders supporting the roof of the rail bridge. But behind it you can see a narrow ledge between the wall and the underside of the tracks rumbling above. It would be just about large enough for a child to hide in, although it would take an extraordinarily determined child to put themselves in that damp, black, claustrophobic and terrifying crack.

Where the Anthropocene began

Alan chuckles to himself at the memory. 'It was the best hiding place,' he remembers fondly.

'It makes sense that Northampton gave the world the Gothic tradition, given this sense of weight and gloom that we have,' he says. 'The Gothic tradition, if you trace it back, comes from James Hervey, the vicar of Weston Favell and Collingtree. He was the most beautiful writer in John Wesley's Holy Club, which was a formative group of Wesley's fellow Methodists. He wrote these brilliant pieces that were mainly about death. They were beautiful invocations about how you can't enter a town without passing a funeral procession, with the cerements blowing in the breeze and things like that. It's beautiful language, but it's all saying, "Flesh dies, people die, flesh is transient, and only god is eternal." That was the original message of James Hervey.

'The Graveyard Poets who came after him thought, Yeah, if you tidied this up and made it rhyme a bit it would be a great form of poetry. They were originally talking about gravestones and skulls and things like that, but they're saying that this was just evidence that flesh is transient, and god is eternal. Then you get the later Graveyard Poets who think, Yeah, this stuff with the owls and the skulls – that's brilliant. I'm not so bothered about all this God stuff.

'After that you get Horace Walpole, who thought, you could do this as a kind of novel, couldn't you? So he wrote *The Castle of Otranto* in 1764, the first Gothic novel, and, from that, the Gothic tradition followed. In fact, I think it's true to say that all genre fiction comes from there, if you trace science fiction back to *Frankenstein* and crime fiction back to *Murders in the Rue Morgue,* and so on. You get every horror writer, crime writer, bodice-ripper writer and science-fiction writer cascading from that point of origin.

'I once asked David J of the band Bauhaus if he was influenced by Walpole or Gothic literature. Bauhaus are from Northampton and they pretty much started goth music in 1979 with *Bela Lugosi's Dead.* And he said, no, they didn't know anything about all that, they just went with the skulls and stuff because they liked them. So, from this, I think you can truthfully say that the Gothic tradition emerged not once but twice from Northampton, and that goth is therefore an emergent property of this place. It's a vertical weight of the past upon a fairly small area in the present.

'This all ties into *Jerusalem* because James Hervey was a big influence on William Blake. He talks about Hervey in his writing and he did that wonderful painting, *Epitome of James Hervey's 'Meditations among the Tombs'* (1820–25). It was a big, black, kind of psychedelic picture of all these figures in alcoves. So Blake, you could say, was a kind of proto-goth. He was taking from the same source as people like

Walpole, so he was as much of a goth as they were. But he was close enough to the origin to know that it was less about death than it was about eternal life.'

We return to Towcester Road, somehow cross a busy roundabout, and walk a short distance up Horse Market. Before we get to the junction with Mare Fair and Gold Street, Alan stops us. We are standing outside an MOT garage called Superior Cars. 'This is it,' says Alan. 'This is the centre of the country.'

Alistair Fruish and Alan Moore at the exact centre of England

A number of places claim to be the exact centre of England. The Ordnance Survey has erected a plaque at its preferred candidate, Lindley Hall Farm, which is further up Watling Street and close to Atherstone. But an 'official' centre is problematic because there are so many different methodologies for working out the centre of this strange-shaped land. You can choose the mid-point from the extremes, the point furthest away from the sea, or the centroid, which is the point underneath which the land would balance on a pin. Given the fractal nature of the coastline, this point would vary depending on the scale of measurement used. Then there are questions about measuring at high tide or low, whether or not to include islands, whether curvature of the earth is included, and which two-dimensional mapping projection to use if not. The centre depends on how you define it, in other words, which means that, in practice, the credibility of each candidate location is defined by the credibility of its supporters. This puts a trusted mapping organisation such as the Ordnance Survey in a strong position. Alan, however, is having none of it.

'An old story tells of a medieval British monk who I've called Peter in *Jerusalem*,' he begins, talking about the monk whose journey we first crossed back at the White Cliffs of Dover. 'Peter was out in the Holy Land digging around Golgotha, which is the hill near the gates of Jerusalem where Jesus was crucified. And he uncovered this stone cross. At that point an angel appeared and told him to take the stone cross to the centre of his own land. Now, that's quite an ask, what with stone crosses being as heavy as they are and with journeys then being undertaken on foot. But it was an angel, so what are you going to do? The monk picks up the cross, lugs it all the way across Europe, gets a boat over to Dover and begins trudging up Watling Street towards the centre of his England, all the while carrying this heavy stone cross.

'Back then, there was a church underneath where that garage is now, called St Gregory's. The monk gets here and another angel appears. This one says, "That's great, you've reached the centre of your land, so good job." Now, I suppose it's also possible that he'd just had enough by that point, that he got as far as here and something about the Northampton atmosphere made him give up. I'm not saying that's impossible, but let's give him the benefit of the doubt. Let's say the angel confirmed that he was definitely, definitely in the centre of England. So he knocks on the church doors and tells them his story, and they put the cross up in an alcove in the church.

'Hitler was another one who thought that Northampton was the centre of England. His invasion plan Operation Sealion came up from the south and ended here, because he reckoned that once he held the heart of England then the rest of the island would surrender. So, yes, if you want to argue that somewhere else is the centre then good luck to you. But be aware that me, God and Hitler all say it is here, and that's basically the dream team.'

The stone cross has long since been lost, but it was very famous in the medieval world. It was known as the Rood in the Wall. 'Rood' was an Old English word for cross or crucifix and was derived from the same root as 'rod'. The word is used in *The Dream of the Rood*, a vision poem that dates back to the eighth century or earlier. Its author is unknown but is possibly Cædmon, the first known poet to work in the English language. He was a lay monk and shepherd who gained the gift of verse, it is said, in a vision of God that came to him while sleeping outside with his animals.

The Dream of the Rood is, as the name suggests, an account of the poet's dream about the crucifix, and the middle section of the poem is told from the perspective of the cross itself. The rood explained how it was indivisible from Jesus. It was once a mighty tree, but it was cut down by the folly of men, mocked and had nails hammered into it. It died and was resurrected as a symbol, re-created throughout the Christian world in gold or silver. The cross and Jesus can no longer be separated, because they are meaningless without each other. The rood and Jesus, ultimately, are the same.

This idea gives us new insight into Blake's 'Jerusalem'. We may be confident that the answer to the question, 'Did those feet in ancient time walk upon England's mountains green?' is 'No'. But if Jesus and the rood are one and the same thing, then the cross coming to this country is to all intents and purposes the same as Jesus arriving. Perhaps that is why the angels tasked the medieval monk with carrying the stone cross to St Gregory's? When the Rood arrived, perhaps the eternal city was indeed built on England's green and pleasant land?

This is the case in Alan Moore's *Jerusalem* as well as William Blake's, although Alan's interpretation of the cross is not Christian in any traditional sense. For him, the cross is a stubby solid plus sign which acts as the centre point of an immense pair of arches that hold up the roof of the British imagination. The cross is the keystone, supported by the arches and in turn supporting them. You can imagine these arches spanning the four corners of the country, with one running from the south-west to the north-east, and the other from the north-west to the south-east. We are underneath the point at which they cross and where the keystone should be, high above the dark heart of the country. These arches aren't physical. They are the product of the history, myths and stories that make up immaterial Britain. From this perspective, the purpose of this lost cross was to support the noosphere.

I ask Alan how his interest in Blake came about.

'My connection with Blake was forged despite the British education system,' he says. 'They managed to put me off of nearly everybody else that I was forced to read for O Level, but not William Blake. And not Shakespeare either, but they really put a crippling dent in my ability to appreciate most of the others. That was when my fascination with Blake began, but it increased as I found out more about him as a person, and discovered the occultist, anarchist and political dimensions of the man. Yeah, morally – I don't think that human beings come a lot better than William Blake.

'I'm a patron of the William Blake society along with Neil Gaiman, and the President is Philip Pullman, which is interesting because I think it was Peter Ackroyd in his biography of Blake who said that today's heirs to Blake were graphic novelists. It was very nice of him to say that, but I think he was probably being a bit over-generous. I don't think that today's graphic novelists are heirs to Blake. They are just both using an integration of imagery and words, but they are using it in very different ways. William Blake didn't do comic strips. But, that said, I would say that in many ways someone like Jack Kirby would have some claim to being a twentieth-century pop-culture American Blake.'

Jack Kirby was a New York-born artist who, while working with the writer and editor Stan Lee at Marvel in the 1960s, co-created characters like the X-Men, the Hulk, the Fantastic Four, Thor, Iron Man and Black Panther. He was particularly known for drawing wild, magical landscapes and cosmic vistas. Whatever superhero character is currently appearing at your local cinema, there's a good chance Jack Kirby had a hand in designing them.

Alan continues: 'Blake and Kirby, they were both surrounded by slums, which Blake was by choice. Blake was born into a well-off family on Golden Square, and was quite a demanding and stubborn little boy. He seemed to gravitate towards living in Lambeth, in poorer areas. Like Blake, Jack Kirby dreamed up all of these god figures with slightly clumsy names, these hosts of eternal archetypal figures. Even in their anatomy, there is something of the statuary-influenced style of William Blake. They have an exaggerated dynamic anatomy. So there are grounds for a couple of comics people who could make that connection with Blake, but only those that see the eternal in the gutter.'

'Is the "eternal in the gutter" what you were aiming to reveal in *Jerusalem*?' I ask.

'It is,' he says, 'although in that book my understanding of eternity rests as much on Einstein as it does on Blake. Einstein was saying that this is a universe of at least four dimensions. Those are physical dimensions, because that's what dimension means. It's not like the Fifth Dimension that Mr Mxyzptlk comes from in Superman comics. It means length, and breadth, and depth; those are dimensions. Einstein said that this universe, this space–time continuum, had four dimensions and it's often said that the fourth dimension is time. That's not strictly accurate. Time is not the fourth dimension, but our perception of time is almost like the shadow of the fourth dimension. The fourth dimension is a physical dimension like all the others, it's just that we perceive it as the passage of time. This would suggest that the entirety of space–time, from beginning to end, is a massive solid. It's got height, it's got depth, it's got breadth. And it's got longevity. Our human consciousness is embedded, fixed, within this massive solid, although it appears to us that it is moving down the time axis until it reaches the end of our allotted span.

'Since that solid we were talking about is fixed and unchanging then, as far as I can see, everything that makes up that solid is eternal and unchanging. This includes our physical existence. This includes our consciousness. Wittgenstein, I think it was, said that a thought was an event in space and time. Which is a bold and anti-scientific statement, but I think he is absolutely right. There is nowhere for the past to go. In Einstein's hypothesis, it is part of this solid. It is coterminous with everything else in this giant hyper-moment that is existence, where every moment is all happening at once – the big bang, the big crunch and everything in between.

'In that construction time does not exist, but the past does. Time, perceived in the normal sense, is this annihilating wave that erases everything, and I'm not sure how that works physically. I'm not sure how you can get rid of all the energy in the universe and re-create it again every split second. Do we only exist in this thin, unbelievably thin sheet of paper that is the now, where there is nothing in the future, there is nothing in the past? That is a bit frightening and precarious. The idea that there is just this single moment and beyond that, absolute nothingness, yeah, I suppose that could be what it is, but it doesn't feel like that is what it is. Whereas I think the idea of a solid space–time continuum, with only our consciousness moving, is very satisfying. It means that every moment exists always.

'There's a Zen kōan that Steve Moore introduced me to, about these two monks in a garden at a monastery. Being monks they haven't got much to do, so they fall into arguing. They are arguing about a flag. One of them says, "The flag is moving." The other one says, "No, it's not. It's the wind that's moving". So they're having this row, when one of their masters walks into the courtyard. They say, "Can you sort this out for us? We're having a bit of a disagreement. I say the flag's moving. He says it's the wind that's moving. Which is it?" And the master says,

"It is neither flag nor wind, but mind that moves." Which is very close to the hypothesis that I've read into Einstein's theory.

'There's a quote from Einstein himself, shortly before his death, when he was consoling the widow of a fellow physicist, that describes this brilliantly. Actually, I found the real quote and it's not as good as the commonly repeated one, so I'll tell you the invented one. Einstein said, for physicists such as ourselves, death isn't really a major issue because we understand "the persistent illusion of transience". That is probably the single phrase that a lot of *Jerusalem* rests upon: the persistent illusion of transience. The buildings that we love have been pulled down, the people that we loved have gone, you don't get anything decent on a Saturday night on the telly any more, they don't make Spangles... all of this roster of loss that is our lives, it doesn't matter. It's all fine. It's all back down the road. You'll probably be experiencing it again, and again, because there's nowhere else for your consciousness to go.

'This means that you should never do anything that you can't live with eternally, which I think is a good rule for life. It also means that Heaven and Hell exist. They're just not places that are elsewhere. They are here now. They are your life.'

For Alan Moore, the destruction of the Boroughs echoes the loss of the medieval keystone and the collapse of those arches that support the national imagination. England's dreamtime has come crashing down. We are stranded in a world devoid of original stories, where adults retreat into Harry Potter books and Hollywood adapts fifty-year-old children's superhero stories because they are the last-known sparks of imagination. This is the world of 3 Hammers cider, empty churches and Dunstable shopping centre, where all films are remakes and all music has been heard before. The immaterial arches of the English dreamtime were places of meaning and purpose. They were our home. They will take some work to rebuild.

And so, over ten years and 615,000 words, Alan Moore began rebuilding the lost territory underneath this arch, brick by brick, story by story, life by life. The Boroughs may be gone and the keystone of the English dreamtime lost, but Alan Moore is a stubborn bugger. *Jerusalem* is an act of will, an insistence that, no matter what all others say, the vanished Boroughs were the blazing eternal city at the exact centre of the nation and they will always be.

When Alan looks across our current zombie culture, where dead stories shamble ever onwards and there seems to be no purpose or inspiration in our imagination, he sees a bleak and hopeless place. But that is the view from his perspective. When the rest of us look at our culture we see that it contains Alan Moore, working away with his snake cane in his hand, bloody-mindedly rebuilding the immaterial arches of our dreamtime, and suddenly it doesn't look quite so bad.

11.

RUGBY

Who makes the rules?

My decision to journey along Watling Street was not the result of careful research or prior knowledge. It may be that other prehistoric tracks, such as the Fosse Way, the Great North Road or the Ridgeway, have greater stories to tell. I set out to cross Britain with a head full of purpose and good intent, but when I chose Watling Street as my route I didn't know the road's story or even where it went. I just liked the name.

It is a very British name, understated and unshowy. It's not a name that is trying to attract attention to itself, but it grabbed me nonetheless. It was some time later that I realised its route, from North Wales down to the south-east coast via London, neatly mapped the course of my life. Once I had noticed this, the story of the road and the story of my life became increasingly difficult to separate. In the end, I gave up trying. Watling Street is not a museum exhibit, carefully preserved behind glass for tourists to observe from a distance. The hundreds of thousands of people who travel along it every day are an integral part of its story, just as it is of theirs. It is we who keep it an active, living thing. That my life is roughly strung along its length like a sparse collection of beads is as good an example of this as any.

I was born just outside Rugby, in Warwickshire, in a house four and half miles from Watling Street. This places it inside my self-imposed limit of not going anywhere more than five miles from the road, so I'm going to take a quick look at the house I was born in. Assuming, of course, that I can find it. We moved from Rugby to North Wales when I was three, after my dad died. The generation of my family who would remember the house are no longer with us. I thought the address of my birth had been lost with them, until my brother provided the solution. 'Look on your birth certificate,' he suggested.

As I drive out towards the address of my birth, neatly recorded for me by the Warwickshire Registrar of Births, I try to recall what memories I have from the time I lived here. Psychologists tell us that adults are unable to recall their earliest years. Our earliest accessible memories form between the ages of two and four, typically a little earlier in girls than boys. Most of the memories we think we recall from our first years are false, and the act of trying to remember can inadvertently cause us to imagine false details which we then mistake for real ones. Attempting to recall where you lived up until the age of three is, in these circumstances, something of a minefield.

Yet there is an image of a house in my head, with a small lawn and a busy main road in front. On the opposite side of the road from the house are fields. When I get to the road, it is reassuring to see that it is indeed a fast A-road, with fields on the other side. The importance of keeping away from this dangerous road was, I suspect, drilled into my toddler self.

Hang on. That house. That house on the right. That was it. That was exactly the house.

Shocked and excited, I wait for a break in the traffic and pull over on the right. How strange it is when one of your deepest memories appears before you, unchanged after so many years. I walk back down the road towards it, glancing at the number of the nearest house as I do so. It is close to the number I was looking for, so it seems like I have recognised it correctly.

Then I check the number of the next house. The number has gone down, when it should have gone up. Something is not right here. I reach the house from my memory. It is a lovely 1930s detached home, set back from the road. It matches my memory in every detail, but the house number is wrong. It's not the house I was born in.

I retrace my steps back up the road. The correctly numbered house, to my surprise, is the one that I've parked directly outside. It is semi-detached, considerably smaller, and much closer to the road. Instead of having a lawn outside, there is a small patch of gravel. It is nothing like how I remember it.

To be presented with a concrete demonstration that your memories are false is always a shock. Our earliest memories are like prehistory. It is our foundation, regardless of whether it is myth or fact that we glimpse through the thick fog.

That said, even after being confronted with the reality of false memories, I'm still convinced I have two or three real memories from within that house. I recall sending a Tonka truck down the stairs and being amazed that it broke, for I had believed that a Tonka truck could never be broken. It was probably television adverts that lied about that. This memory feels particularly convincing because I spent the rest of my childhood in a bungalow, so I never again had stairs to play on. I still retain the suspicion that there is something exotic and cosmopolitan about a staircase.

Mulling the problem of false memories over, I go for a walk around the local streets. There was an alternative life to be had growing up in these streets, had my father not been killed in a car accident and my mother not moved us to North Wales to be close to her parents. It is a past that never happened, like an unobserved quantum superposition. But walking these streets gives hints of what it would have been like to have explored them, as a child on a bike. The railway line at the back would have formed a boundary in my mental world, and the tall grey chimneys of the cement plant that rise up to the east, like a misplaced glimpse of a future cyberpunk world, would have worked their way into my imagination. It would have been, I think, an okay place to grow up.

I walk past a primary school and a memory suddenly hits. I was much lower than I am now, sitting in a pushchair, with my mother talking to somebody behind me. From that perspective, I was looking through the metal fence surrounding this school playing field. My brother would have attended this primary school, and I had the sense that we were waiting to pick him up at home time. The memory is incredibly vivid, despite the fact that I now tower over the fence and can no longer peer through it.

I immediately fear contaminating this memory by overthinking it. False memories, I know, are slippery and seductive. If this one was true, I wonder, how long had it been buried in the foundations of my long-term memory? As far as I can recall, that memory was last accessed in early childhood, when I was perhaps seven or eight years old. I was in a primary school in North Wales, and had just been told that the game of rugby had been invented at Rugby School in Rugby. This is what had last triggered that memory of waiting in my buggy for my brother outside the school gates. Rugby! I had thought. I used to live in Rugby. If I still lived there, I would have gone to Rugby School.

I didn't know then that Long Lawford Primary School was not Rugby School. I certainly didn't know that even if I had grown up in Rugby I would never have gone to Rugby School, because it is one of the most expensive private schools in the country.

When I was growing up, the private-school system was something of a mystery. I knew that if a story in a book or on TV was set in a school, then that school would be very different to my North Wales comprehensive. From *Tom Brown's Schooldays* through to Mallory Towers, St Trinian's or Billy Bunter's Greyfriars, the schools of fiction, with the honourable exception of *Grange Hill*, were all independent institutions. I didn't understand why this was. Who would want to watch that arcane world of fagging, snobbishness, power games, gender segregation and a bizarre insistence on calling children by their surname? Even the 1940s-style school in the *Beano*'s 'Bash Street Kids' felt more relevant, despite its being set in a long-gone world of mortar boards and canings. The kids attending it may have been freakish caricatures, but they were closer to children I knew because they didn't consider themselves superior to others.

I know now that the writers and BBC producers behind those stories were typically 'old boys' themselves, but as a child I was unaware of the extent to which the privately educated were more likely to become TV producers and writers. When only one small slice of society becomes storytellers our cultural image of schooldays, and indeed all other parts of life, is greatly affected, in a similar way to how our folk heroes were claimed by the nobility or how dragons became fall guys for making rich lords look good.

Growing up in the 1970s and 1980s, I found privately educated adults bewildering and unreal, as if they were trapped in an unhealthy state of arrested development. The adult character Lord Sebastian Flyte, who was always clutching a teddy bear in Granada TV's adaptation of Evelyn Waugh's *Brideshead Revisited*, was an obvious example. There was something inherently creepy about adults who kept talking about their school, or asking other adults where they went to school. The gender-segregated, power- and status-obsessed atmosphere of public schools did not seem the healthiest location to receive the lifelong psychological imprint of a first sexual experience.

Having now reached an age where I have seen more of the world, my understanding of people who went to private schools is no longer the simplistic stereotype it once was. Yet I must confess that, even today, debates in Parliament make it difficult to completely shake the impression that there is something wrong with the privately educated. Those in the Westminster bubble, politicians and commentators alike, do not act embarrassed by the schoolboy braying and taunting in the chamber. They sound almost proud of it, talking about it as part of the 'theatre' of politics. They don't seem to understand the impression it leaves on fully formed, emotionally healthy adults, especially those who would lose their jobs if they behaved that way at work. Amazingly, they remain blind to the extent to which it damages trust in the political system.

Private education declined over most of the post-war period. During the 1970s and 1980s it was commonly seen by the wider population as antiquated, dysfunctional and embarrassing. Yet that decline stopped at some point in the mid-1990s, and for a host of reasons, ranging from political and economic changes, concerns about inner-city comprehensives, and the appeal of the Harry Potter books, it once again began to grow. An increasing number of parents are choosing to send their kids to independent schools. Private education is now seen less as something damaging and more as a passport to success.

We're just outside Rugby, so I finally have an excuse to visit the school I never would have gone to. But it is worth taking a little detour beforehand, and heading a further twenty-three miles up Watling Street to the small town of Atherstone. Here we'll find a remnant of medieval culture that will put Rugby School's greatest achievement in a little context.

It is 2.30 p.m. on Tuesday, 8 February 2016. Atherstone is a long, thin town that grew up around a short stretch of Watling Street. Direction signs on the wall of a bakery in the middle of the main street point left to Holyhead and right to London. This main street has been given the nicely literal name of Long Street. It is lined with shops along both sides, and the owners of these shops are currently bringing out large sheets of plywood, which they use to board up their windows. The atmosphere in the street is calm, but there is a sense of gathering anticipation.

It is Shrove Tuesday, the day before the start of Lent. Historically this was a day for using the last of your eggs, milk and fat before the coming fast, a tradition still with us in the form of Pancake Day. It was also a day for letting off steam before the season of self-denial. The medieval version of letting off steam was considerably more riotous than just gorging on pancakes. An early-seventeenth-century book records the tradition of drunken apprentices trashing brothels on this day, to give one example, and Shrove Tuesday was always a holiday for apprentices and schoolboys. It was also an unfortunate day to be a cockerel, because games such as cock fighting, cock threshing and cock throwing were all popular.

Cock throwing, or throwing at cocks, was the simplest of these. A bird would be tied to a stake on the floor, and people would throw things at it. Usually the owner of the cock would charge a penny for the privilege, and whoever killed the bird won it. Cock threshing, meanwhile, involved burying the cock with only its head above ground. Blindfold people were then spun around, and attempted to kill the cock by swinging a club or flail at wherever they thought its head might be. A version of the game is still played to this day but, luckily for bird lovers, it has evolved into the less bloodthirsty Pin the Tail on the Donkey. Compared to cock fighting, as practised back in Ye Olde Fighting Cocks, these were not sophisticated pastimes. Cock throwing and threshing lacked the careful breeding, elaborate betting and sharpened beaks that were part and parcel of the cock-fighting world.

It took some time, but all games or sports based around killing or maiming animals for pleasure are now illegal in the UK. Cock threshing and throwing were the first to go, being slowly outlawed from the 1730s onwards. Cock fighting continued until 1835, as the elaborate rules and rituals which had grown up around it allowed its practitioners to claim it was more than simple cruelty. Fox hunting, which was more elaborate and ritualistic still, was not outlawed until 2005. When it comes to blood sports, the more rules and ritual they have the more respectable and defendable they are claimed to be.

As well as giving a day off for feasting, drinking, trashing brothels and killing chickens, Shrove Tuesday was also the traditional date for a community ball game. These medieval ball games evolved into today's football and rugby, as well as their international variants, like Australian Rules football or American football. This tradition has survived in Atherstone, which is why the shopkeepers are boarding up their windows.

Long Street is starting to fill up. The local schools have given the children the afternoon off. A mix of families, eager young men and smiling senior citizens are starting to gather outside Barclays Bank. By the time the Atherstone ball game begins, at 3 p.m. sharp, there will be 2,000 people in this one street.

Atherstone spectators

'Looks like nice weather for the Atherstone Ball Game today!' tweets the local Conservative MP, Craig Tracey. '800+ year tradition which is very important to local community!' This belief that their ball game dates back over 800 years is commonly held locally. There is very little evidence to back it up, but it is plausible. It appears to be a surviving example of the very earliest form of the medieval game for one very simple reason: it doesn't have any rules.

Other surviving Tudor and medieval ball games preserve the game at a more advanced state in its evolution. A Shrove Tuesday game in

Ashbourne, Derbyshire, involves two teams, traditionally those from the north of the River Henmore (the Up'ards) and those to the south (the Down'ards). The teams can be of any size, and the goals are three miles apart. In the game at Alnwick in Northumberland the two teams were originally married and unmarried freemen, but later became the parishioners of St Michael's and the parishioners of St Paul's. These games preserve a tradition of the sport from the point where it had evolved to have both teams and goals. The Atherstone version doesn't have anything like that. It has a long street with 2,000 people in it, a large heavy ball and, basically, that's it.

The crowd continues to grow, and everyone is in good spirits. The game will start at 3 p.m., when the ball will be thrown from the upstairs window of Barclays Bank. A sign hanging outside the bank reads, 'Shrovetide Atherstone Ball Game. Believed to date back to the reign of King John, 1199–1216. Still as mad as hatters!'

The start time approaches, and local dignitaries can be seen moving about inside the bank. A vicar leans out of the top-floor window and begins photographing the crowd below with a green iPhone. People throw handfuls of individually wrapped sweets out of the window, to the delight of the children in the crowd.

A man with a broken megaphone appears at the window and, after a few failed efforts at communicating, resorts to shouting. Today the ball will be thrown out by Leicester City's Marc Albrighton, he informs the delighted crowd. Albrighton appears at the window to great applause. He holds a huge tan-coloured ball that looks like a leather spacehopper. The Premier League footballer is a local celebrity born only a few miles further up Watling Street, in Tamworth. 'We'll have no trouble,' shouts the megaphone man. 'We don't want the police to stop the game. That means you lot!' As far as I can see there are about seven police officers to police this crowd of 2,000, none of whom look like they intend to spoil the crowd's fun.

At 3 p.m. it is time for the game to begin. Marc Albrighton hurls the ball out of the window like a Premier League version of the Greek goddess Eris tossing the golden apple of discord. It falls into the crowd at the far side of the street, is immediately pounced on by the swarm of players and disappears under a wild sea of laughing bodies.

Atherstone scrum

The rest of the crowd wait, patiently. I wonder what will happen next. The written records of medieval and Tudor ball games are devoid of details about the game itself, but instead focus on its antisocial and violent aspects. In *Playing at Football upon the Sabbath and other Days in England*, for example, written by Philip Stubbes in 1595, we read that 'as concerning football playing, I protest unto you, it may rather be called a [...] bloody and murdering practice, than a fellowly sport or pastime. [...] Sometimes their necks are broken, sometimes their backs, sometimes their legs, sometime their arms, sometime one part thrust out of joint, sometime another, sometimes their noses gush out with blood, sometimes their eyes start out of their heads [...] If this is to do to another, as we would wish another to do unto us, God make us more careful over the bodies of our brethren.'

This lack of knowledge about what went on in the medieval games themselves is part of what makes Atherstone's ball game so valuable. In a sense, it is a form of experimental sporting archaeology. If you want to find out how the game was originally played, you throw a ball at a couple of thousand people in a confined urban area and see what they do.

A number of stocky middle-aged men in fluorescent vests make their way through the crowd to the scrum that has formed where the ball fell. These are the game marshals, and it is their job to separate the bodies. The ball is somewhere under a mound of young men dressed in jeans, trainers and dark sweatshirts or rugby shirts. At the bottom of this pile a man is discovered clinging to the ball for dear life, and he is judged to have won the ball. The crowd step back, giving him room and allowing him to regain his feet. There were a few ribbons attached to the ball when it was thrown out of the window, which players attempt to get hold of, but all of these have already been claimed.

Atherstone ball game

Spotting a small child nearby, the man with the ball holds it out and gives the child the honour of touching it. He then runs forward and kicks the ball down the street in the direction of London, where it immediately disappears underneath another pile of people.

Play continues in this manner. The ball is repeatedly kicked down the road, only to disappear underneath bodies who need to be painstakingly untangled in order to see who has the greatest claim. That proud person then kicks it further down the street. In this way the ball gradually makes its way down Long Street towards London, until someone with the ball feels that it has gone far enough and reverses direction. The ball then makes its way back up the street, in the direction of Holyhead. This ritual continues throughout the afternoon, with the ball going up and down Long Street in alternate kicks and scrums.

It quickly becomes clear that only young men, typically big lads in their twenties with short hair and large shoulders, are really playing the game. Everyone else is just enjoying the challenge of keeping out of the way. It is as if the crowd of a modern rugby match left their seats and walked onto the pitch in order to get a better view. The more serious players are recognised quickly. Many are soon bleeding from the forehead, as heads collide with the street during the struggles for the ball.

It is 3.40 p.m. when the game first turns violent. After a scrum a punch is thrown, its impact on the crowd like a shot from a starting pistol. It causes an immediate flurry of limbs, and arms and legs flail in all directions. There's a sudden blitzkrieg of fists, although it is hard to work out who is attacking who. This is not play fighting: anger and hate are etched onto male faces and their fists jab with force and land with horrible accuracy. People flee from the danger, children scream and mothers panic. A girl of about five or six wearing a fake fur hat with cat ears is picked up by her sister, a girl of about ten with pigtails and a red checked shirt, who blindly carries her away. A mother runs in the same direction, one hand pushing her babe in a buggy in front of her with the other pulling a second child, a girl in school uniform and backpack.

A man in a ripped blue shirt is being protected by marshals. They help him up from the ground and away from the crowd. They then sit him on the pavement, where he looks vacantly around, seemingly concussed. From different directions there are still shouts and challenges, and people being pushed, but the fists have stopped flying.

Then the game continues as before.

The dispersed crowd regroup in Long Street, and the briefly forgotten ball is launched further along the road. Smiles return, and the heavy ball is kicked, thrown and fought over up and down the street for the rest of the cold February afternoon. Long Street has a number of raised flower beds along the pavement and I notice a sign on one which reads, 'Don't destroy, enjoy!'

The Atherstone ball game prides itself on having no rules but it did, at some point lost in history, gain a solitary rule. This rule is quite brilliant. It is not a rule found anywhere else, and sadly none of the global ball games which have evolved from medieval football have included it. The rule is this: after 4.30 p.m. you can end the game by hiding the ball. This is traditionally achieved by stabbing it with a knife and smuggling the deflated remains away inside your clothing. If anyone was to try this before 4.30 there would be a riot, but after 4.30 it would be applauded. International football and rugby would be greatly changed if they too allowed the hiding of the ball, although I am probably in a minority for thinking it would be for the better.

No one smuggles the ball out of play today, however. The game continues until 5 p.m., at which point the crowd leaves the street and enters the pubs. This year's winner, and I confess I'm not entirely sure how this was judged, is announced as Jonathan Slesser, a member of Atherstone RFC.

The game is over for another year. At 3 p.m. on Shrove Tuesday next year a new ball will be thrown out of the upstairs window of Barclays Bank. I suspect this will be true for many years to come. The

Atherstone ball game may be dangerous, pointless and totally mad, but it's great fun.

We can't say with certainty that the game is over 800 years old. Perhaps, if it continues far enough into the future, one day we will be able to make that claim. What we can say is that it is a vital fossil in our understanding of the evolution of sport. It shows us the origins of our national game in a wild, gleeful mob who, over centuries, imposed rules onto chaos.

In my earliest childhood memories, Rugby is vast. It is like Gotham, a sprawling metropolis of towering buildings, noise and energy with criminals and costumed vigilantes around every corner. But, once again, the memory cheats. When I visit friends there now, I am always surprised to find that Rugby is a small market town. It has a lot of great pubs, but it doesn't have a whole lot else.

Because the name ends in '-by' it is tempting to assume the town is of Viking origins. 'By' is a Scandinavian word for settlement, and 'rug-by' would also suggest the town was originally founded by a Viking with the brilliant name of Rug. But this does not seem to be the true, for Rugby predates the Viking era. It was occupied through the early Anglo-Saxon era, as far back as the Iron Age.

The fact that Rugby is a small town of pubs and charity shops makes the position of its world-famous school more incongruous. The school lies a short walk south from the main shopping precinct, a timeless, impressive Tudor building of red-and-white bricks dominated by a tall octagonal tower. Or at least that's how the architecturally inclined would describe it. Others might say that the heart of Rugby School is its green, well-kept rugby pitch, around which a number of school buildings happen to cluster.

In front of the school is a statue of its most famous pupil, William Webb Ellis. Other elite schools have statues of their famous alumni, but they are statues of them as adults after they have left school and achieved great things. The statue of Webb Ellis traps him for ever as a small boy, dressed in the elaborate formal school uniform, with a large odd-shaped ball under his arm. He is frozen mid-stride, running with his head up, his eyes on the horizon and his curly hair blowing behind him. As the nearby plaque says, this was the moment in 1823 when he, 'with a fine disregard for the rules', picked up the ball in a game of football and ran with it. This moment, captured by the statue, is the creation myth for the game of rugby.

Webb Ellis statue

For lovers of rugby, this story is hard to avoid. It was dramatised during the opening ceremony of the 2015 Rugby World Cup, and the winner's trophy of that tournament is called the Webb Ellis cup. It's rare for a sport to have a foundation myth, so this is a situation worth taking advantage of. But sport historians have a great deal of scepticism about the story. It only emerged four years after Webb Ellis's death and was based on uncorroborated hearsay. Running with the ball may have been banned at Rugby in Webb Ellis's day, but games like Atherstone show that it was an integral part of the game's origins. It was about the most obvious thing to do with the ball, until rules were established to prevent it, especially when balls were not properly round and didn't roll well. The idea that Webb Ellis 'invented' it makes very little sense.

There is no sign of running forward with the ball in the lengthy description of a school rugby match in Thomas Hughes's semi-autobiographical novel, *Tom Brown's Schooldays*. This describes a match that took place at Rugby School in 1834, eleven years after Webb Ellis left, and it is far closer to the medieval ball game than the sport we know today. It featured around 200 players, none of whom had specific team uniforms. Unlike Atherstone, there were two teams involved, one representing a specific school house and the other containing the rest of the school. This meant that the sizes of the two teams were uneven, with about fifty or sixty players pitted against a team of about 150. The smaller team, though, was better drilled, and led by an inspirational captain called Old Brooke. As the novel's schoolboy narrator describes him, 'His face is earnest and careful as he glances a last time over his array, but full of pluck and hope, the sort of look I hope to see in my general when I go out to fight.'

In *Tom Brown's Schooldays*, the ball game at Rugby School was the direct midpoint between the community fun of Atherstone and the imperial battlefields of the nineteenth century. It was not the case, as the book makes clear, that rugby football was just a 'struggling mass of boys' pointlessly chasing after 'a leather ball, which seemed to excite them to a great fury, as a red rag does a bull'. This was a game that prepared the schoolboys for the wars of the British Empire. 'A battle would look much the same to you, except that the boys would be men, and the balls iron,' it explains.

The primary purpose of nineteenth-century public schools, and Rugby in particular, was not to educate boys academically. As Hughes says, 'The object of all schools is not to ram Latin and Greek into boys, but to make them good English boys, good future citizens.' The headmaster of Rugby in Hughes's time was Dr Thomas Arnold. He wrote that the priority of his school was 'first, religious and moral principles; secondly, gentlemanly conduct; thirdly, intellectual ability'. After his death in 1842, Arnold's ideas became hugely influential. His imperial Christian approach to education led to him being regarded as the moral architect of the Victorian public-school system, and his ideas and sermons helped define the 'Victorian values' that became so prevalent in the latter half of the nineteenth century. His depiction in Hughes's novel was a large part of that process, to the extent that the value of team sports for personal development became associated with his approach. It was Hughes, not Arnold, who valued sport, but after *Tom Brown's Schooldays* it became seen as an integral aspect in Arnold's approach to making a gentleman.

The boys in *Tom Brown's Schooldays* 'feared the Doctor with all our hearts, and very little besides in heaven or earth', for he was a great believer in the role of a 'good sound thrashing before the whole house'. This helped transform the child, he believed, into the kind of morally correct good citizen he so admired. Arnold certainly made an impression on Thomas Hughes when he was a pupil. He wrote that 'Perhaps [Rugby School under Dr Arnold] is the only little corner of the British Empire which is thoroughly, wisely, and strongly ruled just now. I'm more and more thankful every day of my life that I came here to be under him.'

It was his deep admiration of Arnold that motivated Hughes, fifteen years after he left Rugby School, to write *Tom Brown's Schooldays*, a book that stresses the value of Arnold's methods and world view. As Hughes makes clear in a preface to a later edition, 'Several persons, for whose judgment I have the highest respect, while saying very kind things about this book, have added that the great fault of it is "too much preaching"; but they hope I shall amend in this matter should I ever write again. Now this I most distinctly decline to do. Why, my whole object in writing at all was to get the chance of preaching!' The impact of Arnold's teaching on Hughes's philosophy was clear in the marvellous title of a later book he wrote, *The Manliness of Christ*.

Hughes's preaching of Arnoldian philosophy had an unexpected side effect. *Tom Brown's Schooldays* was the first school novel and, as a result, it laid down a clear template for all school-based fiction to come. Despite how different a moralising Victorian Christian novel like *Tom Brown's Schooldays* might appear compared to a pagan magical fantasy like *Harry Potter and the Philosopher's Stone*, it is striking how much of the basic template remains unchanged nearly 150 years later.

Both books, for example, begin with their boy heroes, Tom Brown and Harry Potter, unaware that they are special. Harry does not realise that he is a wizard and Tom does not realise he is privileged, for he grew up 'playing with the village boys, without the idea of equality or inequality (except in wrestling, running and climbing) ever entering their heads'. Both boys also grew up apart from their parents, although Tom's story is not the tragedy that Harry's is. He was raised by nannies and guardians because that was the social norm.

Both books take over eighty pages before their heroes arrive at the special schools that will transform them into adults with power over the material world. Both of their initial journeys from London to these schools are memorable and magical. Tom's pre-dawn coach ride along Watling Street is a vivid description of the golden years of coach travel in the pre-rail days, hurtling along on top of the coach as dawn breaks over the English countryside. The young boy, separated from his guardian for the first time, encounters such delights as breakfast tables groaning with food in coaching inns and the warming pleasure of a glass of purl, a mixture of warm beer and gin. He has a purse of money to spend for the first time. So does Harry, who also splashes out on a feast on his first journey to school. He buys treats like Chocolate Frogs and Bertie Bott's Every-Flavour Beans from the sweet trolley of the Hogwarts Express.

The first boy whom Tom and Harry meet ('Scud' East and Ron Weasley respectively) becomes their best friend throughout the school adventures to follow. They both encounter a bully (Flashman and Malfoy), whom they have to overcome, and they prove their worth to the wider school, as much for their bravery and heart as their skill, through their efforts at sport (rugby and Quidditch).

Perhaps most importantly, both boys learn to admire the wisdom and example of their headmasters (Dr Arnold, the real Rugby headmaster in what is otherwise a work of fiction, and Professor Dumbledore). Neither of these headmasters provides what we would now think of as 'normal' lessons for their pupils. There is no maths or geography at Hogwarts, while Arnold wrote about his pride in not teaching the physical sciences: 'I would gladly have [my child] think that the sun went round the earth, and that the stars were so many spangles set in the bright blue firmament. Surely the one thing needful for a Christian and an Englishman to study is Christian and moral and political philosophy'. What both of these headmasters teach Tom and Harry is how to grow up and become a man who will choose good over evil. Both boys initially fear their stern educators, but they soon begin to idolise them. They both mourn them when they die, as the laws of narrative cruelly demand they must.

Both boys strongly desire the magical power that their schools promise. Harry Potter has been ignorant of the existence of magic until the arrival of the giant groundskeeper, Hagrid, who casts a spell that makes Harry's cousin Dudley grow a pig's tail. From that point on, he never questions his desire to learn the magical arts himself. Tom Brown, on the other hand, is struck by the superior air of public schoolboys the moment he arrives at Rugby, and finds it intoxicating. He notes the 'patronising air' of a new friend, who was 'gifted with the most transcendent coolness and assurance, which Tom felt to be aggravating and hard to bear, but couldn't for the life of him help admiring and envying – especially when young my lord begins hectoring two or three long loafing fellows'. Tom 'felt friends with him at once, and began sucking in all his ways and prejudices, as fast as he could understand them'. From here on in he begins to think of himself as superior, set apart from the 'wrong sort'.

Both boys understand the need to fight, and fighting plays a pivotal role in their transformations. Harry secretly trains himself in magical combat in order to survive attacks from evil wizards and witches who intend to destroy him. Tom is in an environment where 'fighting with fists is the natural and English way for English boys to settle their quarrels'. Bullying is frowned upon, but complaining about bullying is frowned upon far more. He was a Brown, and 'the Browns are a fighting family'. Fighting was part and parcel of the Christian struggle, because life was 'a battle-field ordained from of old'. This Christian struggle is at the heart of *Tom Brown's Schooldays*, because it plays a vital role in Tom Brown's ability to see himself as superior. By struggling to do the Christian thing he became a good person, and a good person, logically, was superior to others.

The theme of superiority can make *Tom Brown's Schooldays* feel dated and irrelevant to twenty-first-century readers, but our culture has modern equivalents. It's instructive to compare the book to a song such as 'I Am a God' by Kanye West, on his *Yeezus* album. Proclaiming that you are a god is, of course, the ultimate expression of belief in your own superiority. Kanye is not one to shirk from doing this.

As well as declarations of his own divinity, large parts of the lyrics are taken up with Kanye berating his staff, or people in service industries. 'Get the Porsche out of the damn garage,' he raps, along with the unintentionally hilarious line, 'Hurry up with my damn croissants'. This mixture of exaggerated self-worth with horrible behaviour is familiar to anyone who has come across the harsher satires of the English public-school system. Kanye uses the words 'my niggas' and 'bitches' throughout his work, in a way almost interchangeable with the public school concepts of 'fags' and 'oiks' (or 'louts' at Rugby, which is their accepted dismissive term for non-public-school people). None of these terms are respectful, but 'fags' and 'my niggas' indicate accepted insiders while 'oiks' and 'bitches' indicate outsiders of little worth.

A more telling comparison, however, is Kanye's insistence on his spiritual humility. In the song he is simultaneously a man of God and a god himself. He talks to Jesus while he counts his millions, and declares that while Jesus is 'the most high' Kanye himself is 'a close high'. This is a necessary perspective to achieve in order not to be troubled by his wealth, privilege or lack of empathy. As long as he orientates himself by God, the omphalos of universal divinity, then he is a good person who is perfectly within his rights to bully those serving him. And if he is a good person, then it stands to reason that he is indeed superior. As far as Kanye and Tom Brown are concerned, that's just logical.

In 1940, George Orwell wrote an essay called 'Boys' Weeklies', in which he questioned the attitudes of the public-school stories which were so common in publications aimed at children. His essay was published in the March edition of *Horizon* magazine.

In magazines like *Gem* and *Magnet*, Orwell complained, 'the supposed "glamour" of public-school life is played for all it is worth. There is all the usual paraphernalia — lock-up, roll-call, house matches, fagging, prefects, cosy teas round the study fire, etc. etc. [...] As for the snob-appeal, it is completely shameless. Each school has a titled boy or two whose titles are constantly thrust in the reader's face; other boys have the names of well-known aristocratic families, Talbot, Manners, Lowther. We are for ever being reminded that Gussy is the Honourable Arthur A. D'Arcy, son of Lord Eastwood, that Jack Blake is heir to "broad acres", that Hurree Jamset Ram Singh (nicknamed Inky) is the Nabob of Bhanipur, that Vernon-Smith's father is a millionaire.' This focus on the wealth of the family is why public schoolboys traditionally address each other by their surname.

Orwell contrasts the approving portrayals of the privileged boys with the depiction of the 'oiks', or the non-public-school characters. These stories' 'basic political assumptions are two: nothing ever changes, and foreigners are funny. In the *Gem* of 1939 Frenchmen are still Froggies and Italians are still Dagoes. [...] The working classes only enter into the *Gem* and *Magnet* as comics or semi-villains (race-course touts, etc.).' Orwell assumed that these stories were written by a team of writers following a strict house style, because it didn't seem feasible that single writers could be so prolific. 'The stories in the *Magnet* are signed "Frank Richards" and those in the *Gem*, "Martin Clifford",' he noted, 'but a series lasting thirty years could hardly be the work of the same person every week.'

Frank Richards and Martin Clifford were indeed pen-names, but not ones used by teams of writers. They were two of around twenty aliases used by a single man, the remarkable Charles Hamilton, the most prolific writer in history. He is estimated to have written around 100 million words over his career, the equivalent of about 1,200 novels. His stories were predominantly Thomas Hughes-inspired public-school adventure stories, and his most famous creation was the overweight anti-hero Billy Bunter. Hamilton was not pleased by Orwell's critical essay and wrote a response that was published a few weeks later.

Richards made a number of astute responses to Orwell's comments, not least to the idea that they were too much work for one man. 'Mr Orwell finds it difficult to believe that a series running for thirty years can possibly have been written by one and the same person,' he wrote. 'In the presence of such authority, I speak with diffidence: and only say that, to the best of my knowledge and belief, I am only one person, and have never been two or three.'

His response to the perceived superiority of his public-school characters, however, was less convincing. 'As for foreigners being funny,' he wrote, 'I must shock Mr Orwell by telling him that foreigners *are* funny. They lack the sense of humour which is a special gift of our chosen nation: and people without a sense of humour are always unconsciously funny.' The belief that the English were better than other nationalities had been so ingrained in Richards's psyche during his education that he could see nothing wrong with making that statement. And just as the English were superior, so the privileged English were superior to the non-privileged English. 'It is an actual fact that,' he wrote, 'in this country at least, noblemen generally are better than commoners.'

A proclamation like that seems so ridiculous now that it is tempting to dismiss it as just a product of its time. But the idea that people should be judged on the wealth of their parents, rather than their intelligence, creativity, commitment or endurance, is an idea that is still unconsciously accepted and unquestioned by many. It is the core delusion that lies at the heart of the private-education system and it remains endemic in this country because it is drilled into the young, generation after generation. You can see evidence for it in people who are unable to believe that the relatively uneducated Shakespeare could be a genius, who dismiss immense talents like Tommy Flowers, and in literary critics who write endless think pieces about people they went to school with instead of getting the train from London to Northampton to get to grips with Alan Moore. Few people in this country have difficulty imagining a black prime minister, a gay prime minister or a female prime minister, but many are unable to imagine a poor prime minister.

This is the reason why the upper classes evolved their elaborate system of personal titles. Back at Bletchley Park, we encountered the wartime codebreaker the Honourable Sarah Baring. Thanks to her valuable work at Bletchley it seems reasonable to call Baring 'honourable', and indeed many other words of praise. The title, however, claims that she was 'Honourable' not for what she had done, but because of who her parents were.

It is easy to find the use of titles like this funny. They are like human versions of vanity registration plates, expensive and used by those unable to see themselves through the eyes of others. But to those raised to believe that people should be judged on their parents' wealth, not on their own achievements, titles like that appear to have genuine value.

The idea that the privileged are superior is the central tenet of the public-school reality tunnel. An elaborate, but entirely arbitrary, system of social rules and signifiers is employed in an attempt to support it and make it appear believable. It is the one belief that cannot be questioned because, without it, the entire system falls apart. Private education can have some positive effects on children, from the beneficial impact of small class sizes to the nurturing of confidence and self-worth, but the idea that private education endows children with a magical quality of superiority is an illusion. That magical cloak does not exist. Deep down, we all know it.

The result of falling for this illusion is a comic archetype which runs from the loveable but hapless Bertie Wooster, through the Upper-Class Twits of *Monty Python* to comic characters like Harry Enfield's Tim Nice But Dim or Will the Intern from the BBC satire *W1A*. These are not bad people, on the whole. They just believe themselves to be more capable than they are, and this lack of awareness makes them comedic.

Of course, the privately educated do not want to be surrounded with people who see them as inherently funny. This becomes problematic when, once in positions of responsibility, they disproportionally hire people from similar backgrounds to their own.

Research published in 2015 makes the situation clear. In that survey, the 7 per cent of the population that were privately educated make up 61 per cent of top doctors, 50 per cent of the cabinet, 48 per cent of the senior civil service, 74 per cent of the top judiciary and 51 per cent of leading journalists. In the military, 88 per cent of senior officers attended a selective school. Even previously disreputable creative careers such as acting and pop music are becoming increasingly dominated by the alumni of independent schools, including 42 per cent of British winners in the main BAFTA categories and 19 per cent of Brit Award winners, due in part to financial support in the early stages of a career. The privately educated also earn more, with privately educated graduates earning an average of £4,500 more a year than state-educated graduates after only three years in the workplace. Although few would publicly state a belief in the superiority of the privately educated as openly as Charles Hamilton did, the cold evidence of statistics such as these show that his belief has not gone away. An A* grade GCSE from a state school is the same record of ability and achievement as an A* GCSE from an independent school, but there are many who subconsciously believe otherwise.

This is a touchy subject which no one wants to talk about. The 7 per cent of the population with a public-school background fear it causes their work and effort to be overlooked, and that it creates the false assumption that all they gained in life was simply handed to them. Criticism of the school system, in these circumstances, seems like veiled class war, a chip on the shoulder of the bitter and jealous. Public-school children are, ultimately, just children. They are in no way responsible for the social circles they were born into or the education choices of their parents. To them, criticism of their advantage is to damn them for things they had no say in.

The 93 per cent of the population from a state background, meanwhile, also have little desire to discuss the subject. To them, it is just depressing. It is self-evident that privilege, rather than talent, is a passport to the top jobs, so what more is there to say?

The sport of rugby is an example of how the public-school system ripples out beyond education and comes to define aspects of the country. In 2014 61 per cent of players in the top rugby-union leagues went to an independent school. Compare this to the football league, where 6 per cent of players are privately educated, roughly in line with the country.

Love of football covers the whole of Britain, more or less, but interest in rugby is geographically sporadic. One reason for this is an important part of rugby history known as the 'great schism'.

Rugby football continued to evolve in the decades after William Webb Ellis and Thomas Hughes. The game spread beyond the school, and in 1871 an agreed set of rules was written down by the clubs of the fledgling Rugby Football Union. An important proviso at the time was that professionalism, the payment of players, was not acceptable. Rugby old boys saw themselves as gentlemen, and playing for other reasons than the honour of your team was entirely vulgar.

As the game grew in the 1870s and 1880s it attracted working-class players, particularly in the north. Many of those could not afford to lose a day's pay in order to play so they had to be compensated by their teams. To the Rugby Football Union these payments amounted to professionalism and could not be tolerated as a matter of honour. If fear of being beaten by working-class players was factored into this thinking, it was not explicitly stated. When faced with the uncompromising position that rugby should only be played by those who didn't need to work, many northern clubs had no choice but to walk away from the union and set up a league of their own. It was this great schism of 1895 that led to the separate evolution of rugby union and rugby league.

The year 1895 was also when Rugby School held an enquiry into the claims that William Webb Ellis first ran with the ball in 1823. Thomas Hughes was among the many ex-students who gave evidence to this enquiry. Because this occurred at the same time as the great schism, the enquiry is seen as an attempt to reinforce the moral ownership of the game by gentlemen, rather than players. But the enquiry couldn't find any evidence to support the Webb Ellis story and had to conclude that it was apocryphal.

But time passes, and memory cheats, and we all have false memories among our foundations. To young sports fans around the world, who hear the famous creation myth as they avidly follow the Rugby World Cup, this statue outside Rugby School is their history. It is how the sport remembers its past. Whether or not something is real isn't always what matters because if enough people believe something to be true, then the world will behave as if that were the case. Believing or even pretending to believe has an effect, which is how those sent to a public school can believe they are superior and somehow see that reflected and reinforced by the wider world.

Hiding the ball and smuggling it out of play is always an option on the Warwickshire stretch of Watling Street. It's a place where not following the accepted tradition can, just occasionally, be enough to make you a hero. Here lives a mix of stories about both the rules of sport, and the denial of the rules of sport. Belief in these games can be valuable, but it is not compulsory. Ultimately if it's not your game, there's no reason to believe in it.

12.

BOSWORTH FIELD TO WESTON PARK

Lloyd George's question

A field of gently swaying green and yellow barley stretches away in front of me. Beyond is a band of woodland and, behind the trees, distant hills look purple underneath the wet, troubled sky. It is quiet, for the wind is still and the birds are silent. I am looking down from

Bosworth Field

287

Ambion Hill in Leicestershire at a landscape where, over 500 years ago, the crown of England was found on a hawthorn bush. You would not think it now, but thousands of men killed each other in these fields.

There are no shortages of battlefields on or near Watling Street. Battles, after all, take place in locations that armies can travel to. The most obvious battlefield to visit would have been the Battle of Watling Street, where Queen Boudica and her rebel tribes were wiped out by a heavily outnumbered Roman army. According to Tacitus, 80,000 Britons were killed in that battle and only 400 Romans. If this is true, it would have been the most people killed on a single day in history until the First World War. The later Roman writer Dio claimed that Boudica's forces had numbered 230,000. Even assuming that Tacitus and Dio exaggerated, it was still likely to have been the single biggest gathering of people in prehistoric Britain.

That the Battle of Watling Street may have produced the greatest slaughter of pre-modern history is usually explained as a well-trained, professional Roman fighting force slicing through a poorly armed rabble, after cleverly choosing a battlefield that minimised the effectiveness of the Britons' fearsome chariots. There is, no doubt, a lot of truth in this, but the defeat still seems odd. Boudica's forces had proven themselves to be highly effective. They had destroyed the Roman cities that we now call Colchester, London and St Albans. They had easily defeated the Spanish Ninth Legion, commanded by the future governor Quintus Petillius Cerialis, after the Romans made a disastrous attempt to relieve Colchester. The British were motivated because they were fighting to free their lands from foreign invaders, and they had momentum on their side. Their total collapse at the hands of the Gemini Fourteenth Legion, in this context, is surprising.

Perhaps the psychological impact of recent events on Anglesey, an island off north-west Wales, affected the battle? Julius Caesar, who knew the Druids in Gaul, wrote that those enigmatic Celtic warrior magicians' 'rule of life' had been developed in Britain, and that those who wanted most diligently to study it travelled to these islands to do so. Anglesey, many believe, was the prehistoric equivalent of Canterbury Cathedral or Westminster Abbey. It was the part of Britain associated with knowledge and teaching, the Druid version of Oxford or Cambridge. And the Roman army facing Boudica's troops was returning from comprehensively wiping it out.

Tacitus reports that the Romans destroyed the Druids' sanctuaries and sacred groves. This is striking, for it was not usual for the Romans to attack native religious sites in this way. It is also unusual to hear of the Druids in battle, for they were typically described more like advisers, lawyers or travelling magicians than as soldiers. Details like these support the idea that Anglesey was the Druids' 'last stand' in their most sacred heartland, and that the Roman attack was intended to end their influence on British civic life once and for all.

For the Romans, the organising force they feared most in Britannia had been overcome. For the Britons, their previous way of life had been wiped away. The British may have trashed Roman cities, but the Romans trashed the British noosphere. This, I suspect, would have been an influence on their collapse and slaughter at the Battle of Watling Street. Before the battle had begun, the British had already lost.

We cannot visit this battlefield, unfortunately, because its exact location along the road has been lost to time. It may have occurred as far north as these Leicestershire fields, near Atherstone, or as far south as Dunstable. But there are no shortages of other battlefields along this road. A particularly important one next to Watling Street was the Battle of Naseby. It was there, in June 1645, that King Charles I was defeated by Oliver Cromwell's and Thomas Fairfax's New Model Army. This was not the final battle in the English Civil Wars, but it was the decisive one. More than 80 per cent of Charles's army was killed, including all his artillery and many of his infantrymen and officers. The king lived to fight on, but the idea he was fighting for did not. Charles believed in the divine right of kings. He thought that he was king because God willed it so, and that whatever he did was God's wish. The defeat at Naseby could only be explained by rejecting that idea. God, the evidence suggested, had more invested in the divine right of king-slayers.

But I am at Bosworth Field, where Richard III, the last Plantagenet, went down horseless and fighting in the marsh. This was the place where the Welsh contender, Henry Tudor, placed his family line on the throne and ushered in what is now considered something of a Golden Age.

Henry landed at Pembroke on 7 August 1485. He marched his army under his red-dragon banner up to Watling Street and then travelled along it until he reached these quintessentially English fields. Here, he fought the forces flying the banner of a white boar. In these fields, the crown of England passed from a French family to a Welsh one.

It is one of those strange quirks of history that ever since Harold went down with an arrow in his eye at Hastings in 1066, no English dynasty has ever taken the English throne. Following the Norman and Plantagenet dynasties, who came from what is now France, the crown passed to the Welsh Tudors, the Scottish Stuarts, the Dutch William of Orange and the German Hanoverians and Saxe-Coburg-Gothas. The House of Saxe-Coburg-Gotha, however, did declare itself to be English in 1917, due to the anti-German sentiment of the First World War era. From that point on, the dynasty explained, they wished to be known as the Windsors. Our acceptance of this was an early example of the progressive identity politics more usually associated with transgender issues. If the Royal family wishes to identify as English, then we will respect their choice and consider them English.

King Richard's dead body was stripped, abused and carried on the back of a horse to Leicester, where it was discovered, 530 years later, underneath a large letter 'R' painted on the ground in a car park. The crown was found in a hawthorn bush and given to Henry Tudor, who became King Henry VII. This was the conclusion of the bitter Wars of the Roses, a violent clash between two ambitious branches of the House of Plantagenet. The two sides were the House of York, who used the symbol of a white rose, and the House of Lancaster, who, a little ahistorically, are now symbolised by a red rose.

The practice of nobility being referred to by place names can make English history a little confusing. History books casually mention names like Essex or Warwick, and assume that we understand that these are people and not places. The origins of this practice can be traced back to the Norman Conquest. Before then, English people did not use surnames, although some Saxon nobility followed the Celtic practice of referring to themselves as the 'son of' their father. If Bill was the child of Ben, for example, they might be called Bill O'Ben in Irish, Bill ap Ben in Welsh or Bill McBen in Scottish Gaelic.

The Norman invaders, in contrast, often used the name of their French home town as a sort of proto-surname. After William took all English land by right of conquest and gifted sections of it to his Norman allies, dukes and earls began to refer to each other by the names of their new lands. This was a natural evolution of their use of ancestral homes as names, as well as a conspicuous display of wealth. It was as if, to reinforce their right of ownership, they were declaring that the land and its owner had in some way become one and the same thing. The lord and the land shared one name. It also made it clear to the people who lived in those lands that they had no claim to them.

From this began the complicated system of peerages and titles linked to land. As the practice of using a family name indicated high status, it was eventually emulated by those lower down the social ranks. Lacking land, the names the Saxons used were commonly based on occupations, such as 'Baker' or 'Cooper'. In this way, around the thirteenth century, 'Sir names' evolved into surnames. In the origin of surnames, the English define themselves by what they do, the Celts define themselves by their ancestors, and the nobility define themselves by what they own.

The Wars of the Roses were a clash between York and Lancaster, by which we mean the dynasties who historically had claimed ownership of those two places. Curiously, it is not typically regarded as a civil war, which is odd, because a civil war is an internal war waged between two sides from the same country in order to claim power. The difference, perhaps, is that the Wars of the Roses were not fought to change the political hierarchy, but simply to decide who should sit on top of it. A 'proper' civil war, such as the conflict that led to Naseby or the American Civil War, was fought over how authority and the political system were to be defined. They were as much struggles in the noosphere as they were battles in the biosphere. The Norman invasion, Boudica's rebellion and English Civil War are examples of wars fought not just to run the country, but to define it. The Yorkists and Lancastrians, in contrast, had a simpler conflict. They were just landowners who wanted more.

It might have looked like there was little hope of the Wars of the Roses ever coming to an end after so much blood had been spilt and decades of bitterness had accumulated. The enmity between the two sides looked too deep to offer hope of reconciliation. But Henry Tudor united the country and the two feuding houses when he married Elizabeth of York, the niece of the defeated Richard III. To symbolise this union, the Tudors used a piece of very powerful iconography called the Tudor Rose. This was the white rose of York at the centre of a red rose, which was retroactively said to symbolise the house of Lancaster. The name 'Wars of the Roses' was applied much later, only coming into common use in the nineteenth century.

The Tudor Rose did not get rid of the symbols of York and Lancaster. It did not elevate one above the other. It simply accepted them both and declared them to both be part of a larger whole. In this it was the Good Friday Agreement of Tudor England.

When violence splits a group of people, this is the only way in which reconciliation can be achieved. Both halves need to be seen from a higher vantage point that doesn't favour either but which transcends both. When Europe was split by the violence of the Second World War, the political institutions that developed into the European Union were the greater perspective needed to heal those wounds. For those who voted to leave the EU the gamble was that this had worked, and that the divisions had been so thoroughly healed that there was no longer any risk of war between European countries.

In Belfast in 1980, in England in the 1470s, and in Poland in 1943 it must have looked like reconciliation was impossible. And yet, in all those cases, reconciliation did occur. It just needed all involved to see themselves as part of something larger. That might take a vast political bureaucracy like the EU, or a single multilateral agreement like the Good Friday Agreement. Or it might just take something as simple as a symbol, perhaps even one as slight and as English as a rose within a rose.

Heading west along Watling Street, past Tamworth, where Leicester City's Marc Albrighton grew up, we find a reminder that old roads were the principal means by which soldiers could move around.

The M6 Toll road was opened in 2003, and it snakes around and across Watling Street for much of its length. It was an experiment in introducing road charging, but traffic levels have been less than expected and this has undercut the argument for more toll roads in Britain. That the M6 Toll follows Watling Street is apt, however, because Watling Street was a toll road for much of the seventeenth and eighteenth centuries. It was operated by a turnpike trust, and the money collected paid for repairs to the road caused by carriages.

Not long after the M6 Toll road opened, a family driving along saw what they first interpreted as animals in the road. Drawing nearer, they realised that they were looking at the ghosts of about twenty Roman soldiers. This sighting was near Lichfield in Staffordshire, which is where the M6 Toll crosses over the old Roman road section of Watling Street. Intriguingly, the ghosts' legs weren't visible, and they waded 'through the tarmac as you would through water', according to one of the witnesses, Sue Cowley, from Coleshill, Warwickshire.

When the M6 Toll opened, the building supplies company Tarmac Group announced that its surface was made out of asphalt, tarmac and 'two and a half million pulped Mills & Boon novels'. Those Roman ghosts were not just wading through the physical accumulation of centuries, but the immaterial accumulation as well: the road is literally built out of stories. Populist, throwaway stories, admittedly, but romance is the best genre to build roads from.

Having driven this section of the road countless times, I can unhappily report that I have yet to see Roman ghosts on the M6 Toll. My theory is that ever since they put the price up to over a fiver on weekdays the ghosts take a different route.

It is two days after my visit to Bosworth Field, and I stand in front of a different landscape. This is Weston Park, a 1,000-acre country estate in Shropshire, to the west of the M6 Toll road. The view is very English, but in a different way to Bosworth Field. Bosworth was working farmland. Where once armoured knights on horseback hacked at one another, now hay bales in black polythene dot the fields. But here, at Weston Park, the grass stretches away to the horizon in one unbroken vista while, behind me, the woods I've walked through contain a rich variety of trees, including oak, hornbeam, sweet chestnut and sycamore. The landscape could not be more perfect, which is in itself a clue that it is not entirely natural.

The view out to the horizon is designed to appear unbroken, but an eight-foot-deep ditch runs right across it. The ditch is invisible from this position only, because it is here that the landowner would have stood, surveying or showing off his property. The purpose of the ditch is to keep livestock away from the house. It allows you to gaze out at a field of sheep or deer without the risk of those animals coming close enough to bother you. The ditch is called a ha-ha, because anyone who didn't know that it was there was in danger of falling into it and breaking their neck. Landowners found that funny.

The trees behind me have also been selected for effect. This part of the grounds, Temple Wood, was laid out by the great engineer of the English landscape, Lancelot 'Capability' Brown. It was Brown who built the ha-ha.

British garden design at the start of the eighteenth century copied the formal, structured style of the French and the Dutch, with their straight lines, symmetrical topiary and elaborate fountains. Continental formal gardens like these had been copied in Britain since Tudor days, and a small area of Weston Park, in front of the house, is still kept in this style. But even though they can be admired as expressions of the gardener's skill, formal gardens never really looked like they belonged in this country, in much the same way that the straight Roman line was less 'us' than the rolling drunken road.

For some reason, trees in this country somehow lose their power when you plant them in a straight line. In a garden like Versailles the natural world is organised and controlled. This is inherently political, a statement of man's mastery over nature that is intended to symbolise the power of the garden's owner. To the British eye, however, to control nature is to lose what makes it vital. The moment you line trees up in a long row, be they London Planes along Midsummer Boulevard in Milton Keynes or chestnuts along a drive to a country estate, you somehow neuter them. With their intrinsic nature tamed, their spell is broken. A neat row of trees fails to inspire us in the way that a more natural clump of trees can do.

So, across the eighteenth century, a move away from the continental style of gardening began. At first this was done in a rococo style, where landscapes became littered with statues, urns, obelisks and classical temples. Quirky follies, built in faux Gothic, Turkish and Chinese styles, became commonplace in English estates. This was due to the influence of the Grand Tour, where young upper-class gentlemen explored the Mediterranean and sites of antiquity during a form of proto-gap year. On their return, they placed classical statues and temples around their family homes in order to build their own Arcadias. Landscape became a story, but one only intended to be read by the sufficiently educated. The garden at Stourhead in Wiltshire had a temple engraved with the warning of the Cumaean Sybil, 'Begone, you who are uninitiated, begone!'

To walk around a rococo garden was to indulge in al fresco play-acting. A nineteenth-century guidebook to Stourhead advised visitors that they would 'associate for a time with only the gods and heroes of antiquity'. It was an early form of live-action role-playing for the nobility. These well-educated landowners were behaving not unlike Steve Moore, except they had land, gardeners and architects at their disposal, whereas Steve had only his imagination.

Rococo gardens cleared away the earlier Franco-Dutch formality in favour of uniting the noosphere with the biosphere. But this was the classical noosphere, rather than the British one, and so it remained something of an awkward fit. It was Capability Brown who removed these classical allusions, and in doing so created a fully English tradition of landscape gardening. By the end of the eighteenth century Sir Horace Walpole, the politician and author of the first Gothic novel, declared that 'We have reached the peak of perfection. We have given the true model of gardening to the world; let other countries corrupt or mimic our taste, but let it reign here on its verdant throne, original in its elegant simplicity.' As he predicted, continental gardeners did copy the *jardin anglais*. Capability Brown's vision of the landscape became internationally recognised as the ideal of what England is supposed to look like.

Brown came from a family of Northumbrian yeoman-farmers and became a gardener at his local estate, Kirkharle Hall, when he was sixteen. Well-connected and hardworking, he worked his way up to become Master Gardener to George III. Over his thirty-five years as a landscape designer, he worked on more than 170 properties, across the length and breadth of England. His style was to enhance nature, rather than overwrite it. He aimed to simplify and remove artifice. He even hoped to remove the maze from Hampton Court but was overruled by the king. His nickname came from his reputation for quickly sniffing out the 'capability' of a landscape; after only an hour's ride around an estate, he would be able to produce a design that brought the best out of the landscape.

English poets always knew that paradise was natural, not artificial. In *Paradise Lost*, Milton described Eden as containing 'Flow'rs worthy of Paradise, which not nice art / In beds and curious knots, but Nature boon / Powrd forth profuse on hill and dale and plain'. Alexander Pope explained his opinion on garden design in a 1713 Epistle, where he wrote, 'To rear the Column, or the Arch to bend, To swell the terrace, or to sink the Grot; In all, let *Nature* never be forgot... Consult the *Genius* of the *Place* in all.' This approach was the key to Brown's work. He did not start with a blank page and wipe away the existing landscape. As Brown saw it, he was like an editor of a manuscript, rather than the author. As he described his work in 1782, 'Now *there* I make a comma, and there, where a more decided turn is proper, I make a colon; at another part, where an interruption is desirable to break the view, a parenthesis; now a full stop, and then I begin another subject.' His designs of sweeping lawns, perfectly placed clumps of trees and curving lakes were designed to look entirely natural, even though they were not. Brown was more of a cosmetic surgeon than a sculptor. He was still the rolling drunken road rather than the straight Roman line, but he was a rolling drunken road that had been tastefully tidied up. Such is the aesthetic of England.

I arrive early at Weston Park, shortly after it has opened for the day. Having paid my £7.20 entrance fee, I am able to wander around Brown's work before the bulk of the day's visitors arrive. It's far from quiet, but the noises are all natural: the flapping of ducks' wings hitting the lake, the breeze through the leaves, the cooing of doves in the tops of the trees. A low, background rumble turns out not to be planes or traffic along Watling Street, but a small waterfall where one lake drains into another. For all the simplicity of appearance, Brown's work could include very sophisticated drainage and hydraulic engineering.

Walking over a gently arched stone bridge at the far end of the lake, I find a sign on a post with a black exclamation mark inside a yellow triangle. 'Warning', it reads underneath, 'Beware of moving vehicles'. It is the sort of sign you'd walk past without a second thought in towns and cities, but here it jumps out like a mobile phone ringing in a church; the visual equivalent of noise pollution. In the rest of Brown's landscape, there are no voices controlling you or making demands. Near the lake is a summerhouse called the Temple of Diana, which a notice describes as a 'luxury holiday let'. It has a fence around it to keep day visitors away. That fence, like the warning sign, also feels like a crack in Brown's spell. Jolted by these abrupt controlling intrusions, I understand why Brown went to the expense of building a ha-ha rather than a fence.

Capability Brown gardens

Looking over images of Brown's landscapes, it is striking how unpopulated they are. Modern photographs of his work are usually entirely devoid of people. Paintings from the eighteenth and nineteenth century might have a well-dressed couple in the near foreground, as if for scale, and there might be a farm worker visible in the far distance, to add rural authenticity without troubling the strolling nobility, but the landscape would otherwise be empty. The England of Capability

Brown was a church of solitude and peace, a retreat to calm the souls of the landed gentry.

Some of Brown's improvements were explicitly designed to increase this sense of solitude. When farm buildings or kitchen gardens interfered with a view, he would plant a clump of trees in front to hide them. At times, such as at Stowe, Croome and Houghton, he destroyed entire villages that were in the way of the lord of the manor's views. When the work was completed and the villagers evicted, it was as if these ancient settlements had never existed. As the poet Oliver Goldsmith wrote in 'The Deserted Village':

> ... the man of wealth and pride
> Takes up a space that many poor supplied;
> Space for his lake, his park's extended bounds,
> Space for his horses, equipage and hounds.

Capability Brown's English landscape tradition has become so globally synonymous with how England should look that it is easy to forget how artificial it is. If it was left up to nature, Britain would be predominantly forest, as it was for most of its history. If the ever-present Watling Street itself was abandoned, it would only take fifty years for it to also become woodland. The requirements of agriculture have created new landscapes that, in time, have come to be thought of as quintessentially English, from the regular field systems of the Middle Ages to the large-scale agriculture of the Garden of England. The image of England is not fixed. It fluctuates as our technology and needs evolve.

But Brown's alternative landscapes were created for a different reason to those farming-defined landscapes. Landowners enhanced and improved their estates not as an agricultural necessity, but because they claimed it was their duty. Landowning was a burden and a responsibility, they said. It required refined and careful stewardship for land to be elevated to an almost spiritual level. Such a justification was unlikely to impress those evicted from their villages. Rural people knew that finding a feeling of spiritual connection to the natural world was really not that hard. It didn't require the removal of people and the emptying of hundreds of acres.

Nevertheless, the history of the great estates of Britain is a history of constant attempts by landowners to justify their ownership of the land they inherited. Hiring Brown to improve the look of their estates was one way to do this.

One common way in which owners of country estates get money from their land is by hosting a festival, and Weston Park is no exception. Virgin Media's V Festival was held at Weston Park in August 2016, and boasted Justin Bieber and Rihanna as headline acts.

This brings to mind a conversation I had with C. J. Stone at the Port Eliot Festival in Cornwall in 2014. As we wandered around the grounds he told me about the time he had spent in Romania and how much he loved the Romanian landscape.

'What's strange about it,' he said, 'is that you look out and you suddenly realise there are no fences. Well, you might see a scattering of cottages with small, fenced enclosures, but beyond those, in the wider landscape, you expect to see fences and they're just not there. You look out and see maybe a valley, with drifting wood smoke and some small barns, and a few of those characteristic Romanian haystacks dotted about, the ones that look like witches' bonnets. But the landscape isn't owned, there's no one claiming it's their property.

'It's genuinely wild. There are bears and wolves in the woods and things. And it's hard to explain, but when you've lived all your life in a place like England, that's shocking. It's as if the landscape owns the people and the creatures in it, rather than being owned by them. Once you've looked at the land through those eyes, you can no longer take the notion of a landscape as someone's property seriously. Really it's vanity to claim that land is your personal property. In a few hundred years you'll be forgotten and the land will have shrugged you off as if nothing has happened.

'If you look at words like possession, belonging, occupation, words like that, they're all curious words. Land is occupied when a foreign army takes it, but a person is occupied when they work. So if someone is farming land or planting seeds or cultivating an orchard, we say they are occupied by the land. We occupy the land, and the land occupies us. It's the same word, but the meaning is very different. Saying the land belongs to you is very different to belonging to the land, and possessing the land is very different to the land possessing you. When we use those words to claim ownership of the landscape they remove us from it, but when we use them to talk about our relationship with that place, making no claim of ownership, then the same words describe something much more meaningful.'

The festival Chris and I were exploring was an example of what the comedian Robin Ince calls 'the Waitrose Festivals'. These are increasingly common events targeted at a more financially comfortable audience than festivals of previous years. Where you might expect to find burger vans, this festival had a Fortnum and Mason stall, for example. It had all the trappings of British festivals, from healing fields to yurts, but it also had a stall that sold golliwogs. I found this very disorientating.

What made this evolution in festivals so striking was the talk that Chris gave there. He had spoken about the history of the free-festivals movement in Britain in the 1970s, and how this had developed into the thriving festival scene up and down the country we have today. He told the history of the pioneers of these festivals – people like Bill Dwyer, Phil Russell and Andrew Kerr – who had all been driven by a spiritual vision.

The commercial direction that festivals have evolved in would have horrified these pioneers. And yet there were thousands of people of all ages at this festival, all enjoying the beautiful landscaped grounds on a glorious summer long weekend. It was hard to be cynical about this when so many people were clearly having such a good time. The role of the counterculture, perhaps, is to be a form of research and development department for the wider culture. Many of its experiments fail, yet it constantly produces new ideas which enrich generations to come. When the products of the counterculture are co-opted by the mainstream, as the best ones always are, it just shrugs and continues to experiment.

Chris had explained how the festival pioneers were influenced by men like Gerald Winstanley. Winstanley was a founder of a group known as the Diggers, or the True Levellers, who were active in the turmoil after the English Civil War. The Diggers occupied and planted crops on unused common land that had been enclosed by landowners. They shared possessions and did not recognise the authority of the nobility.

'When you look at men like Bill Dwyer, Phil Russell and Andrew Kerr,' Chris had said, 'what drove them was absolutely the exact same thinking you find in Winstanley. It was the same sense of insisting that land is common land, and that the coming together of people in the landscape was a necessary consciousness-raising event. Those first festivals were all driven by a spiritual mandate which declared that we were not just dispossessed consumers, but that our lives had meaning and we belonged here in the land. It was about confronting landowners and saying, I don't care what the law says, that landscape is not your possession and deep down in your heart you know this to be true.

'The political class don't know how to react to things like that. When Winstanley met with the lords, he refused to remove his hat and show deference, because he did not believe they were his superiors. He called them his "fellow creatures", like he called everybody else. He told them that their ancestors took their land by murder and theft, and that although they did not themselves kill, by benefiting from the sin they had taken the sin onto themselves, and that they would pass it on to their children unless they admitted the land was common. What could they say to that?'

*

Bosworth Field and Weston Park, the battlefield and the estate, are always linked in Britain. When you follow claims of land ownership back through history, you find they are all based on conquest.

The island of Great Britain consists of 52 million acres of land emerging from the Atlantic. William the Bastard of Normandy wanted all of those 52 million acres for himself, so he killed anyone who stood in his way. After he defeated King Harold near Hastings in 1066 and gained the more impressive title of William the Conqueror, he granted estates of this land to his Norman supporters. They used this land as a source of wealth and power, by extracting rent from tenants under the feudal system.

Weston Park dates back to Norman times. The land is mentioned in the Domesday Book of 1086, and it was recorded as being in the possession of the de Weston family in 1150. Since then it has been passed down along a series of complicated family trees until it reached Richard Bridgeman, the seventh earl of Bradford, who gifted the estate to the nation in 1986 under the stewardship of the Weston Park

Weston Hall

Foundation. Bridgeman later ran for political office, unsuccessfully, as a UKIP candidate.

The story of Weston Park's ownership is far from unusual. Despite huge changes in land use over the twentieth century, Britain still has the most concentrated land ownership in Europe. A third of the UK is owned by 1,200 aristocrats and their families. Thirty-six thousand people, or 0.6 per cent of the population, own half of the rural land in England. Despite the widely held belief that Britain is 'full' and that it is in danger of being 'concreted over', only 6 per cent of the UK's land use is classed as urban, with 94 per cent rural.

Land ownership in Britain remains a remarkably murky business. The Land Registry Act of 1925 tasked the Land Registry with producing a record of who owns what, but as of July 2012 it had only managed to register ownership of 80 per cent of England and Wales. We have no way of knowing who owns the remaining 20 per cent. Registration is only compulsory when land and properties are sold, and the missing land has not technically changed ownership over the past century. It is tied up in complicated trusts that allow ownership to remain in families over generations without troubling the taxman. An example of this occurred after the death of Gerald Grosvenor, the sixth Duke of Westminster, in August 2016. Grosvenor was the UK's third-richest man and one of the country's largest landowners. His title and the bulk of his £9-billion wealth passed to his 25-year-old son Hugh in the form of a trust that was not liable for inheritance tax. Hugh received the untaxed inheritance instead of his older siblings, incidentally, because his older siblings were female.

The trust is an example of how the Grosvenor family have often been skilled at avoiding tax. When the fourth duke, Colonel Gerald Hugh Grosvenor, died in 1967, his family convinced the taxman that his estate should not be taxed on the grounds that the duke died of wounds he received on active service in the Second World War. In this they must have been remarkably persuasive, given that the duke lived for another twenty-two years after the war and eventually died of cancer.

Land ownership can bring large subsidies from the European Union's Common Agricultural Policy. The Common Agricultural Policy, which accounts for around 40 per cent of all EU spending, is intended to support food production, but you do not need to produce food in order to receive it. You just need to own land that is in a condition where it could be farmed. The more land you own, the more money you receive. Because of this, Russian oligarchs, Saudi princes and Wall Street bankers have all bought European land, and the secretive nature of British land ownership makes it very attractive to overseas investors attempting to hide assets. Rural acres are now a better investment than property in Mayfair, with the price of prime arable land rising by 277 per cent in the decade to 2014, compared to a 127 per cent increase in the price of prime London property over the same period.

Land is a finite resource, and demand outstrips supply. In the 1970s about 500,000 acres per year were put up for sale, but that figure is now down to about 100,000–150,000 acres. For young farmers, this has made establishing their own farms prohibitively expensive, to the extent that the average age of UK farmers is now estimated to be well over sixty. Land speculation means that builders can sometimes make more money by sitting on land rather than building homes on it, which is one of the reasons behind our current housing crisis. Wherever you look, the laws surrounding our land seem in need of a major overhaul. To give one troubling example, 57 per cent of Grade 1 agricultural land lies on flood plains and is at risk from climate change. That we can't even say who owns some of this presents difficulties in effective planning.

Given the power of the landed gentry, political attempts to reform land laws have been few and far between. The post-war Labour government, which built the NHS and the modern welfare state, originally intended to nationalise the land but was ultimately unable to do so.

Instead, it produced the Town and Country Planning Act of 1947. This was quietly whittled away by the 2010–15 coalition government.

The most successful attempt at land reform was the 1910 'People's Budget' of David Lloyd George. Lloyd George famously asked, 'Who made 10,000 people owners of the land and the rest of us trespassers in the land of our birth?' It's a question that brings to mind the French novelist Honoré de Balzac, who said that 'The secret of great fortunes without apparent cause is a crime forgotten, for it was properly done.' Balzac's words are more famously known in the simplified form they take as the epigraph to Mario Puzo's novel *The Godfather*: 'Behind every great fortune there is a crime.' Land ownership in Britain always traces back to death on a battlefield and the taking of land by force. This was the reason for the Digger Gerald Winstanley's belief that landowners took the sin of the land's original theft onto themselves when they benefited from the land, and that they passed on that sin when they passed land to their children. As he put it, 'The buying and selling of land, and the fruits on it, one to another, is the cursed thing.'

You do not need to go as far as Winstanley, and believe in the transference of sin, to feel that Lloyd George's question is still a pertinent one. Nor do you have to be as radical as the post-war Labour Party, who wished to nationalise the land. There is a simple solution to the problem, which does not require anything as radical as rescinding property rights. It's called a Land Value Tax. What is particularly interesting about this solution is that you never hear anyone talking about it.

Many places in the world use variations on land-value taxation, including Australia and Denmark. It has been shown to work well, in that it makes the land market more stable and efficient. It is less bureaucratic and it is one of the hardest taxes to avoid, because you can't hide land. Perhaps more importantly, it is generally seen as fair and has broad popular support among voters. Of course, as with all laws and taxes, there will be winners and losers, but I doubt there is a law that would have more winners and fewer losers than British land reform.

It works like this: those who own land pay a yearly tax, which is based on the amount of land they own and not how it is developed. That fee is based on the local market price of land, which would encourage economic growth and land use in the north, where land is cheaper. The idea is to prevent people hoarding land, as something to pass down to as yet unborn ancestors, and instead make it available for those who have need of it now, such as young farmers or entrepreneurs. A Land Value Tax would replace other taxes, such as income or inheritance, rather than being an additional tax. It would be eased in, small at first, but it could ultimately become a significant source of government income.

A Land Value Tax turns land into something you can use and develop, for a yearly fee, rather than a speculative asset to be hoarded. But I think its greatest value is psychological. A Land Value Tax erodes the belief that someone owns the land and reminds us all that we are only using it. Our country should support us all, rather than exclude us. It should be something that occupies us, rather than which we occupy. The immaterial world of geographic identity, as we have seen, has roots that sink down into the physical island itself, but the deep historic injustice that keeps us excluded from the land prevents us from being nourished by these roots. Hundreds of years have passed, and yet that inequality still remains a fracture in our noosphere. The political arguments for a Land Value Tax naturally centre on practical measures like helping new farmers and easing our housing crisis, but it would also help heal the rift between the noosphere and the geosphere.

Looking at our largest landowners, such as the new young Duke of Westminster, the Duke of Buccleuch or Prince Charles, I cannot honestly say that I believe they 'own' the land they claim in any meaningful way, except legally. I am sure that deep down they recognise this too. They are still unable to provide a good answer to David Lloyd George's hundred-year-old question, 'Who made 10,000 people owners of the land and the rest of us trespassers in the land of our birth?' That doubt cannot be a healthy thing to carry.

The need for land reform is recognised in Scotland, where it is a current political issue. As the First Minister, Nicola Sturgeon, told the Scottish Parliament in November 2014, 'Scotland's land must be an asset that benefits the many, not the few.' But south of the border, the subject remains absent from the national conversation.

Could this be about to change? The political power of French farmers means that reform of the Common Agricultural Policy is unlikely but, by leaving the European Union, the UK is leaving that policy behind. Farmers are still going to need subsidising, but it will be difficult to justify creating a new system that also pays people to own land rather than one that pays them to produce food. Taking advantage of 'European money' is viewed differently to taking money directly from the British taxpayer, even if ultimately they are the same thing. Paul Dacre, the editor of the *Daily Mail*, for example, received £460,000 from the EU between 2011 and 2016 for his ownership of a Scottish grouse-shooting and fishing estate, plus a second estate in Sussex. His readers may turn a blind eye to exploiting European money, but they do not take kindly to those who 'scrounge' from the British taxpayer.

The Common Agricultural Policy was almost entirely absent from media coverage of the EU referendum. This is not surprising. The few who benefit from our land laws have a disproportionate voice in politics and media. Yet one striking thing about a Land Value Tax is that, as a policy, it is possible to imagine it being proposed by any of our main political parties, be that UKIP, the Greens, Labour, the Liberal Democrats or the Theresa May-era Conservatives. It is a policy that will become politically coloured by the first party to properly promote it. When a new system to replace European farming subsidies is debated, the subject of land reform and a Land Value Tax may finally be exposed to light.

Many who campaigned to leave the European Union did so because they wanted to 'take their country back'. There is one perspective from which that slogan becomes meaningful and one way that it could be achieved. A hundred years after Lloyd George's question, perhaps there is now a small chance that we will finally get an answer.

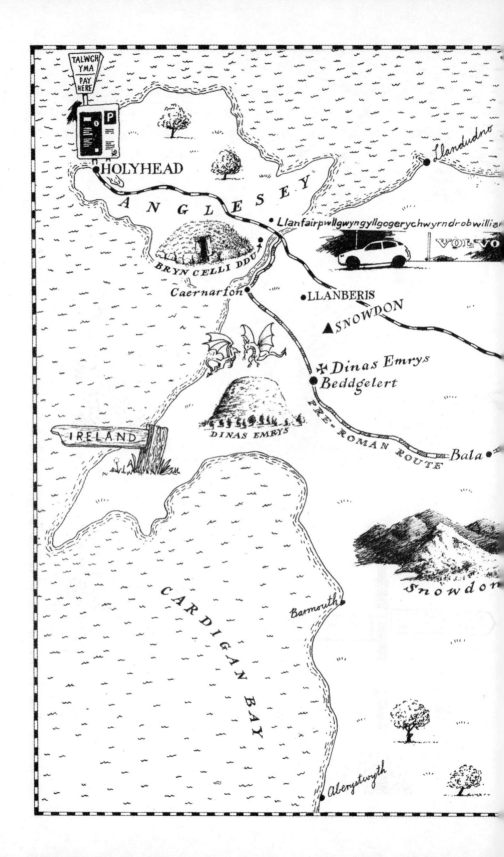

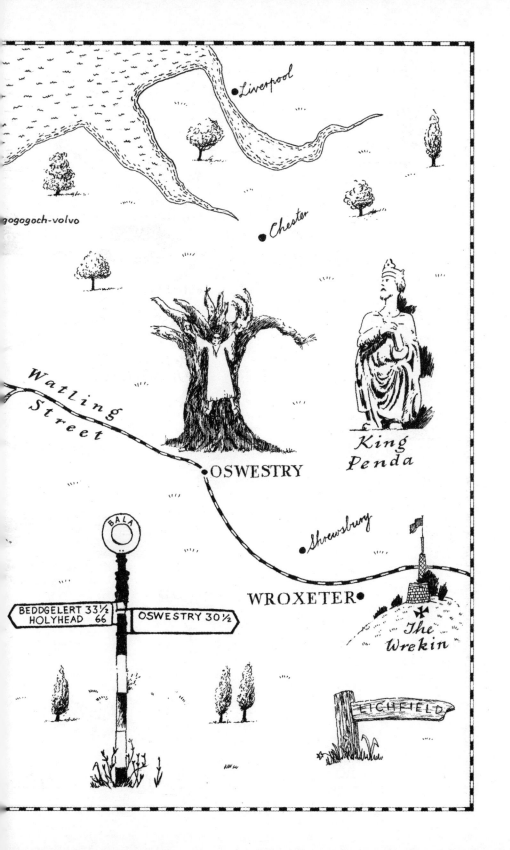

gogogoch-volvo

• Liverpool

• Chester

Watling Street

OSWESTRY

King Penda

• Shrewsbury

WROXETER •

The Wrekin

BALA

BEDDGELERT 33½
HOLYHEAD 66

OSWESTRY 30½

LICHFIELD

13.

WROXETER TO SNOWDONIA
All borderland, no borders

Where does this road take us? According to some descriptions of Watling Street, I am now heading towards its end.

If you go west from Weston Park along ever-straight Watling Street, there are moments when the ground falls away and an unnatural-looking hill stands directly ahead in the distance. It looms up as if from nothing, a single lonely hill rather than a peak in a mountain range like a northern Glastonbury Tor. It is called the Wrekin, and when you drive towards it, it looks for all the world like the intended destination of Watling Street.

The associations that have attached themselves to the Wrekin have none of the other-worldly romance of Glastonbury Tor. The Labour leader, Jeremy Corbyn, climbed the hill when he was a member of the Wrekin Young Socialists, for example, in order to plant the red flag on the top on May Day. The comedian Stewart Lee included a reference in one of his routines to orienteering around the Wrekin with members of the grindcore band Napalm Death. It is mentioned in passing in the Half-Man Half-Biscuit song 'Rod Hull Is Alive – Why?' (1987). These associations may seem slim pickings compared to the Arthurian and Christian tales attached to Glastonbury Tor, but they tell us that the Wrekin looms large in the imaginations of the local young. It just shrugs off their attempts to nail meaning to it.

But the road is not heading to the Wrekin. It is heading just beyond it to Viroconium Cornoviorum, which was at one point the fourth-largest town in Roman Britain. It is now a collection of ruins near the Shropshire village of Wroxeter. Viroconium is said to translate as 'place of the werewolves', which perhaps gives an indication of how the Roman army saw the Celtic Cornovii tribe who originally lived here. Watling Street turns southwards to enter Viroconium and runs through the centre of the town. From here a path leads to an important ford over the River Severn, which is the reason why the Romans built here.

A visitor centre stands by the ruins now. Visitors can explore a selection of ruins, including a large wall from an impressive bath house, as well as a Roman villa recently built using traditional tools and materials. There is an audioguide tour that mentions Watling Street, now a narrow road to Wroxeter running through the ruins, and explains how this nondescript road is the end of an immense ancient route that runs all the way to Rome itself.

Wroxeter Roman Villa

Accounts are contradictory about the route of Watling Street from this point. Many take the safe option of simply saying that it ends here. But now that I am here, the idea that this is the end of Watling Street doesn't make sense. We have come a long way to stop at a ford in the river. You travel to a ford in order to cross it. You don't just stop on one side. The original road, surely, must have continued.

The earliest English description of the route, by the medieval St Albans monk Matthew Paris, claimed that the road from here turned north and ran to Chester. This pleased me personally because I grew up just ten miles from Chester, on the other side of the England/Wales border, and I have many happy memories of hanging out there in my pre-responsibility teenage years. But now that I am at Viroconium, I begin to question this abrupt turn north. I look to the horizon, and at the mountains in front of me. It seems wrong to travel to a ford and not cross it. And it makes little sense to ford the Severn if you intend to travel north.

The road existed before the Romans paved it, and our best description of its original Celtic route is the *Itinerary of Antoninus*, which was written by an officer of the imperial court around 150 CE. The *Itinerary* says that the road split in two directions after the River Severn, one of which went to Chester. This has been used to support the argument that the Roman road to Chester is part of the original route. But the *Itinerary of Antoninus* also makes clear that the ancient route split in west Wales, rather than Viroconium, and this route is unrelated to the Roman Chester road. The original road, if you look past the Roman complications, did the obvious thing. It crossed the ford and continued on across North Wales to the Druid heartland of Anglesey.

The route described in the *Itinerary of Antoninus* goes to Anglesey via Bala, Beddgelert and Caernarfon. This sounds about as scenic a journey as you will find on this island, although it is not one that bears much relation to the modern road network. The modern A5 runs roughly parallel with this route, but usually a little to the north.

This was originally the route of one of the great engineering feats of the nineteenth century, Thomas Telford's Trans-British Highway, which was designed to speed up travel between Dublin and London, particularly for Irish MPs.

The journey across North Wales had previously been perilous, with sections described as 'a miserable track, circuitous and craggy, full of terrible jolts, round bogs and over rocks where horses broke their legs'. Telford built terraces that allowed his new road to cling to the side of mountains. Where previously the journey had meant tackling gradients as steep as 1 in 6, Telford's new road was never steeper than 1 in 17. The journey now became practical for carriages. The present A5 still uses some of these terraces, and in many sections the new road surface was built directly on top of Telford's.

Chester will have to wait for another day. The road has other ideas. It wants us to follow it into North Wales. It wants us to go even deeper into the past.

Wales is not just the place to the west of England. Wales is also what is underneath England. It just becomes less obscured the further west you go.

There is no one point where Englishness stops and Welshness begins. Land borders are arbitrary; they exist in order to make paperwork easier. While there is a certain logic to river and coastal borders, political land borders are the historic limits of some wealthy lord's army. They are the nobility bragging about how much they own, the historic equivalent of a merchant banker's stock portfolio.

Having grown up in borderlands, I know that there is no real difference between one side of a line and the other. People may treat them differently, but that doesn't mean that they are different. Everywhere is a shifting blend of the places that surround it, and our geographic identity comes from squinting at the woozy patchwork quilt of our differing regions. Everywhere is betwixt and between. Nowhere is an island unto itself. Borders may not be real, but everywhere is borderland.

Believing in borders can play havoc with people's sense of self-worth. It is not healthy if your sense of pride is based not on what you have done, but on which side of the field you started on. A tragic example can be found in the book *Bred of Heaven*, by the *Daily Telegraph* journalist Jasper Rees. Rees is English, but he wished to connect more fully with the Welsh heritage of his grandparents. His book is an account of his attempts to become fully Welsh. His journey starts off open and positive, but slowly nationalism gets its claws in him and he ends the book standing on top of Offa's Dyke pissing onto England. The siren call of nationalism always demands an opponent in order to strengthen itself. That never ends well.

Before the A5 enters Wales, it reaches the pretty market town of Oswestry, on the unreal border between England and Wales. Oswestry was where the Northumbrian king Oswald was defeated and killed by the Mercian king Penda in 642 CE, in a doomed attempt to extend his own borders, wealth and bragging rights. Oswald was also a great promoter of Christianity and later became Saint Oswald. Penda, in contrast, was the last pagan king of the Britons. Legend has it that after Oswald was captured, Penda had him nailed to a tree in a mock crucifixion. From this we get the name Oswestry, a corruption of 'Oswald's tree'. Another version of the story claims that after Oswald was killed and dismembered, a raven carried his arm into an ash tree. This tree became associated with healing after Oswald became a Christian saint.

Penda inspired the extraordinary BBC television film *Penda's Fen*, which was directed by Alan Clarke. *Penda's Fen* was, by anyone's standards, a very weird film. It was produced by BBC Pebble Mill in Birmingham, and as such the London BBC drama department paid it little attention during its production. Left alone and free from interference, the filmmakers produced something unique, important and strange. It was like an episode of *Songs of Praise* directed by David Lynch. It was broadcast without warning on BBC One on a Thursday evening in March 1974, after the *Nine O'Clock News*, as part of the *Play for Today* series.

Penda's Fen tells the story of a sanctimonious English grammar school boy called Stephen. His father is the local vicar, and at the start of the film Stephen blindly accepts the conservative, Christian world view of his family and school. But Stephen also loves the pastoral English music of Elgar, and in particular his oratorio *The Dream of Gerontius*, a piece of music which climaxes with a vision of God. The impact of *The Dream of Gerontius* combines with Stephen's sexual awakening and reveals a world where the divine does not descend as a gift from above, but instead oozes up from the land itself.

Stephen has visions of angels and demons, and Elgar himself, before finally encountering the spirit of King Penda and receiving a blessing from the last pagan king of England. In the process, his childhood understanding of the world evaporates. Stephen discovers he is adopted, has Welsh heritage and comes to accept that he is gay. The film climaxes high on the Malvern Hills with an astonishing speech in which he raves, 'No, no! I am nothing pure, nothing pure! My race is mixed! My sex is mixed! I am woman and man, light with darkness, mixed, mixed, I am nothing special, nothing pure! I am mud and flame!'

Then the film finished. A programme presented by Ludovic Kennedy began as if nothing unusual had happened. In the days before video recorders or streaming, the programme was gone, seemingly never to be repeated or explained. To give credit to Leonard Buckley, the television reviewer of *The Times*, he immediately recognised the importance of what he had seen. 'Make no mistake,' he wrote, 'we had a major work of television last night. [Screenwriter David] Rudkin gave us something that had beauty, imagination and depth.' But many in the audience probably spent the next few days in a bit of a daze, strangely affected by what they had seen but quite unable to talk about what it actually was. It didn't help that the film was directed by the social realist Alan Clarke, who is better known for films like *Scum* (1977) and *Rita, Sue and Bob Too* (1987). Clarke's naturalistic camera grounded the visions of angels and demons in present-day England in a way that was far more troubling than anything a more fantastical director would have achieved.

The film received a sort of stunned silence, but the memory of it lingered. In the decades that followed, the question would occasionally be asked, usually late at night and after a lot of drink, 'Do you remember a weird film on the telly years ago?' A repeat on Channel Four in the 1980s was videotaped, and this tape was uploaded to a video-sharing website in the early twenty-first century. The recording rolls and distorts in places, especially towards the end, which makes watching the film an even stranger experience. Nevertheless, word spread, and in 2011 *Time Out London* declared it to be one of the 100 Best British Films. It was finally released on DVD in 2016.

The history of the film, in many ways, echoes its own plot. King Penda was forgotten in time and sunk into the ground but, being of vital spirit, he was always destined to rise and be remembered. Like the Winchester Geese, who revealed themselves to a poet raised here in Oswestry, *Penda's Fen* was not so much damned but patient, waiting to be remembered and understood.

I cross the meaningless border and head into Wales.

Just north of Beddgelert, next to the route of pre-Roman Watling Street, stands a rocky wooded hillock in the southern foothills of Mount Snowdon. It is called Dinas Emrys. At its summit are the remains of a number of Dark Ages fortresses, with a pool in the middle. This was the setting for a story about our old friend King Vortigern.

When we last met Vortigern, back in Kent, he had given the Isle of Thanet to the Jutes and in doing so had inadvertently triggered the Anglo-Saxon invasion. Many adventures followed. To give one example, he attempted to seal a peace treaty between the British and the Saxons at a meeting in a large tent on Salisbury plain. Weapons were left outside. The chieftains entered the tent and sat in a circle, with British chieftains next to Saxon chieftains. After a number of speeches, the Saxon leader Hengist gave a pre-arranged cry of '*Eu nimet saxas!*'

('Hey! Draw your swords!'), and the Saxon chiefs reached into their boots and pulled out hidden knives. They then butchered the unarmed Britons. Vortigern was taken prisoner and eventually ransomed. This event became known as the treachery of the long knives, and it was a story often used by the Celtic British as evidence of Saxon treachery.

Vortigern then moved into Wales and decided to build a fortress on Dinas Emrys. Construction began, but every morning when the workers returned to the site they found that the previous day's work had mysteriously collapsed. Confused, Vortigern consulted a magician, who informed him that the tower would only stand if he sacrificed a fatherless boy and sprinkled his blood on the walls.

Word went out to find a fatherless boy and, as luck would have it, one soon turned up. According to Geoffrey of Monmouth's *History of the Kings of Britain*, this boy was Merlin. His mother was summoned to explain his conception. She explained to the king that she had never lain with a man. She had, admittedly, been visited by a strange entity who was sometimes invisible and sometimes in the shape of a handsome young man, and things had got pretty intimate. But as for a human father, Merlin had none. This makes Merlin a member of the illustrious ranks of protagonists of world mythology without a mortal father, along with Hercules, Jesus Christ and Darth Vader.

Merlin did not want to be sacrificed to help Vortigern build his tower. Although he was still young, he dismissed the king's magicians as worthless and told Vortigern that if he dug down from the summit he would find a pool, and in the pool would be two stone jars. The contents of these jars were the cause of his tower's collapse. Workers began digging, and the pool and the jars were discovered just as he had foretold.

The jars were opened. From one flew a red dragon and from the other a white dragon. The two dragons immediately began fighting, swooping through the air and around the Welsh mountains with fire billowing from their jaws. The red dragon, Merlin told Vortigern, was the spirit of the British people, and the white dragon represented the

Anglo-Saxons he had invited into the country. These were dragons as the Chinese understand them, vital spirits rather than the hapless fall-guys and victims of various lords that the post-Norman establishment defined them as. The fight between these two dragons was the reason Vortigern's tower would never stand.

At this point Merlin, with tears in his eyes, began to utter a wild, bewildering prophecy. In *History of the Kings of Britain*, the account of this prophecy is a breathless rant that lasts for twelve pages. It is full of great stuff. Some of what Merlin prophesies seems like a safe bet: 'Men shall be drunk with wine'; 'An owl shall build her nest upon the walls of Gloucester'; 'Women shall become serpents in their gait, and all their motions shall be full of pride'; 'Pleasures shall effeminate the princes, and they shall suddenly be changed into beasts'. Other parts seem less likely: 'The River Thames shall be turned into blood. The monks shall be forced to marry'; 'The malignity of the star Saturn shall fall down in rain, and slay mankind with a crooked sickle'; 'The roots and branches will change their places, and the novelty of the thing shall pass for a miracle'. Merlin's prophecies, Geoffrey of Monmouth tells us, 'caused in all that were present an admiration at the ambiguity of his expressions'.

Vortigern asked Merlin what his future held, and Merlin told him he would soon die. According to some versions of the story, Vortigern then fled to the Llŷn Peninsula to the west and built a wooden tower. But this was burnt down with a single burning arrow by Uther Pen-dragon and his brother Ambrosius, who had tracked down Vortigern and intended to make him pay for his many sins. Uther, of course, would later be an acclaimed king and have a son named Arthur. Vortigern escaped the tower and ran across the clifftops. With his pursuers closing in, he leapt to his death onto the rocks below. The place where he is said to have died is still called Nant Gwrtheryn (Vortigern's Creek). From what we can glimpse of Vortigern from the many stories about him, his life makes *Game of Thrones* seem like a documentary.

Stories like these were once very well known. Geoffrey of Monmouth wrote *History of the Kings of Britain* around 1136 CE, and hundreds of hand-copied editions were produced. They reached all the capital cities of Europe, and Geoffrey's tales of Arthur and Merlin made a big impact on European culture. The book has been described as the first 'bestseller' of all time, apart from the Bible. But early historians gradually came to the conclusion that what Geoffrey had written was more myth than history. It would be far more acceptable to study truthful books instead, they thought, such as the Bible. In this way, our myths became neglected in favour of the myths of others.

Yet the influence of this early British mythology, of which this north-west corner of Wales has more than its fair share, is still found in surprising places. When Queen Elizabeth I wanted to follow the example of Spain and Portugal and claim Tudor dominion over parts of the New World, she needed to justify English claims to any new territories. For this, she turned to Dr John Dee, the brilliant mathematician, polymath and sorcerer who was almost certainly the inspiration for Prospero in *The Tempest*. Dee was a spy who signed his name with the code '007', a codename borrowed by Ian Fleming when he created James Bond. Dee also spoke with spirits and received the language of the angels, but that's a story for another day.

Dr Dee searched his extensive library for some way to justify the Queen's desire for North American territory, and eventually found what he needed in the Tudor dynasty's Welsh roots. Elizabeth claimed descent from King Arthur, who, Dee argued, had at some point in his glorious career conquered Iceland, Greenland and much of the north-eastern coast of North America. Dee admitted that many of the stories about Arthur were myths, but he was certain that he definitely owned America. Further justification came from the story of the Welsh prince Madoc, who left his home in Snowdonia and sailed west in the year 1170. He was never heard of again, but later stories claimed he landed in America and married a native princess.

Because Dee's justification was based on Welsh or British stories, rather than English or Anglo-Saxon ones, he did not talk about an 'English Empire'. That might have been the expected name for Tudor colonialism, especially as the union with Scotland was still many years in the future. Instead, Dr Dee coined the phrase 'British Empire'.

Hundreds of years later, this decision has come to define how much of the wider world feels about the word 'British'. To give one example, Dee's choice of words proves awkward for Ireland. Politically, Ireland is definitely not a British isle, but technically it is one of the British Isles and has been since long before words like 'England', 'Scotland' and 'Ireland' existed. This is confusing, and has made referring to these islands awkward in Irish political and diplomatic circles. The usual solution to the problem is, I think, very pleasing. In documents drawn up jointly by the Irish and British government, they simply use the words 'these islands'. It's quite a lovely solution, but one that would not have been necessary if it had not been for the deep influence of ancient Welsh myths.

Those paying attention will have noticed that in our travels we have now encountered three different and contradictory explanations as to why Ian Fleming gave James Bond the codename '007'.

At the beginning of our journey, at the White Cliffs of Dover, it was said that Fleming took the number from the 007 coach route which ran from London along Watling Street to his home on the south Kent coast. In the middle of our journey, at Bletchley Park, we heard that Fleming was in Naval Intelligence during the war and was inspired by the famous German 0075 cipher from the First World War. Here at the end of our journey, as the Tudors raid the Welsh myths, we encounter a famous Elizabethan spy who signed correspondence with the code 007.

All three explanations seem plausible. Any one of them could be true. Or possibly none of them are true. Or a combination of two or three of them could have led to the name. Or it could have been something entirely different that we don't know about.

We simply don't know. Fleming explained very clearly that he borrowed the name James Bond from an American ornithologist, but he never definitively explained where 007 came from. It's possible that he didn't know himself, that he was typing away and it just popped into his head and he liked the sound of it.

Much of history is like this. There's not always a definitive reason for why something happened or what people were thinking. When one plausible explanation is offered up, it is often assumed to be the truth, even though it may not be. But when more than one plausible explanation is available, things start to get messy.

The problem typically gets worse the further back in time you look. When you are dealing with second- and third-hand accounts written down perhaps hundreds of years after the event, allowing for bias and political prejudice, then the border between what we call history and what we call myth, like all borders, is arbitrary, or at the very least porous. Just as with the land, there are no firm borders, and everywhere is borderland.

Our best evidence suggests that Vortigern, Hereward the Wake and Dun the Outlaw all existed, even if the stories we tell about them are myth, while King Arthur, Robin Hood and King Belinus never existed, even if some of the stories we tell about them may be based distantly on fact. That is the general opinion now, but it was different in the past and it is entirely possible that it will be different in the future.

It might be tempting to dismiss all our three explanations for the name 007 and simply say we don't know where the name came from. Yet while those three explanations are not certain, they are not worthless. They give insight into the background and influences of Fleming, and reveal possible aspects of the circumstances that led to the creation of James Bond. They are nice little stories in themselves, and that has some value. They are also all we have. A foggy uncertainty is better than an empty void.

Geoffrey of Monmouth's *History of the Kings of Britain* is myth, and for that reason those stories are largely unknown. We are not told, as children, about Brutus defeating the giants of Albion and founding

London, or about the red dragon and the white dragon that were hidden in the pool underneath Dinas Emrys. But these first stories are the roots of modern Britain. They are the earliest accounts of what made us who we are, and there may be a glimmer of truth in there somewhere, even if we can't put our finger on it.

In Geoffrey's account of the events at Dinas Emrys, the two dragons disappear off over the mountains, fighting as they go. They are last seen flying over the mountain lake Llyn Dinas, at which point they disappear from sight. As to what happened to them after that, the old books are silent.

This seems a disappointing way to leave our two air-bound spirits. If we leave them for ever at each other's throats, our myths offer only an unresolved division of the people on this island. Their story needs a conclusion or a continuation, I decide, because the dragons must have gone somewhere. I decide to follow them and take the road alongside Llyn Dinas, then up past Llanberis, as I head to Anglesey.

It's hard to concentrate on this drunken rolling road, because the landscape is mesmerising. It is gnarled, crumpled and mysterious, like the Scottish Highlands' wizened grandmother. After driving for an unknown amount of time I have to pull over and stop the car, because I need to stare. Only one place in Britain was included in Lonely Planet's top 10 Best in Travel 2017 list of top regions, and it does not surprise me that it was North Wales. It is often remarked upon that houses in North Wales are frequently squat and ugly, but when the landscape looks like this there is no point competing on appearance. It is better to give up on visual aesthetics and concentrate on becoming a land of song instead.

The notion strikes me that if I scramble up the mountain a little, I will find a place where the modern world can no longer be seen or heard. I will find myself alone in a landscape indistinguishable from the one where Puck, our first Palaeolithic explorer, made the first footfalls on what would become Watling Street. I start walking, away from the car, up the mountain in front of me. It is early evening, and the light falling on the moss and gravel I scramble over is warm and golden. I look away from the sun and notice there is also a crescent moon in the sky, barely visible against the blue sky behind me. The combination of the sun and the moon together reminds me of Selene and Belinus, and the lunar and solar aspects of Watling Street. I stop climbing and sit down to take in the view. The moment my hand touches the ground all desire to continue climbing ceases. I don't need to find Puck's landscape. I am content exactly where I am.

The act of a hand touching the ground has significance in Buddhism. A demon tried to get the Buddha away from the tree under which he achieved enlightenment by claiming he had no right to be there. The Buddha responded by simply touching the ground. This small act was enough for the spirit of the earth to confirm that the Buddha was exactly where he should be. Touch the ground anywhere, and that's where you are. Sat halfway up that Welsh mountain, with the road snaking north up the valley below me, and the sun and moon both hanging in the evening sky, is exactly where I should be. In Alan Moore's view of the universe, I am always here.

Growing up in Wales, I always thought of the Welsh as being the quintessential Celtic people. The Welsh were typically small and dark, so therefore the Celts were small and dark. Of course, the Scots were quintessential Celts as well. They were tall and red-haired, so therefore Celts were tall and ginger. The Irish were also Celts, and they were small and ginger. The Gauls were as Celtic as they come, and they were tall and blonde. It took me some time to notice the flaw in all of this.

It is easy to think of the Celts as a single group of people. They spoke the Celtic group of languages. They had a very distinctive style of ornamental art, full of swirling and spiralling knot work devoid of straight lines and with very little symmetry. They had a distinctive style of fashion and wore a rigid metal ring around their necks, usually open at the front, called a torc. These details, however, are all culture, not biology. In the biosphere, there was no single type of Celtic people.

There was a whole bunch of different people all living in north-west Europe, who shared a single noosphere. Being Celtic was not the result of blood. It was the result of ideas.

A few hundred years ago, colonialists left Britain and other European countries and went forth to claim new lands. The people they encountered were very different to those back home, and it was thought that this meant they were different biologically. Humans, the colonialists believed, came in different types, or races. The idea that there were different races was very useful in justifying colonialism, because if races were different it was easy to claim that some were better than others.

Thanks to genetic science, we now know that we had this all wrong. Human DNA is essentially the same the planet over, with only minor statistical differences here and there. 'Race' is a largely meaningless term in human biology, for there is only one race: the human race. There are, of course, variations in details such as hair colour, skin colour and eye colour, and there are geographical clusters of such details, but that is not enough to define separate races. There are, admittedly, many people who have yet to grasp this, but the real source of the differences that the colonialists encountered was cultural, not biological. The real differences lay in the noosphere.

Biologically, the British are the cumulative sum of the original aboriginal British plus the Celts, Romans, Jutes, Angles, Saxons, Danes, Normans, French, Irish, Norwegians, West Indian, Indian, African, Pakistani, Polish and, now that we're living in a time of affordable long-distance flight, everywhere else on the planet. Anyone who believes they are 'pure British' will be in for a shock if they have a DNA test.

This hasn't stopped the people of this island from retaining a distinct personality. The bawdy humour first recorded as long ago as Chaucer, for example, is still alive and well in the twenty-first century. One generation after the first immigrants from the West Indies arrived in post-war Britain, their children were making music the likes of which had never been heard before anywhere in the world, from the multicultural 2 Tone punk-ska of The Specials to the proto-grime of the Ruthless Rap Assassins. But that music, to the outside world, was definitely British. If our history tells us anything it is that Britishness is cultural, not genetic. Aliens from far-off galaxies, if they settled in Ipswich, would be down the pub moaning about the weather in a generation or two. Indeed, it is noticeable that the pre-Celtic aboriginal British are all but invisible in any discussion of our identity. We are such mongrels now, and that mongrel nature is so British, that the original aboriginal Brits are paradoxically overlooked for being in some way un-British.

Like dragon-loving Japan, we are an island that absorbs things from beyond our shores and somehow makes them distinctly our own. The drinking of tea is an obvious example, as are the French words in our language or the royals from the house of Saxe-Coburg and Gotha we now call the Windsors. On the level of DNA, the British Isles contains very little evidence of the Roman and Norman invasions, but their presence is unavoidable on the level of ideas. The Anglo-Saxon invasion contributed only about 5 per cent of the English gene pool. For all that the arrival of the Anglo-Saxons changed England drastically, it was far more an invasion of culture than it was of people. As a result, the operating system of our noosphere became the flexible, adaptable English language. Perhaps this is why we are now so good at absorbing new things.

All this is healthy, because a culture must keep evolving if it is to remain a vivid and living thing. As a physicist would say, entropy increases in a closed system. No generation wants to grow up in a culture frozen before their time into a heritage-park version of how their country once was. The noosphere must be fed with a constant supply of new ideas, and these can be grown internally, absorbed from the wider world, or be a mixture of both. The country does not adopt every idea that arrives on these shores, of course. Some things, like straight Roman roads and rococo gardens, will not flourish here. And nor does every cultural idea want to be absorbed. Some things will fight against the process and try to remain true to their place of origin. This can be painful, as it only drags out the inevitable.

Yet it is also true that a factor in the EU referendum was a rejection of those seen as foreign. How large a factor is a matter for debate, but there were many who voted to prevent immigration into the UK, and even some who voted leave in the belief that this would mean that 'foreigners' would be deported. Boris Johnson, the public face of the official 'leave' campaign, often seems to view the world through nineteenth-century-colonial eyes. As editor of the *Spectator*, he published articles claiming that blacks had lower IQs than other races, and the less said about the column he wrote for the *Telegraph*, in which he talked about 'flag-waving piccaninnies' and tribal warriors with 'watermelon smiles', the better. His comments during the EU campaign about President Obama's Kenyan ancestry were widely condemned as dog-whistle racism. Johnson does not see himself as racist, of course. He is a reminder that teaching children to judge people by the wealth of their parents can bring a darkness to our sense of geographic identity. When that idea is applied by the privileged to large groups of people, the results can get ugly.

Racism is a real problem in this island as it is elsewhere, both structurally and in individuals. But anyone who lives on this island, regardless of their geographic ancestry, can follow the example of the Buddha and place their hand on the ground and know that they are where they are supposed to be. The story of Britain is the story of the people on this island. It follows that if someone is on this island, then they are part of that story. That applies to everyone, from the lowly Winchester Geese who the church wouldn't even bury, to those who are born to inherit large country estates. It applies to those who embrace change and those who find it difficult. It applies equally to those who voted to leave and to those who voted to remain. They are all expressions of the island's story.

The difference between leave and remain voters is much discussed. It is currently the division that most preoccupies those worried about the state of Britain. But the line between leave and remain voters is only one of the lines that can be drawn through our population. Just as you can divide the British into leave voters and remain voters, you can divide them into the wealthy and the disadvantaged; into traditionalists and progressives; into the South and the rest; into the Scots and the English; into the English and the Welsh; into the securely employed and the insecure; into the young and the old; into owners and renters; into the healthy and the sick; into the well-educated and the less educated; into the connected and the unconnected; into the Celts and the Anglo-Saxons; into the immigrants and the native-born; into creators and critics; into men and women; into able-bodied and people of disability; into gay and straight; into left-wing and right-wing; into carers and non-carers; into Yorkshire and non-Yorkshire.

We can keep going. You can divide the British into privately educated and state-educated; into voters and non-voters; into urban and rural; into introverts and extroverts; into those who recycle and those who don't; into Christian and non-Christian; into the bilingual and the monolingual; into those who read books and those who don't; into the Welsh and the *Cymraeg*; into vegetarians and meat eaters; into rugby union and rugby league; into those who connect to Saint George and those who don't; into smokers and non-smokers; into the famous and the crowd; into the well dressed and the casual; into the aristocracy and the commoners; into those on social media and those who aren't; into those who follow political authority and those who follow spiritual authority; into coders and those who can't code; into drivers and non-drivers; into those who live by the coast and those who live inland; into those with mental-health difficulties and those without; into *Daily Mail* readers and non-*Daily Mail* readers; into the politically active and the non-politically active; into those on benefits and those who aren't on benefits; into atheists and believers; into BBC viewers and ITV viewers; into the active and the sedentary; into the patriotic and the non-patriotic; into the metropolitan elite and the rest of the country; into white-collar workers and blue-collar workers;

into the retired and the workforce; into soldiers and civilians; into those who feel European and those who don't; into criminals and the law-abiding; into those who feel certain and those who doubt; into the red dragon and the white dragon; into us and into them.

We can keep going, but if the point isn't clear by now it never will be. Yes, you can draw a line across a country and divide it. But not just one line. Keep going and, if you have sufficient imagination, you need never stop. Line after line, divide after divide, split after split: if you do this for long enough you realise that the country isn't being fractured by all those lines you cast on it. It remains whole but is just being perceived from different perspectives. Individuals that you define as being different under one divide are defined as being the same under another. So, are those people the same or different? The answer you choose reveals more about what you are focusing on than about the people themselves.

All those lines are mental projections. They are useful tools to help grasp particular problems, but they are ultimately arbitrary and im-material. The true population is chaotic, an ever-varied soup of differ-ence and similarity. There is no us and them, there is just everything and the helpful shortcuts we use to try and make sense of everything. To divide them into two is only possible if you simplify them massively, and strip out all their noise and colour. It can be useful to do this, of course, but it's not good to confuse the resulting model with the real world itself. To do so is to miss out on the big picture.

The big picture is immense. You can't look at it for too long because it's just too much. Sometimes you need to make a simpler model of the island and its culture just to get anything done. You need to mark out some borders, and throw down some dividing lines, and dismiss huge chunks as 'them'. But you also need to remember this is what you are doing, and that the big picture doesn't go away when you intellectually abstract it out of view. Every now and again it is necessary to look up from our models and abstractions and prejudices and just lie back and stare at the blazing giant sun of the Albion noosphere.

The Albion noosphere is practically infinite. You do not need to define yourself by the parts imposed on you. You do not need to start your history with 1066, or take people who judge others by their parents' wealth seriously. Some people, such as Steve Moore and Alan Moore, stay in their place of birth and find that soil rich enough to sustain them. I have moved, but I can make sense of the places I have lived by abstracting them into the journey I've just taken you on. You don't need to adopt this story, or any other narrative that suits others. If you dig, you will find a story meaningful enough to sustain you. That is guaranteed, for such is the richness of the soil.

We found three explanations for Ian Fleming's use of the codename 007 when we dug in the Albion noosphere. We could hold that up as proof that we are excavating fertile territory, but remember that we found those three things when we were only looking along one road. Who knows what else is out there? And, rather neatly, we found those things at the very start, the end and the middle of our journey, spaced out perfectly so those multiple explanations wouldn't be too obvious. What are the chances of that? It does feel almost as if whatever you need to find, you will find.

Brexit, the ending of our political union with the European Union, is happening. I don't know what the impact of that will be, but it's possible we will think less about the outside world and become more of an inward-looking island. If so, what will we see when we look inside? If we just see what is imposed on us then our sense of division will not heal. But if we remember to lie back occasionally and look up at the full extent of the living Albion noosphere, with all our fiction and our history, our science and our magic, our crimes and our kindness, then I don't think a period of introspection will do us any harm. We may see the past alive in the present. We may all touch the ground and know we are where we are supposed to be. We may even be able to produce an answer to Lloyd George's question. The noosphere rests on the biosphere, which rests on the geosphere. This island is damp and strange, but there are rich lives to be lived here.

Sitting on this mountain, I imagine the red and white dragons flying in from the south, fighting as they tumble through the skies. I imagine them circling above, their cries harsh and powerful, the heat from their fire singeing the grass and moss. They continue to circle, getting closer all the time, and then their cries stop. I wonder for a moment what they are doing. The white dragon is curled up in the centre, with the red dragon going around it. There they stop, hanging in the sky above me. I realise they are re-creating the Tudor rose, where neither of the sides of the divide are wiped away or held above the other. Instead, they transcend their division. They both understand they are part of something larger. Like the twin personalities in a tulpamancer's head, the division is not necessarily an illness. It may be a necessary step towards a deeper understanding.

I stare up at this Tudor rose of dragons, suspended between the crescent moon and the setting sun, for I don't know how long.

'That would make a great tattoo,' I think.

We are nearly at journey's end. The last stop is Anglesey.

14.

ANGLESEY

Tyrd, troedia donnau amser

I am at the car park at the end of the road.

The Blackbridge pay-and-display car park (£3.50 for twelve hours) is at the very end of the A5, just before it enters Holyhead port in the north-west of Anglesey. It is a triangular slab of grey asphalt that runs alongside the end of the railway line, with a red-brick bridge running

Car park at the end of the road

along its southern end. The road over that bridge is called London Road, a name both accurate and an indication that, around a port, the focus is on the far distance. The pubs around here, for example, have names like the Dublin Packet, Holland Inn, the Edinburgh Castle and the Boston.

Is this the end of my journey? I look at the weather-beaten buildings, the signage that promises a new Aldi superstore is coming soon and the drinkers smoking outside the pubs, and something seems to be missing. I'm not sure exactly what I was looking to find at the end of my travels, but I don't think I'm seeing it.

Exploring further, I notice some Welsh words cut into the metal edges of a raised walkway at the other side of the railway station: *Tyrd, troedia donnau amser* ('Come, tread the tides of time'). After travelling all this way along Watling Street, from the port of Dover to the port of Holyhead, it is hard not to see 'Come, tread the tides of time' as an invitation to embark on that journey again, but this time in the opposite direction. I wonder if the people of Dover could be persuaded to erect a sign with those very words outside their port. *Tyrd, troedia donnau amser*; I can't help but think that it is trying to send me back.

The road across Anglesey to the Blackbridge pay-and-display car park was the quietest part of my journey. A number of Thomas Telford's hexagonal toll booths still stand along the road, showing that the road had once been a major route for freight. The old toll prices are visible on a sign outside the Llanfair toll gate: four pence for 'every horse, mule or other cattle drawing any coach or other carriage with springs', for example, and double tolls for wheels with 'tyres fastened with nails projecting and not countersunk'. But in 2001 a modern dual carriageway was built alongside the route, and keeps the freight lorries travelling to and from Holyhead port away from the small villages along the A5. As a result, there were traffic-free periods with no living soul in sight. At one point my solitude ended when I saw a middle-aged woman on a mobility scooter coming towards me on this long, isolated, pavement-free stretch of the A5, trundling along at perhaps

5 mph. It was like a Welsh version of the David Lynch film *A Straight Story*. I admired her spirit, although I feared for her battery.

If only I could shake the feeling that I've missed something. Where is the deep past of Anglesey, as glimpsed in the writings of the Roman historian Tacitus? This was a sacred island that witnessed the last stand of the British Druids, before they were slaughtered by the Romans during the time of Boudica's rebellion. Tacitus documented the fear Roman troops felt at the sight of the wild pagan horde, when the Roman and native British armies faced each other across the Menai Strait: 'The enemy lined the shore: a dense host of armed men, interspersed with women clothed in black, like the Furies, with their hair hanging down, and holding torches in their hands. Round these were the Druids, uttering dire curses, and stretching out their hands towards heaven. These strange sights terrified our soldiers. They stood motionless, as if paralysed, offering their bodies to the blows.' Anglesey is a very different place now, even if a few pubs in Bangor still match Tacitus' description. If you were raised to unconsciously judge people by the wealth of their parents, you are likely to identify with the Romans when you hear that story, but it was the wild pagan horde who were our ancestors.

The Druids had an oral tradition and left no written record of their acts or beliefs. They didn't build churches and held their ceremonies out of doors in sacred groves deep within thick British forests. This struck Roman and Greek writers as deeply unusual, and not a little frightening. But the Druids are long gone, and their groves are no more. Anglesey is largely treeless now. The road has led us here for a reason, but that reason seems lost as the Winchester Geese before the coming of the Jubilee Line extension.

But then, a thought hits me. A grove is a natural clearing in the woods, but I recall seeing the word used in a different context. I pull out a map of Anglesey and search for a site called Bryn Celli Ddu. This name translates as the mound, or house, of the dark grove. This is an underground Neolithic burial chamber, many thousands of years old, built by the pre-Celtic aboriginal Brits. I had begun this journey by going underground into the White Cliffs, why not end it by taking a passage underground into this 'dark grove'?

I find Bryn Celli Ddu on the map, and smile when I realise how close to the A5 it is. It is a short drive from the toll house I passed earlier at Llanfairpwllgwyngyllgogerychwyrndrobwllllantysiliogogogoch. I am a great admirer of the place name Llanfairpwllgwyngyllgogerychwyrndrobwllllantysiliogogogoch, as you can probably tell. Being able to pronounce it is about the only achievement of mine which impresses my kids. The name was extended into the longest place name in Britain in the 1860s as a gimmick, but this mischief does not damage its charm. It still speaks of a culture very different to that which named settlements things like Bath, York or Leeds. Personally I'm particularly fond of the sign outside the local car dealership, which reads Llanfairpwllgwyngyllgogerychwyrndrobwllllantysiliogogogoch Volvo.

I'm going to double back. The Druids may have been wiped off the map, but there are older roots under the ground.

The walk to Bryn Celli Ddu is idyllic. It lies within farmland perhaps half a kilometre from the road. The hedgerows along the path are a riot of variety. There are hawthorn, holly, blueberries, redcurrants, thistle, blackberries, raspberries, thorn and bramble. There are fruit and leaf and flower and a slow-running stream alongside, with cattle and horses in the neighbouring fields.

The monument itself is an artificial mound about three metres tall. It was already a couple of thousand years old when the Romans arrived, and the site had been used for ritual purposes for a couple of thousand years before the monument was built. 'Ritual purposes' is, of course, the preferred historical term for purposes unknown, but which seem to be above and beyond the needs of basic human survival. 'Ritual purposes' are the foundations of our present noosphere.

The culture that built this was as unknowable and mysterious to the Druids as the Druids are to us, yet there are still connections that link us all. The chamber's entrance is aligned to sunrise on the summer solstice in the same way that the streets of Milton Keynes are. Glastonbury Festival marks the same annual event that the mound in front of me was designed to do. The people who built this chamber were born, lived, grew and died on this damp green island, exactly like the Druids did thousands of years later, and exactly like we do today. We would not be here if they hadn't. This should be blindingly obvious and hardly worth saying, but such is the extent that we identify with the Romans and Normans that it can sound surprising.

Bryn Celli Ddu

I walk around the mound to find the entrance in the north-east corner. I can see why the 'ritual purposes' of places like this are often linked to fertility. The mound looks like a pregnant belly, as if the field itself was about to give birth. This makes the narrow stone entrance appear labial, waiting to be penetrated by the rays of the sun god at the allotted time of the year. Freud would have loved it.

I step past the rocks that surround the mound like a kerb, approach the narrow stone entrance and peer into the darkness beyond. It is smaller than you would expect, and I will have to crouch low to enter. Fear washes over me, and I consider turning back. That fear seems natural at the portal to a burial chamber of such antiquity, until I suddenly realise where it comes from. That fear was engineered on Elstree sound stages, a long way back down Watling Street. Looking into this underground passage, I am expecting *Indiana Jones*-style snakes and spiders and traps that trigger rolling boulders. I am unconsciously expecting Darth Vader to emerge from the Dagobah cave in slow motion.

I lower my head and walk in.

The passage is narrow, and the ceiling is low. It is a reminder of how much smaller people were in the past. The notion that the 'little people' used to live in these islands suddenly doesn't seem so fanciful.

After a few metres the passageway opens into the central chamber, and the ceiling becomes high enough for me to be able to stand once again. I can also see. After archaeologists excavated the site in the twentieth century, they rebuilt only part of the covering mound in order to leave a hole where natural light enters the chamber. The practical side of my nature thanks them for this, while my romantic side curses them.

Even with a little sunlight filtering in, it takes my eyes a moment to adjust to the gloom. I am in a roughly circular chamber, a couple of metres across. The walls are made from rock. Some of these rocks are huge megaliths that you cannot imagine people ever being able to move, while others are smaller, intricately positioned stones of various sizes that fit tightly together. It is like a cross between a drystone wall and an igloo. Previous visitors have left offerings in here. Two apples sit on a ledge, and a sprig of rosemary has been placed in a crevice.

I am not alone.

In the centre of the chamber stands a round stone pillar, a little under six feet tall. The information board outside the monument refers to it as a 'sentinel', a conscious guard watching over the remains of the dead. They are being poetic, but it has a presence and encountering it in these circumstances does feel like meeting more than stone.

The pillar is a replica. The original is currently in a museum in Cardiff, but knowing this does not lessen the impact of finding it here. When it comes to Neolithic burial chambers, location matters. Encountering a replica down a narrow tunnel in a burial chamber in a field in Anglesey is an experience that walking past the original in a brightly lit museum display is not going to match. Like Banksy's *Kissing Coppers*, the replica in the original location retains what is lost when the original is cut away.

There is some uncertainty about what the sentinel pillar actually is. It was originally assumed to be a carved rock, but some now think it might be a fossilised tree trunk. It seems that, in certain circumstances and given enough time, solid rock and living wood can become indistinguishable. A tree trunk is a product of the biosphere, while a deliberately carved pillar is an expression of culture and hence a product of the noosphere. Perhaps the boundaries between the geosphere, biosphere and noosphere will fade into nothing, given enough time. A plant can become a rock, and a rock can become culture. Like London Stone, sometimes the material and the immaterial become inseparable, as with Jesus and the Rood.

This sentinel has been watching over these islands, perhaps, since the Albion noosphere first emerged. It has remained a constant presence throughout millennia. It represents both culture and also how culture ultimately emerges from the geosphere. I doubt I could find a single object which symbolises what I have discovered on this journey better than this half-buried pillar. To me, the sentinel is the physical embodiment of the indivisible union between the physical and immaterial halves of Albion. I know that really it's just a chunk of stone that some scientists from Cardiff left here not long ago, but I'll overlook that if you will.

Looking around, I notice that the stone walls are not the simple grey slabs I first assumed. There are different colours in them; greens, reds, blues and even white. This part of Anglesey is formed from a rock called blueschist. It is globally famous among geologists, and UNESCO has designated the entire island as a Global Geopark. Most of the blueschist in the world is less than 250 million years old, but Anglesey's is 570 million years old.

If the sentinel is a fossilised tree, it would be unthinkably old. When our ancestors found it, and erected it like a totem to watch over the remains of their loved ones, they could not have understood just how long it had waited in the ground for them. When the tree was alive, there would have been no people to see it or climb it. The years recorded in the rings of its trunk passed long before mankind entered Anglesey, or Britain, or Europe, and possibly before humans evolved in Africa. It may have been a sprightly young thing compared to the world the monument builders lived in, dominated by the mountains, the blueschist rock and the stars above. But as an object in the culture of our ancestors, the sentinel was a physical manifestation of eternity.

A culture that buried its dead is a culture that felt loss. It knew those no longer with them not as a physical presence, but as a physical ache. This monument, built over countless hours by countless hands, would protect what was precious and valuable, even if what was precious and valuable was only memory. The dead who are not forgotten are part of the living. Entering this chamber and meeting this sentinel is to enter a place put aside for the dead. It is to be reminded of eternity, and to be shown your place in it.

I lean forward and place my hands on the dirt floor. At that moment I suddenly realise I am on my knees in front of the totem; I had not noticed myself going down to the ground. With shock I realise that, for perhaps the first time in my life, I am praying. It was an unconscious gesture, unplanned and automatic. What has got hold of me? I immediately decide to blame C. J. Stone for this embarrassment. Only he could have placed the idea in my head.

Perhaps it is appropriate? Was this how the monument builders greeted the sentinel, lowering themselves in front of it in an act of worship? As I'm down here, in the mud, perhaps I should continue? I make an attempt to do so, but now that I've become aware of what I'm doing I can't take it seriously. I raise my head and look up at the pillar. It looms over me like a prehistoric blueprint for the black monolith from *2001: A Space Odyssey*. This isn't right.

I stand, rising up to the height of the pillar and then, just fractionally, over it. Our shorter ancestors looked up to this sentinel, but here in the twenty-first century we're taller now. We have grown so that we can meet this guardian of the past, this physical embodiment of both the material and the immaterial Albion, and stand eye-to-eye with it.

We face each other as equals.

Worshipping this physical embodiment of our past, lowering myself on my knees in the dirt, does not feel appropriate any more. But some gesture still seems necessary. It stands in front of me, nearly six feet tall and maybe a foot across. I make the decision to hug it.

It is the perfect size. My arms fit around it comfortably. If it was a tree, it was never climbed by people when it was alive, and it was never hugged. I rest my cheek against its cold flat face. I feel incredibly fortunate to be able to do this; to be at peace with such a perfect physical symbol of all that is immaterial; to recognise its value and to demonstrate my gratitude. We are opposite and equal, time and space, the present and the eternal, the living and the dead. And here, on this quiet autumn afternoon in a wild and remote landscape, deep inside the dark grove, we hug.

For a time, we are not separate. All is silent. Then I step back, aware of the separation that act creates, temporary as it is. I back away, a living thing. I look around the chamber one last time, aware of the moment, a resident of the present. I crawl back out through the passage, awkward and uncomfortable, and I think I hear a strange high-pitched voice singing 'going up', not unlike the theme tune to *Are You Being Served?* For some reason, that doesn't seem odd.

I emerge into the afternoon, blinking, able to feel the warmth from the sun, subtle though it is. A small blond boy in blue wellies, aged about three, is singing and running around the monument. He does the obvious and sensible thing for a child confronted with a mound – he runs to the top. His dad follows him, protectively. The boy surveys the world from his elevated position, standing on the shoulders of giants, to borrow a phrase from Newton. In the field to my left a black-and-white farm kitten is hiding in the grass, studying me, thinking it is invisible.

The Albion noosphere is not a fixed object handed down to us like a family heirloom. It is something we enact, a story we continue to create through the choices we make. It continues to evolve as we choose which parts of it to shape into our geographic identity. It is alive, and we make it so by our actions. The aim of the game is to do this well.

If you don't identify with the national myth, this is a sign that your voice is not being heard. Change your focus and listen again; it is in there somewhere.

I head back alongside the stream to the empty lane, then I walk along the middle of the road in the approximate direction of the future.

NOTES AND SOURCES

Introduction: A Milton Keynes solstice

Derek Walker's obituary appeared in the *Guardian*, Saturday, 23 May 2015, and I'm grateful to Jason Arnopp for sending me the article. The public artwork *Light Pyramid* is by Liliane Lijn.

1. The White Cliffs of Dover

In Douglas Coupland's *Shampoo Planet*, the character of Tyler expresses his fear of 'overdosing on history' in a postcard written during a visit to France on p. 95 of that novel. The concept of the noosphere was jointly developed by Pierre Teilhard de Chardin, Édouard Le Roy and Vladimir Vernadsky in the early 1920s, although it appears to be de Chardin who coined the word. The statement that British men and women are 4.3 inches taller than they were a hundred years ago is based on research by the NCD Risk Factor Collaboration network, whose paper 'A century of trends in adult human height' is online at https://elifesciences.org/content/5/e13410. The 1944 Pathé newsreel *Hellfire Corner* can be viewed on the British Pathé website at http://www.britishpathe.com/video/hellfire-corner-aka-hell-fire-corner. The photograph of Jakob Nacken

345

surrendering to Bob Roberts can be seen in a 9 June 2010 *Daily Telegraph* article, 'Tallest German surrenders to short soldier in Second World War picture'. The quote from *King Lear* is from Act 4 Scene 6.

2. Dover to Canterbury

'IT'S THE SUN WOT WON IT' was the front-page headline of the *Sun* on 11 April 1992. The estimate of 150 million to 200 million climate refugees can be found on p. 77 of *The Stern Review: The Economics of Climate Change* (Nicholas Stern, 2006).

The account of the evolution of the English language is based largely on Joseph Piercy's book *The Story of English*. Speculation as to a Germanic influence on the Brittonic language in southern parts of the island can be found in Stephen Oppenheimer's book, *The Origins of the British*. For more on the neurological impact on Greek brains of their two words for blue, see 'Cognitive representation of colour in bilinguals: The case of Greek blues', by Panos Athanasopoulos, pp. 83–95 of the January 2009 edition of *Bilingualism: Language and Cognition*, Volume 12, Issue 1. For more about experiments on the Himba tribe, and the late arrival of a concept of blue in ancient languages, see Kevin Loria's 28 February 2015 article in *Business Insider Australia*, 'No one could see the colour blue until modern times'. That the English language even has a verb for tricking people into watching a Rick Astley video ('rickroll') has been pointed out by the I'm Terrible With Names tumblr at http://shitsuren-chama.tumblr.com/post/146748301996/what-people-think-it-means-when-we-say-language.

The quote about how driving along the M1 was like 'riding in a train without a book [...] safe, comfortable, relaxing and a dreadful bore', comes from p. 33 of *On Roads* by Joe Moran.

3. Canterbury

King Henry's exclamation of 'What miserable drones and traitors have I nurtured and promoted in my household who let their lord be treated with such shameful contempt by a low-born clerk?' is quoted from p. 78

of Dan Jones's *The Plantagenets*. The description of Henry approaching Becket's shrine with 'streaming tears, groans and sighs' comes from the same book (p. 89).

For an account of the Blair government 'not doing God' see Colin Brown's article in the 4 May 2003 *Daily Telegraph*; Campbell interrupted Blair as he spoke of his faith: 'We don't do God.' The ex-Archbishop of Canterbury Rowan Williams is quoted as describing Britain as a 'post-Christian country' in the 26 April 2014 *Daily Telegraph* article: 'Former Archbishop of Canterbury: We are a post-Christian nation', written by Tim Ross, Cole Moreton and James Kirkup. For more information on the decline in identifying as Christian as recorded in the national census, see the article 'Religion in England and Wales 2011' on the Office of National Statistics website, at http://www.ons.gov. uk/peoplepopulationandcommunity/culturalidentity/religion/articles/ religioninenglandandwales2011/2012-12-11. The 10 November 2016 *Daily Mail* Comment, 'America's lesson for all complacent elites', which dismisses the Archbishop of Canterbury as 'a luvvie', did not give a byline to its author, although the *Guardian*'s Roy Greenslade claims it was written by Dominic Sandbrook.

4. Canterbury to London

The description of Miss Havisham's house comes from Chapter 8 of *Great Expectations*. Details of Rod Hull's life are taken from his obituary by Pierre Perrone in the 19 March 1999 edition of the *Independent*. The Debbie Davidson quotation about her father is taken from the 2003 Channel Four documentary *Rod Hull: A Bird in the Hand*, produced by Wark Clements.

Pádraig Ó Méalóid's lengthy and authoritative interview with Steve Moore can be found online at http://www.comicsbeat.com/the-hermit-of-shooters-hill-an-interview-with-steve-moore-part-1/. For more on the cultural differences surrounding hallucinated voices, see 'Differences in voice-hearing experiences of people with psychosis in the USA, India and Ghana' by T. M. Luhrmann, R. Padmavati, H. Tharoor and A. Osei, which was published in the June 2014 issue of *The British Journal of Psychiatry*. For more on the initial academic study of tulpamancers see https://www.academia.edu/8124455/Talking_to_Tulpas_Sentient_Imaginary_Friends_the_Social_Mind_and_Implications_for_Culture_Cognition_and_Mental_Health_Research.

The quotation from *Tom Brown's Schooldays* is from p. 76, and the quote from *Late Night on Watling Street* is from p. 17.

5. Cross Bones

This telling of the story of Mary Overie is taken from John Constable's *Secret Bankside*, which also covers the history of Southwark recounted here. For the history of Cross Bones, see www.crossbones.org. The source for the estimate of 15,000 bodies buried at the site is *The Cross Bones Burial Ground, Redcross Way, Southwark, London* by Megan Brickley and Adrian Miles with Hilary Stainer. For more on Robin Hood's Day and 'merrybegots', see the essay 'Robin Hood's Day: A Medieval May Day Festival', in *The Empire of Things* by C. J. Stone (p. 41).

6. London

For an account of the sale of Banksy's *Kissing Coppers*, see the 19 February 2014 *Guardian* article 'Banksy's *Kissing Coppers* – taken from a pub wall in Brighton – sells for $575,000 in US'. The accounts of London's streets before the Great Fire of London, such as Cannon Street flowing into Watling Street, are taken from *Hollar's Map of the Great Fire of London 1666*, which is in the collection of the Museum of London.

For an overview of the history of London Stone, see Charlotte Higgins's 12 March 2016 *Guardian* article 'Psychogeographers' landmark London Stone goes on show at last'. The accounts of the history of the Tyburn gallows are largely based on *Tyburn: London's Fatal Tree* by Alan Brooke and David Brandon. The quote from Thomas Platter about Tyburn House is found in Nicholas Fogg's *Hidden Shakespeare: A Life*. Angela Merkel's speech to both British Houses of Parliament was delivered on 27

February 2014 and is archived online at www.parliament.uk. The statistic that London generated 22 per cent of UK GDP comes from the Office of National Statistics' report *Regional GVA 2013*, and that it pays 30 per cent of taxes was reported by Philip Inman in his 7 July 2016 *Guardian* article, 'London pays almost a third of UK tax, report finds'.

7. St Albans

For more details about the St Albans Pilgrimage, see www.stalbans cathedral.org or www.enjoystalbans.com. If balance to my anti-George stance is needed, the book *St George: A Saint for All* by Samantha Riches would be a good place to start. For more on the Wantley Dragon, see the BBC Radio 4 documentary *In Search of the Wantley Dragon*, which was broadcast on 5 September 2009. The historical details about the life of Alban are based on *In Search of Saint Alban* by Simon Webb and *Images of Alban* by Eileen Roberts.

8. Dunstable

For more on the 2014 sale of Markyate Cell, see Emma Glanfield's 22 May 2014 *Daily Mail* story 'Highwaywoman's home is a steal at £4.5m'. The house particulars are still available on the rightmove.co.uk website.

For more on the efforts to move the bell Great Paul along Watling Street, and about the Dunstable stretch of Watling Street in general, see Dick Dawson's book *Up the Watling Street*. The Buckley Tivoli episode of *Most Haunted* aired on 4 June 2015 on the UK TV channel Really. I am grateful to the writer Alistair Fruish for telling me of Dunstable's status as the wellspring of English theatre. The figure of 7 million people being in precarious employment is taken from Robert Booth's lengthy look at the gig economy in the *Guardian* from 15 November 2016, 'More than 7 million Britons now in precarious employment'. The figure of 7 million people in poverty from working families comes from a 7 December 2016 report by the Joseph Rowntree Foundation, *Monitoring Poverty and Social Exclusion 2016*.

The tale of the outlaw Dun was published in 1821 in *Dunno's Originals; Containing a Sort of Real, Traditional and Conjectural History of the Antiquities of Dunstable and its Vicinity,* by the anonymous author Dunno. The frontispiece of the 1952 children's book quoted is p. ii of *Robin Hood: Green Lord of the Wildwood* by John Matthews.

9. Bletchley Park

The 1937 auction details are on display to the public in the Bletchley Park mansion. Details about the class issue at Bletchley are drawn from Sinclair McKay's wonderful social history *The Secret Life of Bletchley Park,* and in particular chapter 12, 'Bletchley and the Class Question'. The draft recruitment advertisement quoted appears on p. 123 of that book, the quotation from Hugh Trevor-Roper is from p. 125 and the quotation about 'silly girls' admiring Hitler is on p. 124. The shade thrown on Lord Jenkins's codebreaking skills can be found on p. 263. Details about hiring humanities academics rather than mathematicians come from Stephen Budiansky's essay 'Colossus, codebreaking and the digital age', included in *Colossus: The Secret Life of Bletchley Park's Codebreaking Computers,* edited by B. Jack Copeland.

For more details of the rehabilitation of Turing's reputation, see Quentin Cooper's 18 November 2014 story on the *BBC Future* website, 'Alan Turing: separating the man and the myth'. Bobby Hopper's poem is on display at the Bletchley Park visitor's centre. The account of Tommy Flowers's efforts to build Colossus, including the decryption of Hitler's message to Rommel, are from Flowers's essay 'D-Day at Bletchley Park', in B. Jack Copeland's *Colossus.*

Tony Banks's extraordinary pro-pigeon Early Day Motion (number 1255) can be found on the British Parliament's website, at http://www. parliament.uk/edm/2003-04/1255. An account of the politics dividing the Bletchley Park site can be found in Miranda Prynne's 20 February 2014 *Daily Telegraph* article, ' "Berlin Wall" erected at Bletchley Park as charities fall out'. The quotation from the codebreaker Jack Good about Turing's impact on the war comes from p. 51 of B. Jack Copeland's *Colossus.* Philip

K. Dick's quote about using the *I Ching* comes from an interview he did with *Vertex* magazine, Vol. 1, No. 6, February 1974.

10. Northampton

Details about the history of the Blue Boar services at Watford Gap and the source of the Nick Mason quotation come from pp. 127–9 of Joe Moran's *On Roads: A Hidden History*. The account of Alan Moore's early life given here comes from the author's interview with Moore, but further details can be found in Lance Parkin's *The Extraordinary Life of Alan Moore* and Gary Spencer Millidge's *Alan Moore: Storyteller*. Information as to comic sales figures in 2015, which show Alan Moore's *The Killing Joke* to be the best-selling DC graphic novel, are taken from the website of Diamond Comic Distributors, at http://www.diamondcomics.com/Home/1/1/3/23 7?articleID=173232.

11. Rugby

Details of Shrove Tuesday customs, historic football matches and cock-based blood sports come from Steve Roud's *The English Year*. For an account of the 2016 Atherstone ball game, including a photo of the victor, Jonathan Slesser, see the February 2016 *Tamworth Herald* report, 'Three's the magic number for Jonathan after victory in Atherstone Ball Game 2016', by Sam Jones.

Statistics about the number of privately educated individuals in different professions come from the 24 February 2016 report by The Sutton Trust, *Leading People 2016*, which can be found online at http://www.suttontrust. com/researcharchive/leading-people-2016/. The figures for the number of privately educated players in professional rugby and football are taken from the 14 September 2015 *BBC Sport* article by Ben Dirs, 'Rugby World Cup: Is English rugby union just for posh kids?'

12. Bosworth Field to Weston Park

The claim that the Battle of Watling Street saw the greatest number of people killed on a single day until the First World War, based on Tacitus' report, is on p. 261 of Vanessa Collingridge's *Boudica*. For an account of the Roman ghosts witnessed on the M6 Toll road, see p. 21 of *They Still Serve: A Complete Guide to the Military Ghosts of Britain* by Richard McKenzie. The quote from Sue Crowley is taken from Martin Wainwright's 31 October 2006 *Guardian* article, 'Roman soldiers march on M6, Britain's most haunted road'. The details about the use of Mills and Boon novels in the construction of the M6 Toll road come from Nick Britten's 18 December 2003 *Daily Telegraph* article, 'Toll road built on pulped fiction'.

The quotation from a nineteenth-century guidebook to Stourhead is taken from p. 26 of Laura Mayer's *Capability Brown and the English Landscape Garden*. The Walpole quotation is from p. 59 of that book, and the 1782 Brown quotation, which compared his art to literary composition, is on p. 33. Oliver Goldsmith's poem 'The Deserted Village' was written in 1769 and first published in 1770. The claim that a modern road, such as Watling Street, would become woodland if left for fifty years comes from p. 250 of Joe Moran's *On Roads*.

The claim that Britain has the most concentrated land ownership in Europe was made by Philip Lowe, Professor of Rural Economy at Newcastle University, and is quoted on p. 27 of *Whose Land is Our Land?* by Peter Hetherington. The statistic that 36,000 people, or 0.6 per cent of the population, own half of rural England is on p. 52 of that book. For a good overview of the Grosvenor family and their approach to inheritance tax, see the 23 August 2016 *Moneyweek* article, 'How the Duke of Westminster dodged IHT', which is online at http://money.aol.co.uk/2016/08/23/how-the-duke-of-westminster-dodged-iht/. For details of how investing in land is proving more rewarding than property, see the *Financial Times*'s 18 February 2015 article, 'UK farmland returns more than Mayfair', written by Scheherazade Daneshkhu. For more on the issues surrounding land ownership, see Tamara Cohen's 10 November 2010 *Daily Mail* article, 'Look who owns Britain: A third of the country

STILL belongs to the aristocracy', George Monbiot's 21 June 2016 *Guardian* article, 'The shocking waste of cash even leavers won't condemn', and the 16 November 2010 *Country Life* article, 'Who really owns Britain?'

The claim that the average age of British farmers is estimated at 'well over sixty' is on p. 17 of Peter Hetherington's *Whose Land is Our Land?*, and the comparison between the amount of land for sale in the 1970s and early twenty-first century can be found on p. 33 of that book. The statistic that 57 per cent of Grade 1 agricultural land lies on flood plains comes from the 2010 Foresight report from the Government Office for Science, *Land Use Futures: Making the Most of Our Land in the 21st Century*. The Nicola Sturgeon quotation was part of her 16 November 2014 'Programme of government' speech in the Scottish Parliament.

13. Wroxeter to Snowdonia

For more details on how the modern A5 follows Thomas Telford's Trans-Britain Highway, including the quote about bogs and horses breaking their legs, see David Keys's 5 August 2000 article in the *Independent*, 'Telford highway to Holyhead found intact under the A5'. A good introduction to Saint Oswald can be found on the website of the Parish Church of St Oswald, King and Martyr, Oswestry, at http://www.stoswaldsoswestry. org.uk/church-history/. The prophecy of Merlin takes up all of Book VII of Geoffrey of Monmouth's history. For details of Lonely Planet's top 10 Best in Travel 2017, see their website at https://www.lonelyplanet.com/ best-in-travel/regions.

The claim that the Anglo-Saxon invasion added only 5 per cent of the English gene pool comes from Stephen Oppenheimer's *The Origin of the British*. Boris Johnson wrote about 'piccaninnies' and tribal warriors with 'watermelon smiles' in his 10 January 2002 *Daily Telegraph* column.

BIBLIOGRAPHY

Ackroyd, Peter, *Albion: The Origins of the English Imagination* (Chatto & Windus, 2002)

—, *Chaucer* (Vintage, 2005)

—, *The History of England*, Volume II: *Tudors* (Macmillan, 2012)

—, *The History of England*, Volume III: *Civil War* (Macmillan, 2014)

Beevor, Antony, *The Second World War* (Weidenfeld & Nicolson, 2012)

Belloc, Hilaire, *The Old Road* (Constable, 1911)

Bennett, Arnold, *Teresa of Watling Street* (Echo Library, 2011)

Blake, William, *Poems and Prophecies* (Everyman's Library, 1927)

—, *Songs of Innocence and of Experience* (Oxford University Press, 1967)

Bright, Morris and Paul Burton, *Elstree Studios: A Celebration of Film and Television* (Michael O'Mara, 2015)

Brooke, Alan and David Brandon, *Tyburn: London's Fatal Tree* (The History Press, 2009)

Chaucer, Geoffrey, *The Canterbury Tales: A Selection* (Penguin Books, 1969)

Collingridge, Vanessa, *Boudica* (Ebury Press, 2005)

Constable, John, *Secret Bankside: Walks in the Outlaw Borough* (Oberon Books, 2007)

—, *The Southwark Mysteries* (Oberon Books, 1999)

Copeland, B. Jack (ed.), *Colossus: The Secrets of Bletchley Park's Codebreaking Computers* (Oxford University Press, 2006)

Coupland, Douglas, *Shampoo Planet* (Simon & Schuster, 1993)

Davies, Hugh, *From Trackways to Motorways: 5000 Years of Highway History* (Tempus, 2006)

Davies, John, *A History of Wales* (Penguin Books, 1994)

Dawson, Dick, *Up the Watling Street* (Bright Pen Books, 2013)

Dick, Philip K., *The Man in the High Castle* (Penguin Books, 1965)

Dickens, Charles, *Great Expectations* (Chapman & Hall, 1861)

Fleming, Ian, *Moonraker* (Jonathan Cape, 1955)

Fort, Tom, *The A303: Highway to the Sun* (Simon & Schuster, 2012)

Harris, Paul, *The White Cliffs of Dover* (Amberley Publishing, 2013)

Hetherington, Peter, *Whose Land is Our Land? The Use and Abuse of Britain's Forgotten Acres* (Policy Press, 2015)

Hindle, Paul, *Medieval Roads and Tracks* (Shire Publications, 2013)

Hollar, Wenceslas, *Map of the Great Fire of London 1666* (Old House, 2013)

Hopewell, David, *Roman Roads in North-West Wales* (Gwynedd Archaeological Trust, 2013)

Hughes, Thomas, *Tom Brown's Schooldays* (Oxford World Classics, 1999)

Hutton, Ronald, *Blood & Mistletoe: The History of the Druids in Britain* (Yale University Press, 2009)

Jones, Dan, *The Plantagenets: The Kings Who Made England* (William Collins, 2013)

Kipling, Rudyard, *Puck of Pook's Hill* (Oxford World Classics, 1987)

Macfarlane, Robert, *The Old Ways: A Journey on Foot* (Hamish Hamilton, 2012)

Mackinder, Anthony, *A Romano-British Cemetery on Watling Street: Excavations at 165 Great Dover Street, Southwark, London* (Museum of London Archaeology Service, 2000)

Maddern, Eric, *Snowdonia Folk Tales* (The History Press, 2015)

Manning, William, *A Pocket Guide to Roman Wales* (University of Wales Press, 2001)

Mayall, Roy, *Dear Granny Smith: A Letter from Your Postman* (Shortbooks, 2009)

Mayer, Laura, *Capability Brown and the English Landscape Garden* (Shire Publications, 2011)

McDonald, Fiona, *Gentlemen Rogues & Wicked Ladies: A Guide to British Highwaymen & Highwaywomen* (The History Press, 2012)

McKenzie, Richard, *They Still Serve: A Complete Guide to the Military Ghosts of Britain* (Lulu, 2008)

McKay, Sinclair, *The Secret Life of Bletchley Park: The WWII Codebreaking Centre and the Men and Women Who Worked There* (Aurum Press, 2010)

Millidge, Gary Spencer, *Alan Moore: Storyteller* (Ilex, 2011)

Milligan, Spike, *Robin Hood According to Spike Milligan* (Virgin Publishing Ltd, 1998)

Moore, Alan, *Jerusalem* (Knockabout, 2016)

Moore, Steve, *Somnium* (Strange Attractor Press, 2011)

Moran, Joe, *On Roads: A Hidden History* (Profile Books, 2009)

Mortimer, Ian, *The Time Traveller's Guide to Elizabethan England* (Vintage, 2013)

Naughton, Bill, *Late Night on Watling Street* (Bloomsbury Reader, 2013)

Northampton Arts Development, *In Living Memory: Life in 'The Boroughs'* (Northampton Arts Development, 1987)

Oppenheimer, Stephen, *The Origins of the British: The New Pre-History of Britain: A Genetic Detective Story* (Robinson, 2012)

Parker, Mike, *Mapping the Roads* (AA Publishing, 2013)

Parkin, Lance, *Magic Words: The Extraordinary Life of Alan Moore* (Aurum Press, 2013)

Piercy, Joseph, *The Story of English: How an Obscure Dialect Became the World's Most-Spoken Language* (Michael O'Mara Books, 2012)

Rees, Jasper, *Bred of Heaven* (Profile Books, 2012)

Roberts, Eileen, *Images of Alban: Saint Alban in Art from the Earliest Times to the Present* (The Fraternity of the Friends of St Albans Abbey, 1999)

Robinson, Bruce, *Withnail and I and How to Get Ahead in Advertising* (Bloomsbury, 1989)

BIBLIOGRAPHY

Roud, Steve, *The English Year: A Month-by-Month Guide to the Nation's Customs and Festivals, from May Day to Mischief Night* (Penguin Books, 2006)

Rowling, J. K., *Harry Potter and the Philosopher's Stone* (Bloomsbury, 1997)

Sandbrook, Dominic, *The Great British Dream Factory: The Strange History of Our National Imagination* (Penguin Books, 2015)

Sinclair, Iain, *Lights Out for the Territory* (Granta Books, 1997)

Stone, C. J., *The Empire of Things: Selected Writings 2003–2013* (Gonzo Multimedia, 2013)

Stone, C. J., *Fierce Dancing: Adventures in the Underground* (Faber and Faber, 1996)

Stringer, Chris, *Homo Britannicus: The Incredible Story of Human Life in Britain* (Allen Lane, 2006)

Strohm, Paul, *The Poet's Tale: Chaucer and the Year That Made 'The Canterbury Tales'* (Profile, 2015)

Webb, Simon, *In Search of Saint Alban* (The Langley Press, 2010)

Wilson, Steve, *Robin Hood: The Spirit of the Forest* (Neptune Press, 1993)

ACKNOWLEDGEMENTS

There are many people I need to thank for making this book possible.

I should start with the three visionary writers I sought out to make sense of this country, who were all incredibly generous with their time and support: C. J. Stone, John Constable and Alan Moore.

Then there were the three wise writers who were the first to read the manuscript, and who pointed out its many flaws in the kindest way they could: Joanne Mallon, Alistair Fruish and Jason Arnopp.

And not forgetting the three incorporeal writers who, despite having stubbornly left the playing field in years past, still influence pretty much everything I write: Brian Barritt, Robert Anton Wilson and Steve Moore.

Thanks to Bea Hemming for seeing the potential and to Paul Murphy for bringing it in to land. Thanks to Virginia Woolstencroft, Holly Harley, Alan Samson and all at Weidenfeld & Nicolson.

Huge thanks to Sarah Ballard and all at United Agents.

To the friends and family who got roped in along the way – big love to Lia Higgs, Isaac Higgs, Anna Richardson and Dominique Webb. Thanks also to all the lovely vampires at the Haematology Day Unit of the Royal Sussex County Hospital.

ACKNOWLEDGEMENTS

Thanks to Steve Marking for the cover, to David Atkinson for the maps and to Mike Scott for unwittingly summing up the entire book in a couple of sentences.

And finally, thanks for the much-valued friendship, inspiration and support from Daisy Campbell, Shardcore, David Bramwell, Melinda Gebbie, Greg Wilson, Matt Pearson, Stef Wagstaffe, Alan Edwards, Steve Lowe, Kermit Leveridge, Scott McPherson, Andy Starke, Cat Vincent, Flinton Chalk, Susanna Lafond, Patricia Mallon, Helen Mallon, Brice Dickson, and my brother and sister and their families. Thanks to every strand of the ever-thickening mythos surrounding the Cosmic Trigger crew, Festival 23 Notwork, Super Weird Substance, Odditorium and the NoHo Arts Lab. Remember, if I missed your name off this list, that counts as double and means you are best. X

INDEX